ON THE EMOTIONS

The Ernst Cassirer Lectures, 1991

It is my purpose to explain, not the meanings of words, but the nature of things, and to explain them in such words whose meanings, according to current use, are not debauched by the meaning which I wish to attach to them.

Spinoza, Ethics, Book III, Definition XX

Richard Wollheim

ON THE EMOTIONS

Yale University Press
New Haven and London
1999

Set in Linotron Bembo by Best-set Typesetter Ltd, Hong Kong

Library of Congress Catalog Card Number: 99-65332
ISBN: 0-300-07974-5

10 9 8 7 6 5 4 3 2 1

Printed in Great Britain by Bell & Bain Ltd, Glasgow

TO MY FRIENDS WHO DIED 1991–1997

CONTENTS

PREFACE

This book originated in the Ernst Cassirer lectures delivered in the Philosophy Department at Yale University, in the autumn of 1991. I am deeply grateful to the department, and particularly to Jonathan Lear, for the invitation, and for the hospitality that I received. My philosophical interest in the emotions as such dates from an invitation to deliver a paper to a conference at the University of Michigan on the Emotions in Life and Art, which was organized in 1988 by another friend, to whom I am similarly grateful, Kendall Walton. At the time of the Michigan conference, I delivered, in preparation for it, a three-week seminar on the Emotions at Guelph University. I am grateful to the Guelph Philosophy Department for their invitation to be the Winegrad Professor.

This book is a totally revised, rewritten, and, I need hardly say, massively enlarged, version of the lectures that were delivered in New Haven. Nevertheless most of the views, and the manner of presentation, which was designed more to jog the mind than to convince a more obdurate opposition, are the same. For this reason, I have wanted to call the divisions into which it falls lectures. Readers of this book are bound to feel relief that they never had to listen to my views for the hours that this division suggests.

In the intervening years since 1991, I have benefitted from the opinions and criticisms of others at universities in North America and England, and at psychoanalytic institutes in London, New Haven, and San Francisco, where I have been invited to give talks. I have been extremely fortunate to be able to try out my ideas in a number of seminars offered at the University of California Berkeley, in wonderful circumstances, to wonderful students. I am deeply grateful to the Philosophy Department at Berkeley, and to the university, for a series of annual invitations to teach there, renewed for now over fourteen years.

Amongst my students, I owe most to Steve Arkonovitch and Ariela Lazar, both of whom have read many pages of what I have written, and given me searching, but sympathetic, comments, which have saved me from errors, and allowed me a better understanding of my own views; amongst my colleagues, to Marcia Cavell, Jim Hopkins, Stephen Neale, Sam Scheffler, Barry Stroud, David Wiggins, and Bernard Williams, for criticisms and encouragement over the years; and amongst psychoanalysts, to two old friends, Betty Joseph and Hanna Segal, and to John Steiner, who replied to a talk that I gave at the Freud Museum. I recall illuminating conversations with Rogers Albritton, Malcolm Budd, Myles Burnyeat, David Copp, John Deigh, Philip Fisher, Andrew Forge, Robert Gordon, David Hills, Jeff King, Herbert Morris, David Pears, John Searle, Kayley Vernallis, and Kendall Walton.

I am grateful to various friends whose hospitality I enjoyed while writing this book: Aline and Isaiah Berlin, Susan and Patrick Gardiner, Neiti and Grey Gowrie, George Hellyer and Ira Yaeger, Heike and Kevin O'Hanlon, John Richardson, and Angie Thieriot. I thank my friend Faith Brabenec Hart for her editorial labours and forbearance.

Two passages from Lecture III will, by the time this book is published, have appeared elsewhere: one as 'Emotion and the Malformation of Emotion' in *Reason and Passion: A Celebration of Hanna Segal*, edited by David Bell, the other as 'Emotion, the Malformation of Emotion, and J.-P. Sartre' in *Philosophie in synthetischer Absicht: Festschrift für Dieter Henrich*.

In trying to understand what the philosophy of mind is, I now see that I have derived most from the writings of Montaigne, Hume, and Freud. It is, I believe, no coincidence that these great thinkers were, in their very different ways, paragons of humanity.

I dedicate this book to the memory of several close friends, all known for several decades, most of them for over fifty years, who died in the period of time while it was being written: Isaiah Berlin, Caroline Blackwood, Mark Bonham Carter, Sandra Fisher, Patrick Gardiner, John Gere, Sylvia Guirey, James Joll, and Stephen Spender. The world now seems to me a far emptier place than it was when I lectured at Yale.

INTRODUCTION

THE EMOTIONS

These lectures are lectures in applied philosophy. Applied philosophy is to be contrasted with pure philosophy. The difference between pure and applied philosophy is not nominal, nor is it small. It is real, and major. Pure and applied philosophy differ in at least three broad ways: they differ in method, in aim, and in subject–matter.

In the first place, pure philosophy depends for its method upon conceptual analysis, which in our day has been equated, through erroneous hopes, with linguistic analysis. Applied philosophy, by contrast, employs conceptual analysis and whatever else can serve its needs. It appeals to observation and experiment, to common usage and traditional lore, and the wisdom of the ages is not irrelevant.

Secondly, though both forms of philosophy aim at necessity, they aim at different kinds of necessity. Pure philosophy aims, as its method indicates, at conceptual necessity, or at truths that hold in all possible worlds. Applied philosophy aims at a lower kind of necessity: it aims at theoretical necessity, which has its standards set by the laws of nature.

Thirdly, while pure philosophy takes for its subject–matter things as they must be anywhere, applied philosophy studies merely the more general features of this world, or of some fragment of this world. Identified in this way, applied philosophy evidently blends into scientific theory, and it is a matter more of tact than of observance to recognize where one begins and the other ends.

Much philosophy, perhaps most philosophy as we do it, is applied philosophy, and a certain amount more would be better if it were done as applied philosophy. Moral philosophy is a case in point.

In addition to applied philosophy, there is, I have come to think, substantive philosophy. The difference between the two is a matter of quite how broad or how narrow, quite how general or how specific, a fragment of the world our philosophy sets out to investigate. If aesthetics is applied philosophy, the philosophy of painting would be substantive philosophy, and I think that it may have been an oversight on my part that, when I was writing on the philosophy of painting, I did not appreciate this distinction. But a grave oversight? I think not. And this is because the differences between these two kinds of philosophy are surely only quantitative.

Anyone setting out to write on the emotions is certain to want more assurance than seems forthcoming that there is something, that there is some one thing, there to be studied. Assurance here means prior assurance: prior assurance is to be contrasted with posterior assurance, and it is on posterior assurance that the student of the emotions has to depend.

Why is this? Why is prior assurance seemingly in such short supply?

Before we actually embark on an inquiry into the emotions, there are two sources to which we might look to convince us of the pre-existence of a topic to be inquired into, and in neither case are we much reassured.

In the first place, we might consider the language of the emotions. In these lectures this is not a suggestion that I shall make very often. If we do appeal to the language of the emotions, what do we find? We find the word 'emotion', and then we find a number of words that stand for, or so we assume, the various emotions: 'fear', 'hate', 'love', 'envy', 'jealousy', 'guilt', 'gratitude', 'shame', 'pride', 'resentment', 'despair'. However, if these words are the various determinates of which emotion itself is the determinable, language itself is silent on the matter. The contrast here is with desire or belief. For we have the word 'belief', and then we have a whole way of talking which allows us to refer to the various beliefs we have as the belief that this, or the belief that that, or the belief that the other. Or we have the word 'desire', and then we have another whole way of talking which allows us to refer to the various desires we have – and now the situation is more complex, but certainly not less perspicuous – as the desire that this, or the desire for that, or the desire to be this or to do the other. In this way we gain prior assurance that there is a topic of belief, or a topic of desire.

The second direction in which we might turn for prior assurance is to the literature of the emotions. But, if we start on the most interesting, the most often cited, writers who are regarded as having written on the emotions, we can come away with the idea that there are as many topics lurking under one word as there are writers addressing it. It is not simply that there is a lot of disagreement. I do not know that there is. What is disturbing about the literature is the divergence in starting-point and the infrequency of any intersection.

So much for prior assurance. What then is posterior assurance, and how can we expect it?

If we are to obtain posterior assurance, it must come about in somewhat the following way: First, we survey what we pre-theoretically assume to be the emotions. Next we draw up an account which fits the material as best we can manage. Then we can think of the account as giving us posterior assurance if (one) the fit is reasonably neat, (two) the account coheres with such intuitions as we have about the emotions, and (three) any exceptions to the account that we observe fall into one or other of two categories: either, on further consideration, their claim to be cases of emotion comes to seem less plausible, or their claim continues to hold up but they are evidently emotions of a more complex sort so that it is only to be expected that, if they are to be accommodated, it will be at a later stage of the account.

It cannot be denied that, in any philosophical account of the emotions that is rich enough, there will be an element of stipulation. At the point at which this occurs, the inquiry turns back on itself. Strictly speaking, we can no longer claim to be setting out the truth about the emotions as we find them: from this point onwards, the emotions are whatever our account is true of.

LECTURE ONE

THE ORIGINATING CONDITION

1. What are the emotions?

An emotion is a kind of mental phenomenon, and, in arriving at
a just view of any mental phenomenon, or of any kind of mental
phenomenon, we can best begin by plotting it on an appropriately scaled map of the human mind. On such a map, the most
salient feature will be a broad divide running across it, effecting
a division that is exclusive, though not exhaustive. On one side
of the divide lie *mental states*, on the other *mental dispositions*, and,
since this divide is recognized by a number of philosophers who
by no means see it the same way, let alone the way that I do, I
shall say how I see it.[1]

Mental states are those transient events which make up the
lived part of the life of the mind, or, to use William James's
great phrase, 'the stream of consciousness'.[2] They occur at a time,
though the duration of a mental state seldom admits of precise
determination. Different mental states of the same person can
be successive, or they can overlap, or they can be simultaneous.
Examples of mental states are perceptions, such as hearing
the dawn chorus, or seeing a constellation of stars overhead;
sensations, such as pains, and itches, and pangs of hunger or
thirst; dreams, and daydreams; moments of despair, boredom, or
lust; flashes of inspiration; recollections; images seen in the mind's
eye, and tunes heard in the head; and thoughts, both thoughts
that we think and those uninvited thoughts which drift into the
mind.

Mental dispositions are those more or less persisting
modifications of the mind which underlie this sequence of
mental states. They have histories, and these histories can vary
greatly in length and in complexity. Some will be coextensive

with the life of the person: others will be contained within, sometimes well within, the person's life, starting up some time after birth, or terminating some time before death, or, likeliest of all, both. In the course of its history, a disposition can wax and wane. Examples of mental dispositions are beliefs and desires; knowledge; memories; abilities, powers, and skills; habits; inhibitions, obsessions, and phobias; and virtues and vices.

2. Mental states are different from mental dispositions, but there are *two important facts* that at once unite them and contribute to their both being mental phenomena.

The first fact is that mental dispositions and mental states *interact* in a number of ways that are highly significant. I shall list five of these ways, and illustrate them. There are other ways too.

(One) a mental state can initiate a mental disposition. Waking up and seeing a frog standing on his chest could establish in a boy a lasting terror of frogs. (Two) a mental state can terminate or extinguish a disposition. A moment's dizziness high up in the big tent could destroy for ever a woman's ability to walk the tight-rope. (Three) a mental state can reinforce, alternatively attenuate, a mental disposition. Seeing a frog some years later by the edge of a pond, half-buried in sedge, could, for some boys at any rate, intensify an existing terror of frogs: for others the sight might dispel the terror. And we can readily imagine that the thought, 'Perhaps this will be the last time', suddenly invading the woman's head as she paused high above the crowd, had weakened her confidence some time before her ability deserted her. And (four) a mental disposition can, from time to time, manifest itself in a mental state. A man's desire for revenge might lead him to visualize his rival cringing before him: a woman's memory of a seemingly untroubled childhood might lead her to recall with great vividness the smell of lilac: a child's jealousy of an older brother might erupt in sporadic fits of rage or resentment. We can be, in Hume's phrase, 'possest'[3] with the disposition. And these manifestations will occur, sometimes in response to a stimulus, but sometimes, or so it seems, spontaneously. Sometimes the occurrence of a mental state that manifests a disposition can be explained by reference to something that preceded it or is going on at the time, and sometimes it cannot be.

If we pause to reflect upon these four ways in which mental states and mental dispositions may interact, we observe, in the first three cases, an appropriateness of the mental disposition to the mental state that initiates or terminates it, that reinforces or attenuates it: the mental disposition is of the very kind that, given the content of the mental state, we should expect. In the fourth case, the appropriateness goes the other way round. The mental state is appropriate to the mental disposition that it manifests: the mental state has the content that seems right, given the kind of mental disposition it is. However, in all four cases, for the notion of appropriateness to be altogether clear, we need to grasp another notion, which mediates the connexion: that of the *role* of the disposition. I shall return to this notion.

And now to (five) which is, though the list could be extended, the last interaction that I shall consider. When, as commonly happens, an external event causes a mental state, the causal chain that runs from the first to the second passes through a number of relevant dispositions, which filter the external event. If the external event determines the mental state on which the chain terminates, it does so only in conjunction with these dispositions. A woman, falling on the tennis court, might find the pain in her wrist numbed by her eagerness to win the match, or aggravated by her fear that she is getting too old to play. The eagerness and the fear are dispositions, and they mediate the effect of the fall upon the woman. Or a man, who is driving along in his car when the lights change to red, might be made more attentive to this fact by his long-standing terror of the police, or less attentive by his desire to keep an assignation for which he is already late.

The second fact that unites mental dispositions and mental states is that both possess *psychological reality*. Much philosophy does scant justice to this fact.

In the case of mental states, psychological reality is seldom explicitly denied, but what is ordinarily conceded is something that falls considerably short of what the notion requires. This is because the issue is treated as exclusively an epistemic matter, or a matter of our knowledge of mental states, and the superior access that we have to our own mental states. But that this is not all there is to the issue can be seen from the fact that the asymmetry between the way in which we come to know of our mental states and the way in which we come to know of the mental states of others requires an explanation. We need to know how this asymmetry is brought about, and this is bound to take us back to the structure of mental states, or the mysterious sense in which my mental states are mine, essentially mine. The psychological reality of mental states will figure substantively in any such explanation.

In the case of mental dispositions, psychological reality is more readily, indeed it is frequently, denied them, and the best way of observing this is to consider a view that certainly has such a denial as its consequence. The view that I have in mind is that which equates the ascription of a mental disposition to a person with a general prediction about what that person will do, or would do, in a certain range of circumstances. The disposition itself is taken to be no more than a pattern of such doings. 'Do' here is an all-purpose word, which covers thinking, feeling, acting.

This view, which found classical expression in Gilbert Ryle's *The Concept of Mind*, confronts two major difficulties. (There are further difficulties in Ryle's own version of the view that come from his restricting dispositions to patterns of action, or of things that we do in a narrow sense of that word, but these difficulties are not currently relevant.)

The first difficulty is that the view cannot account for the manner in which we can come to experience our own dispositions, indirectly if not directly. So, for instance, we think of our mental dispositions as having strength or weakness. We say that a desire of ours, or, by extension, a desire of another's, is strong, or that a belief is weak. How can this be so, if the desire or the belief is simply a pattern?[4] By further extension, when two or more of a person's dispositions are more or less of equal or comparable strength, we think of them as entering into conflict, or as leading to inner turmoil. The only interpretation that a view like Ryle's can put upon this phenomenon totally distorts it. For it has to hold that, when an observer ascribes to someone a conflict of dispositions, this merely reflects an uncertainty on the part of the observer about which of two or more predictions to make. Ryle, or anyone who thinks like him, finds himself in effect relocating the conflict from the mind of the person to whom it is attributed, which is its natural site, to the mind of another, who is a mere outsider.[5]

I repeat that the point that I am making does not require that our dispositions are experienced directly, as our mental states clearly can be. But that our dispositions can be experienced indirectly, or through the manifestations that they causally produce, seems to be beyond the power of a view like Ryle's to accommodate.

The second difficulty with which such a view is encumbered is that it can make no sense of the explanatory value that dispositions are ordinarily thought to have. Ordinarily we look to, say, people's beliefs and desires in order to explain how they act, what they feel, the way they see the world. And we do so because we believe that these things are caused by people's beliefs and desires. Now Ryle does not deny all explanatory value to mental dispositions, but he does deny that their explanatory value comes from their being causes. As mere patterns in what people do, dispositions cannot have causal power. In consequence, when we connect what someone does with a disposition of his, and claim that the latter can explain the former, what we do, according to Ryle, is to subsume one thing that the person does under a series of things that he is in the habit of doing, and this is explanatory only in the limited sense that it takes away the oddity that the single happening might otherwise have. As Ryle himself puts it, saying that a person did what he did because of some mental disposition is just 'to say "he *would* do that"'.[6]

If Ryle's view amounts to the denial of psychological reality to mental dispositions, what view respects it?

The view that I espouse is, as I have indicated, the equation of mental dispositions with underlying psychological entities, perhaps ultimately with material entities, and these entities can causally account for what, on a Ryle-like view of the matter, is falsely equated with the dispositions themselves: that is, the manifestations of these dispositions, whether these be thoughts, feelings, sensations, or conduct.

Insistence upon the reality of mental dispositions will be a strong theme running through these lectures. I shall refer to it as the 'psychologization', or the 'repsychologization', of mental dispositions: meaning, of course, the repsychologization of dispositional concepts. Of the two terms, 'repsychologization' is the more precise, for it is only when our thinking has fallen under the sway of philosophy that we are seduced into abandoning the natural, which is the psychological, understanding of mental dispositions, to which we then need to be recalled.

3. Let us return to the differences between mental states and mental dispositions. For these are not fully before us until we introduce three very general properties that qualify mental phenomena. They are – or these are my words for them – *intentionality*, *subjectivity*, and *grades of consciousness*.

Intentionality is the thought-content of a mental phenomenon, and it is intentionality that secures the directedness alike of mental states and mental dispositions.[7] Of mental states: for it is in virtue of its intentionality that, say, a certain perception is a perception of a gathering storm, or that a moment's amusement is amusement at the famous *mot de Saint Denis*, or that a certain recollection is a recollection of a holiday in Worthing. Similarly for mental dispositions: for it is in virtue of its intentionality that a certain belief is a belief about rain tomorrow, or that a certain desire is a desire for good coffee, or that a fear is a fear of frogs. From these examples it should be clear that the thought-content of a mental phenomenon does not have to be what grammarians call a 'complete thought', or logicians a 'proposition': it may be limited to a mere concept.[8]

Subjectivity, unlike intentionality, is a property solely of mental states. (That mental dispositions cannot have subjectivity accounts for the fact, already mentioned, that we cannot experience dispositions directly.) Subjectivity is what older philosophers used to refer to, somewhat metaphorically, as the feel of a mental state, but nowadays it has come to seem illuminating to say that the subjectivity of a mental state is what it is like – like, that is, for the person whose state it is — to be in that state.[9] What it is like to be in pain is different from what it is like to taste something, and what it is like to have a pain in the ankle is different from what it is like to have a pain in the knee, and what it is like to taste raspberries is different from what it is like to taste strawberries, and all these differences, and others like them, are differences in subjectivity. However we must be on our guard against believing, as phenomenalists used to, that we can exhaustively capture, either in words or in thought, the subjectivity of a mental state. We cannot, like copyists in front of a painting, 'square up' our mental states, and then record them, square by square. We cannot do this even for our perceptions. A commitment to subjectivity need not extend to a commitment to what philosophers call 'qualia'.

The intentionality and the subjectivity of a given mental state can be related in many complex ways, but what is invariably wrong is to think, as the Empiricist philosophers of the seventeenth and eighteenth centuries did, that the intentionality of a mental state is wholly constructed out of its subjectivity. The reason why a certain thought is a thought of a horse is not because part of what it is like for the thinker to have such a thought is for him to have the image of a horse.[10]

Nevertheless there may be connexions of dependency between the intentionality and the subjectivity of mental states: not, of course between the concepts, but between the things themselves.[11] So, in some cases, the subjectivity of the mental state largely secures its intentionality. Perceptions, or pains in particular parts of the body, gain their thought-content mostly because of what they are like. In other cases, the intentionality of the mental state largely secures its subjectivity. Being amused by a joke, or terrifying oneself with the prospect of being jabbed in the eye by a needle, are cases where what the mental state is like mostly derives from its thought-content. And, in yet other cases, intentionality and subjectivity are equal partners.

Finally, and not infrequently, intentionality and subjectivity fuse so that, though intellectual analysis can continue to distinguish between them, the two cannot be separated experientially: we cannot indicate where one begins and the other ends. When this happens, I call the fusion of intentionality and subjectivity *phenomenology*.[12] Wittgenstein has shown us that psychological phenomena like the alternating perceptions of a Neckar cube, where at one moment one face of the cube comes towards us, at another moment it recedes from us, or of the duck–rabbit figure, where we see now a duck in the drawing, now a rabbit, cannot be adequately described, let alone explained, solely in terms of changing intentionality or solely in terms of changing subjectivity or even in terms of a mere conjunction of the two. It is only if we recognize the fusion of the two that we get a coherent picture.[13]

From the fact that subjectivity attaches to mental states but does not attach to mental dispositions, it follows that phenomenology attaches only to mental states.

One reason why phenomenology deserves our attention is that not infrequently mental states owe their causal efficacy to their phenomenology, as when a state of terror causes a soldier to run, or hearing the squeal of brakes causes a driver to turn his head.[14]

A residual question is whether there are any mental states that are completely without either subjectivity or intentionality. Some philosophers think so, and typically they press the claims of computations to be mental states without subjectivity, and the claims of pains, or, more plausibly, unlocated pains, to be mental states without intentionality.[15] The issue is not germane to the present discussion.

By *grades of consciousness* I mean the three exclusive and exhaustive properties of being *conscious* (in what I think of as the determinate sense of that term), being *preconscious*, and being *unconscious*. These properties attach both to mental states and to mental dispositions. If, of the two, it is more obvious how mental states possess grades of consciousness, it is more fundamental that mental dispositions do so. Preconscious dispositions are best thought of as dispositions that only with difficulty manifest themselves in conscious mental states, and unconscious dispositions are altogether prevented from doing so, except in heavy disguise.

This map of the mind allows us to plot in a very general way the whereabouts of the emotions. For, if one thing is clear about the emotions, it is that they are mental dispositions. They fit into the general scheme of mental phenomena in just the way that I have proposed for mental dispositions. Emotions are caused by mental states, and emotions can be extinguished by them: mental states can reinforce emotions, and can also attenuate them: emotions will normally manifest themselves in mental states: and, in many circumstances, emotions can be expected to influence which mental states will occur, given the impact of the external world upon the person. Emotions possess intentionality, but, unlike the mental states in which they manifest themselves, they do not possess subjectivity. And emotions can be qualified by all the various grades of consciousness.

4. That emotions are mental dispositions has been anticipated, for, in illustrating how mental dispositions relate to mental states, I could not find convincing examples without using the emotions.

However that emotions are mental dispositions is something that the vocabulary of emotions can easily obscure. For we use the same words to refer to the emotions themselves and to the mental states in which the emotions manifest themselves.[16] When we say that Hamlet was angry with his mother, or that Macbeth was frightened of Banquo's issue, or that the youth Claudio was ashamed of his sin, we might be talking either about one or another of the underlying dispositions of these characters or about certain episodic states of theirs in which these dispositions erupt or originate. The difference between emotions as mental dispositions and emotions as (derivatively) mental states corresponds to no disjointedness in our psychological vocabulary.

There is a way in which, when using an emotion term, we can, up to a point, make it clear that we are referring to a mental state, and that is by replacing the verb 'to be' by the verb 'to feel'. If we say that Hamlet felt angry with his mother, or that Macbeth felt frightened of Banquo's issue, then it is unambiguous that we are referring to what occupied the mind of one as he taunted his mother in her bedroom, or what tormented the other as he heard the witches' prophecy, or was told of Fleance's escape. In such cases the word 'feel' does not retain its normal implication: there is no suggestion of one special kind of mental state – that is, a feeling – rather than of another kind – say, a thought, The only implication is that we are referring, not to a mental disposition, but to a mental state. But note that this way of disambiguating emotion as disposition from emotion as mental state does not seem available to us when we get, as we shall in Lecture III, to shame and guilt. To feel shame (or to feel ashamed), to feel guilt (or to feel guilty), are, it seems, fully ambiguous between the dispositional and the episodic instances of these emotions.

That the same emotion-term can be applied in these two ways is not necessarily objectionable. It need not lead to confusion or misunderstanding: indeed it can be profitably exploited. When Elgar entitled a section of a suite 'Sir John in Love', he took advantage of the ambiguity to let the music evoke both the old knight's deluded cast of mind and those transient thoughts and experiences and dreams of his into which, from time to time, his condition was assumed to overflow.

Some philosophers have drawn large conclusions from the dual appearance of emotion-terms. So it has been asserted that a mental state of a given emotional kind, say feeling angry, cannot occur unless the corresponding emotional disposition, or being angry, is already established, or, an even stronger claim, that the mental state cannot occur except as a manifestation of the corresponding disposition.[17] But to both claims – and these must in turn be distinguished from the more plausible thesis that we cannot understand what 'feeling angry' means without first understanding 'being angry' – there are obvious exceptions. A man, taken off guard, could be momentarily frightened of a snake without having any dispositional fear of snakes. Or he could have a dispositional fear of snakes, and be frightened of the snake before him, yet his current fright have nothing to do with his underlying fear. For he might have momentarily mastered that fear, and what now frightens him is his knowledge that the snake he confronts is no ordinary snake but has been adjusted by a madman to be the carrier of some synthesized venom.

More generally, imagination can induce a particular emotional state in someone who does not have the emotional disposition that that state would ordinarily manifest. A woman might experience a transient attraction to a woman whom she imagines her husband to be in love with, even though, lacking the appropriate sexual orientation, her feelings could never blossom. She has no love for the woman, only jealousy of the man, with whom she momentarily identifies.

Finally, the thesis that emotional states of a given kind are invariably causally dependent upon the corresponding emotional disposition is conclusively refuted by considering how emotional dispositions arise. As we have seen, an emotion can, indeed is likely to, originate in a mental state of the very kind in which the emotion, once established, will characteristically manifest itself. If fright on seeing a frog, which is how fear of frogs is likely to manifest itself, can induce fear of frogs, it follows that fright cannot invariably presuppose fear.

And there are ways in which we use emotion-terms, some of which are little more than quaintnesses, in order to pick out something that is neither a mental disposition nor a mental state, and in fact is not psychological at all. We say that the prisoner is guilty, and we refer to an exclusively legal fact about him. We say, 'I hate to say No', or 'I'm afraid that I can't come, though I'd love to', and these are ways of being polite about, or of apologizing for, something into which hate, fear, and love do not enter. Such idioms are not puzzling, nor are they interesting, and the only thing that is interesting is that it should have been thought that they had anything to teach us about the emotions.[18]

I began this section by referring to those who have been led into error of one kind or another by the tendency of emotion-terms to have two distinct applications. We need to distinguish between such thinkers and those who show no sign of having been misled by language but have, for metaphysical or other reasons, equated emotions exclusively with mental states. Two major thinkers of whom this is true, at least in their more theoretical moments, are William James and Freud, whose views on the nature of emotion have more than a little in common.[19] Other thinkers have arrived at the same conclusion, but more as a matter of philosophical convenience.[20]

5. If emotions are dispositions of a certain kind, what is their kind? How are emotions to be distinguished from other dispositions?[21]

When we set out to identify a kind of disposition, a natural starting-point is with a notion already briefly mentioned: that of the *role* of a disposition.[22] The role of a disposition is what the disposition standardly does for, or the contribution it characteristically makes to, the psychology of the person who houses it.

There is however a distinction within roles, which is important. With some dispositions, their role includes an *end* that the disposition serves: this is true for beliefs and desires. But there are other dispositions whose role does not include an end. These are the instrumental dispositions, and they include thinking, and imagination, and capacities generally. Emotions are, as we shall shortly see, dispositions of the first kind. Their role is connected with an end.

For the identification of most kinds of disposition, the appeal to role suffices. For the emotions, not so. A consideration of their role needs to be supplemented by considering their *history*, or how individual emotions tend to form within the life of the individual. The two methods of identifying dispositions – the appeal to role, the appeal to characteristic history – are interdependent.

I return to role.

6. What is the role of an emotion? Let us contrast it, first with the role of a belief, then with the role of a desire.

Both belief and desire are, at least from one point of view, more primitive phenomena than emotion. Accordingly, I shall ask you, in following these contrasts, to envisage, first, a creature which has beliefs, but as yet no desires and no emotions, then a creature which has beliefs and desires, but as yet no emotions, and, only finally, a creature which has beliefs and desires and emotions. But whatever expository value this thought-experiment may turn out to have, this should not blind us to its artificiality. If, as I hold, desire is posterior to belief, it does not follow that there could be a fully functioning creature that had beliefs but as yet no desires. Only something robotic in nature could be like that. Or, if, as I also hold, emotion is posterior to both belief and desire, any creature that had beliefs and desires but no emotions would not only be highly restricted, it would be highly restricted in the beliefs and desires that it could have. Certainly it is only a creature with all three that we can begin to think of as a person.

The truth is that the chronological, as opposed to the conceptual, dimension to this thought-experiment is negligible, for it is plausible to think that the three kinds of disposition come into existence in rapid succession, and furthermore within the first few hours of human life. The chronological dimension becomes significant – and then not invariably – only when we shift our focus from the origins of belief, desire, and emotion as such to how particular beliefs, particular desires, or particular emotions, come to form.

So to role, and let us start by asking, What is the role of belief?

The role of belief is to provide the creature with *a picture of the world it inhabits*. Not, of course, any picture of the world, but, subject to one proviso, a picture that depicts the world more or less as it is. And with adequate luck, or if the creature has, not only a functioning sensory apparatus, but a broad enough experience of the world, this is just what it will acquire. The proviso, which cannot be omitted from any overall account of belief, is that there is also pressure within the creature to have some picture of the world rather than none. In many circumstances of life, it needs must prefer error to suspended judgment.[23]

That belief has this role is confirmed by three powerful features of the psychology of belief.[24] The first is that beliefs initially arise within us in response to, and are then reinforced by, what we take to be evidence for them. Secondly, when we encounter what we take to be evidence against any belief of ours, then, unless we can somehow suppress this evidence, the belief will tend to dissipate. Unfavourable evidence denies belief the air that it needs to breathe. Thirdly, once we recognize that any two of our beliefs are inconsistent, so that not both can fit into the same picture of the world, they will falter, and we are inevitably led to look for further evidence that will determine which, if either of them, deserves to survive. These three mechanisms, which I have cited because their existence confirms the role that I have assigned to belief, also do much to bring it about that belief fills this role.

Next, desire, and now let us ask, What is the role of desire?

The role of desire is to provide the creature with *objectives*, or with *things at which to aim*. If belief maps the world, desire targets it. And, just as belief presupposes some measure of experience, desire presupposes a certain minimal mobility, or at least the expectation of it.

Another way of formulating the role of desire is to say that desire furnishes the creature with reasons for doing something: and, not just reasons for doing something rather nothing, but reasons for doing this rather than that.[25] Under the urgings of desire, the creature has reason – reason and cause – to bestir itself. Of course, any creature that has one desire will have more than one desire, and just how the different reasons provided by the different desires, as well as those reasons which come from sources other than desire, weigh one against the other is a complex matter, with no simple formula for its resolution. Some of our desires generate reasons that will never be listened to: their voices are too faint, or too discordant. If Dr Johnson was right to say of himself that he 'always felt an inclination to do nothing', it was an inclination to which he seldom turned a listening ear.

Some further observations, still within a minimal characterization of desire, will help to bridge the transition from the role of desire to that of emotion.

Standardly desire commences in unpleasure, and, if things go well, ends in pleasure. However there are two conclusions not to be drawn from this broad connection between desire, on the one hand, and pleasure or unpleasure, on the other. We should not conclude that our desires are necessarily for pleasure rather than for something that is expected to bring pleasure in train: desire is, or appears to be, from the beginning of life, object-directed – a term suitably capacious in scope. Nor should we conclude that desire in itself, or inherently, implies any specific sentiment or attitude, indeed any sentiment or attitude whatsoever, towards what is desired. It cannot be assumed that every desire that we have presupposes some description that we could – perhaps without our being aware of this ability – apply to what we desire, and that would catch why we desire it. The truth is that we might be unable, on any level of consciousness, to give such a 'desirability-characterization', as it has been called, of what we desire.[26] Often we come to find characteristics desirable only because they are instantiated by what we desire.

The point has been made, surely fairly, that desire is not simply a force within us that pushes outwards: it is also a response to something outside us that exercises attraction over us.[27] But this is no objection to the last point. The attraction that a thing has for us need not be, nor is it usually, mediated by some appreciation on our part of what it is about it that attracts us. To bring out what is desirable about what we desire can be a real achievement.

Now the stage is set for the emotions.

This is so, because precisely the role of emotion is to provide the creature – or, as we might now get used to saying, the person – with an *orientation*, or an *attitude to the world*. If belief maps the world, and desire targets it, emotion tints or colours it: it enlivens it or darkens it, as the case may be.

The view, just dismissed, that we desire only those things which instantiate what we regard as desirable acquires such appeal as it has because, often when we reflect upon desire, we think of it with emotion grown up around it. For, envisaged in this way, desire takes on some of the properties of this accompaniment. It gains weight or urgency from the attitude that is essential to emotion. But it remains true that what desire is in itself can be understood without reference to emotion.

That emotion rides into our lives on the back of desire is a crucial fact about emotion, as well as a crucial fact about us. As we shall see in the next section, and then at greater length in the next lecture, the colour with which emotion tints the world is something to be understood only through the origin of emotion in desire.

7. Emotion, I have said, requires for its comprehension an appeal to history as well as to role: an appeal, that is, to the history of an emotion within the life-history of an individual. So I now set out, as I see it, the *characteristic history* of an emotion. Not every emotion follows this course, but to recognize it as the characteristic history of an emotion is crucial to understanding what emotion is. So

(one) *we have a desire*:
(two) *this desire is satisfied or it is frustrated, or it is in prospect of*

being one or the other: alternatively, we merely believe one of these things of it:

(three) we trace the satisfaction or frustration, real or merely believed-in, actual or prospective, to some thing or some fact, which we regard as having precipitated it:

(four) an attitude develops on our part to this precipitating factor:

(five) this attitude will generally be either positive – that is, tinged with pleasure – or negative – that is, tinged with unpleasure – though sometimes it may be neutral. And it will generally be positive if it originates in satisfaction, and negative if it originates in frustration, but this is not exceptionless:

(six) the attitude persists:

(seven) the emotion, as it now is, manifests itself in a number of mental states, and it generates a variety of mental dispositions:

(eight) the emotion tends to find expression in behaviour: and

(nine) it is highly likely that the mental dispositions that the emotion generates will include desires, and, if this is so, and if we possess the necessary worldly information, the emotion may generate action, but only indirectly. 'Indirectly', for what directly generates action, here as elsewhere, is the motivating conjunction of desire and instrumental belief.

There are many elements in this narrative that need to be explicated. The rest of this lecture, and the whole of the next, will be spent in doing so. But, first, two preliminary remarks.

In the first place, even so skeletal a history makes it clear that the connexion of an emotion with its past has an intimacy certainly not to be found in the case of belief, and probably not in that of desire. And that is because the attitude, which is the core of emotion, seldom totally casts off the marks of the situation in which it was formed. Emotion is not a mnemic phenomenon, but it is like one in certain respects, and this ensures that no account of emotion is adequate if it does not refer to history as well as to role.

Secondly, an account of emotion that includes an historical or developmental element is alternative, indeed is rival, to the more customary kind of account, which specifies the criteria of an emotion. Even when the two kinds of account are descriptively equivalent, or when the criteria that one account enumerates correspond to the successive stages that the other account narrates, there are still reasons for finding the historical account superior.

For (one) the historical account supplies a rationale, even if only implicitly, for what the criterial account proposes on the basis of intuition, or by appeal to conceptual, or sometimes just linguistic, observations.

(Two) an historical account can make it plausible how, in a given case, some of the criteria of an emotion might be unsatisfied and yet the emotion be present. For the unsatisfied criteria might correspond to stages in the narrative that have, in this particular case, been jumped over but, for reasons of which the narrative can in turn make sense, without detriment to the formation of the emotion. Within a criterial account, any such exception must either be fatal to the account, or be arbitrarily condoned.

And (three) an historical account has the strength of its vulnerability: that is to say, it invites a broad-based form of scrutiny from which it will, if it passes, only emerge the stronger. For, whereas a criterial account offers us a shopping-list of conditions, whose claim upon our credence is simply the brute fact that they hold, an historical account has the same form, or the same developmental cast, as our broad beliefs about human nature, and it stands or falls by its congruence with our general picture of the continuity through time of the single human mind.

I shall now go over this history, stage by stage. At each stage I shall try to elucidate the concepts and conditions that it deploys.

8. (One) *we have a desire.*

Philosophers, particularly contemporary philosophers, do not set a good example in how to think about *desire*.[28] Even the extension of the concept is often lost sight of, being taken sometimes too narrowly, sometimes too broadly.

As a warning against taking too narrow a view of desire, I offer a reminder of the various categories there are of desire, none of which we can afford to overlook. If some of the names are my own, the categories themselves will be generally familiar. They overlap unobjectionably.

In the first place, there are desires that are conscious, desires that are preconscious, and desires that are unconscious.

Secondly, there are desires that are explicit, and desires that are implicit. What explicit desires are requires no explanation. Implicit desires are desires that we have and that are implied by explicit desires: they are not to be thought of as desires that we don't have but would have if we reflected harder on those which we do have. Implicit desires are a form of closure of explicit desires, but there is no logical notion of consequence that will predict, given our explicit desires, the implicit desires that we have. An implicit desire must meet the general requirements of desire.[29]

Thirdly, there are background desires, which are presupposed, not so much by single desires, or small sets of desires, as by our desires *en masse*. They often provide our lives with broad aims. Background desires may go unrecognized by us until the very moment of their satisfaction or frustration: and, even then, we may be misled and may treat their satisfaction as if it were a happy windfall, or their frustration as if it were a cruel bolt from the blue. Failure to satisfy these desires, or the even deeper failure even to recognize that we have them, can weave through our lives an enduring thread of sadness. It must be insisted upon that background desires too are desires that we actually have: they too must meet the general requirements of desire. Examples would be the desire for peace of mind, or the desire that our desires be relatively harmonious, or the desire for someone to whom we can impart, above all, our most intimate desires.

And, fourthly, we must not overlook those desires – I call them instant desires – which arise only at the moment of their satisfaction or frustration. With instant desires, it isn't, as it can be with background desires, that we do not recognize them until then. They do not exist until then. In a restaurant I might desire oysters only at the moment when the old waiter, muddling the orders, slaps them down in front of me. Desires, like other dispositions, have their histories, and what is distinctive of instant desires is that their histories are very abbreviated.

To many, including myself, these ways of dividing up desires, though of some descriptive interest, are superficial. There are two forms that this objection can take. The first form is the view that what we need is a fundamental, as opposed to a superficial, way of classifying desires into kinds, and the only fundamental way of doing so is in terms of the kind of thing desired. But to this there is the retort that to look for any variety in desire is already to be led astray by appearances. The second form that the objection takes is the claim that there is only one kind of desire, and that any way of subdividing desires is superficial.

I start with the second, or reductive, view. At its core is the conviction that all *ascriptions of desire* can be cast in a single mould, and the form fixed upon for this purpose is

Subject + 'desires' (or 'wants') + 'that' + sentence.

Since, on this view, the object of the desire is given by the sentence that appears in reported speech within the ascription, I call the view the *oratio obliqua thesis*.

The oratio obliqua thesis is often thought to assimilate desire to belief. And so it does in that it claims that, in both cases, the object can be expressed in propositional form, or by means of a sentence.[30] Sometimes this claim is put by saying that both belief and desire are propositional attitudes. However this is ambiguous, and, if it means that, not merely can the objects of both belief and desire be expressed propositionally, but both belief and desire have propositions as their objects, this certainly goes beyond the oratio obliqua thesis, and its content is not clear.[31]

There are two principal arguments advanced in favour of the oratio obliqua thesis. The first is that it allows what is the central fact about desire, or that desire is always directed towards something, to emerge. It certainly does this, for, in any ascription of desire, the sentence in oratio obliqua makes explicit the object of that desire. But, in doing this, the thesis does more. For it claims that what any desire is directed towards is something that can be expressed in a complete sentence. But is there any good reason to believe this further claim?

The second argument, which takes over at this stage, starts from the observed interaction between desires and other psychological phenomena like beliefs, emotions, and wishes, and it maintains that the only way this could occur is through a common sentential content, which, in each case, gives the object of the phenomenon. What inspires this argument, and is then taken to provide the model of such interaction, is the familiar way in which a desire and an instrumental belief interact to generate a further desire. An example: I desire that I have a better understanding of German. I believe that the best way to do so is to read a good German grammar. Therefore I desire that I read a good German grammar.

But underlying this last argument is a thesis about the mind and its workings, which is excessively rationalistic. It is that, whenever two psychological phenomena interact, their interaction can be reconstructed as an example of a valid inferential pattern. What this thesis overlooks – and I shall return to this issue in the next lecture – is the role of the imagination. Imagination can blend two mental phenomena without their having to stand to one another as premisses in an argument.

However, even if the oratio obliqua thesis is true, its significance for the nature of desire is entirely dependent upon a further thesis, dominant over much contemporary philosophy of mind, which I shall call *the linguistic thesis*. According to this thesis, there is a one–one correspondence between the linguistic forms that we use to ascribe mental phenomena and the ways in which such phenomena ought to be classified. There is, for instance, a correspondence between forms of ascription of desire and kinds of desire. I see no obvious reason to believe that this linguistic thesis is true, either in general or in the particular case.[32]

However, rather than argue against the linguistic thesis, I shall prefer a more positive approach. I shall for for the moment bracket both the linguistic thesis and the oratio obliqua thesis, and I shall turn to the view that there is a way of dividing up desires into kinds that is not superficial. This approach has the further advantage that, if it can be pursued, and the claim on which it is based substantiated, we shall have made some progress towards what I have called the repsychologization of desire.

I propose to start from the most plausible way we have of classifying desire that gives us different kinds of desire, and then see just how robust such a classification proves to be. If it survives, the philosophy of mind can benignly ignore the oratio obliqua thesis. The linguistic thesis can then be treated as it always should have been: as broadly directive, or as working when it does.

I have already indicated what I should take the principle of such a classification to be. It would be to classify desires according to the kind of thing desired, or their objects, and the version that suggests itself is one that gives us (one) *desires for some state of affairs*, (two) *act-desires*, or *desires directed on an action*, and (three) *thing-desires*, or *desires directed on to a thing*. Can such a classification hold up?

I shall at the outset concede this much to the upholders of the oratio obliqua thesis: I shall take the existence of desires for states of affairs, which, on my reading, is what they think that all desires are, as beyond dispute. What remains to be established is whether additionally there are act-desires and thing-desires.

First, then, *act-desires*.

Act-desires are desires that have as their objects intentional actions, and what would make them into a distinctive kind of desire is the peculiarly intimate relation in which they stand to their objects, and hence to action generally. The argument for their separate existence unfolds in two separate stages.[33]

Let us first consider a sub-set of act-desires, to be called basic act-desires, or desires to do basic acts.[34] Basic acts at once occur within the person's body and are under the person's immediate control. Examples of such acts would be raising one's arm, or sniffing the air, or swallowing. The feature characteristic of basic act-desires is that they do not require, indeed they could make no use of, instrumental beliefs, or beliefs about the means that have to be pursued if they, the desires, are to be acted upon. Basic actdesires, it has been said, naturally flow into a striving to do that which they are desires to do, 'a striving towards an act of fulfilment'.[35]

In immediate contrast to basic act-desires are desires that, though they are desires to do something, the something either occurs outside the person's body or, though inside the person's body, is not under the person's immediate control. Examples would be the desire to open the door, or to photograph the last rays of the setting sun, or to brush one's teeth. What is characteristic of these desires is that the person must have an instrumental belief if the desires are to issue in action, or even in a striving to act. For this reason, such desires appear to distance themselves from basic act-desires, and so not to belong to the same kind of desire, or be bona fide act-desires.

At this stage, the second part of the argument takes over.

For, once we start to reflect upon what it is for a belief to be instrumental for a given person relative to a certain desire – and the circumstances of the person have always to be taken into account in determining the belief that is required if the desire is to find outlet – the gap between the two kinds of act-desire starts to close up. For a belief to be an instrumental belief, it must satisfy three conditions. The belief must, relative to the circumstances in which the agent currently finds himself, pick out an action that (one) is a means to the realization of his desire, and (two) is within his reach. For an action to be within a person's reach is a broader, or more inclusive, notion than for it to be within the person's immediate control: it is, in a looser sense, something that he can do. But the belief must do more than simply pick out such an action. It must (three) bring the action before the agent's mind, and in such a way as to incite in him a desire to do it.

An example: I have the desire to open the door. Since this is clearly not a basic act-desire, it needs an instrumental belief before it can be acted upon. What suggests itself for this role is the belief that my leaning on the door would be a way of opening it. For that is something that I can do. But for the belief to be instrumental for me, it must also make me want to do it.

Now the way in which an act picked out by an instrumental belief can be within an agent's reach is if either it is a basic act, or the further instrumental belief that must be drawn upon if it is to be done picks out, at one or more removes, a basic act.

It is through chains of this last sort that desires that are not basic act-desires are linked, actually or potentially, with basic act-desires, and the resultant pyramidal structure of desires is what allows us to think of them as all act-desires, and of act-desires as a class apart. What makes them a class apart, or what ensures them

a place in a robust classification of desires into kinds, is their relationship, immediate or mediated, to action.

However the connexion of act-desires with action is still only
incompletely before us. For it is crucial to recognize that act-
desires are not just desires to do something, they are desires to
do that thing intentionally. And, since doing something intentionally is, amongst other things, doing that thing out of the
desire to do it, it follows that an act-desire cannot even be acted
upon, let alone be satisfied, except by something that the agent,
in doing, does under the influence of, or motivated by, that desire.
If I do what I desire to do, but do it through coercion, or inad-
vertently, that is not satisfying my desire. Nor is it acting upon
my desire. By contrast, if I desire that something be the case, there
is no general dependence of the satisfaction of my desire upon
some particular way it comes about.

I desire, say, to cook a good meal for my friend. Now, this
desire of mine is not acted upon in a situation like the following: I am asked to cook a meal for some important people whom
I am told I have to entertain, I do so, I go to some trouble over
it, at the last minute they cry off, then unexpectedly my friend
drops in, and together we eat the lavish dinner that I had prepared. We have an excellent time, I am delighted with the
outcome, but it would be devious of me to claim that I have
done what I wanted to do.

Nor is an act-desire of mine satisfied, when what I desire to
do is done, but is done largely through the intervention of others.
But, in applying this last point, we must be extremely careful to
exclude only those cases where what others do is the very thing
that I desired to do, and not something that is only ancillary to
the object of my desire. Michelangelo wanted to build the church
of San Giovanni dei Fiorentini, but he did not do so because his
drawings were ignored, and the church was built to the designs
of another. His act-desire was not satisfied because another did
the very thing that was the object of his desire. By contrast, Kubla
Khan realized his desire to build a pleasure-dome in Xanadu. He
built it, he built it himself, and no-one else did, for his orders,
and no-one else's, were followed: even though, for this to come
about, many workers slaved away for many years, dragging stone

to the site and laboriously cutting it into shape, and doubtless died in large numbers – but these things were never part of what he had wanted to do. They were ancillary to what he wanted to do, and their being done by others allowed it still to be true of him that he acted upon, and thus satisfied, his act-desire.

It might be thought from this discussion that, contrary to what I have suggested, there is a linguistic marker that indicates act-desires: namely, the use of the infinitive to pick out the object of the desire. But this is not so. For, not only do linguists claim that, at any rate on a deeper level, the infinitive construction is a mere rewrite of the oratio obliqua construction, but we can say such things as 'I desire to live for ever', or 'I desire to gain the confidence of the jury', and the desires thus expressed do not require that they themselves make the appropriate contribution to their realization. They are desires for a state of affairs with no limits imposed on how the state of affairs is brought about. Hence they are not bona fide act-desires.

Secondly, *desires for something*: that is, for some thing, or things.

If, alongside desires for states of affairs, there are thing-desires as well as act-desires, the former, unlike the latter, are not desires that mature persons necessarily have. Certainly they are not a sign of their maturity, whereas without act-desires persons would decline into the condition of Oblomov. Thing-desires are essentially primitive desires: they derive from crude, unreflecting attempts to – as I have been putting it – target the world. We may speculate that originally these desires would have been entertained through the medium of sensations or images, in which what is targetted is experienced as something to be merged with or taken into oneself, or to be engorged or ingested, and in ways that not merely involve but invite confusion.

If, as the foregoing description suggests, such desires are not central to our lives, to our adult lives, they can make a claim to be fundamental.[36] They are fundamental, not only logically in that they resist reduction, but also developmentally: they are proto-typical of human desire. They are the chrysalis out of which other kinds of desire break free.

Most contemporary philosophers of mind, partly through an indifference to such genetic considerations, reject the claim of thing-desires to be a class apart. However their criticism of them is generally expressed in a way to which I am not likely to respond favourably. It is generally expressed as an adverse reflexion upon the linguistic form that, it is assumed, ascriptions of such desires would take: that is, one in which the object of the desire is picked out by means of a noun, or noun-phrase, say, a nominalization. In deciding whether the rejection of thing-desires is cogent, it will be necessary to cut away the tendrils of the linguistic thesis with which it is entwined.

Criticism that is not based on purely lingistic considerations characteristically pursues the following track: Given that, when a person says that he desires a thing, he does not desire the mere existence of the thing – though what difference it would make if he did is not made clear – what he must desire is always to stand in some relation to the thing. Therefore, if he is to make his desire explicit, he must say what the desired relation is.[37] So, for instance, he says that he desires a hammer, or a Canaletto, or a bodyguard, and these desires do not receive proper formulation until they are re-expressed as the desire that he have the use of a hammer, or that he own the Canaletto, or that he have the services of a bodyguard. And, when there are several relations in which a person might conceivably stand, and might conceivably desire to stand, to the thing, but only one in which he actually desires to do so, this reformulation of the desire is not just better, it is imperative. For instance, both the homeless person and the person who provides food for the homeless could say of himself that he wants food. But, unless each person specifies whether he wants to eat food or to have food at his disposal, he leaves the object of his desire woefully uncertain. Once the uncertainty is removed, the argument concludes, all such desires will turn out to be desires for states of affairs.

That some desires where, in the ascription, a noun, or noun-phrase, is familiarly used to pick out what is desired are not really thing-desires is incontrovertible. However, what is true of some not necessarily being true of all, whether there are bona fide thing-desires remains undecided.

It certainly looks as though we can have desires that we distort if we insist that, in addition to the thing that attracts us, or to which we are drawn, there is some specifiable relation in which we desire to stand to that thing. Consider the following case: A middle-aged man, after a life of moderate dissipation, has a desire for a child: for a child, as he might put it, of his own. Fathering it is unlikely to be all that he desires: and he may well want the child despite, rather than because of, having to bring it up. What, in his case, is the desired relation? Or now consider the case of an orphan boy, two or three years old, perhaps the very child with whom the middle-aged man will finish up, who has a desire for a father. It is too late in the day for us to say that he wants to be born of a father, and far too specific to say that he wants to be adopted by a father. What, in this case, is the desired relation? In both cases, how each, man and child, is to get on with the other if either is to get out of the situation what he is looking for is likely to remain, not just an experimental matter, but genuinely an open question until, say, the man is dead or the boy grown up.

Or, on the darker side of life, there are those cases to which we shall return in the next lecture, where envy directs us towards things that others have, things whose goodness we recognize, but whose function, or role in life, eludes us, so that were we somehow able to prize them away from their owners, there is not likely to be a relation in which our desires would have us stand to them. Even the desire to destroy what we desire, which is taken by some to be central to envy,[38] may arise for lack of anything better.

Where the present criticism of thing-desires has gone astray is in its failure to recognize that, if there are certain features of desire that fail to show up in my account of these desires, this may suggest a deficiency, not so much in my account, as in the desires themselves. In other words, there may be desires that are too primitive to have these features.

It might now be countered that, when I said of some thing-desires, and explicitly of early ones, that their objects are characteristically experienced as something to be merged with, or ingested, or taken into oneself, I in effect conceded the point that I now appear to be contesting. I conceded that, even with primitive desire, there will always be some relation, if itself a primitive relation, in which we desire to stand to what we desire. Merging, taking into oneself, ingesting, are the names of such relations. But this would be a misunderstanding. For these highly concretized, highly corporealized, relations are the ways in which we experience primitive desire rather than the ways in which we desire to stand to what we primitively desire. They belong to the representation of desire itself, rather than to the representation of what is desired. The desire is felt to be a form of merging with an object, as opposed to being a desire to merge with its object.

Staying for a while longer with the criticism of thing-desires, we shall hear it said that, if a person merely says that he desires some thing, if he says that and no more, we shall (one) not know what will satisfy the person's desire, and (two) not have before us the reason that the person has for his desire, or what he wants the desired thing for.[39] But these further considerations should weigh with us only if we believe that both what will satisfy a person's desire, and the reason that he has for his desire, are somehow part of the object of a person's desire. For it is exclusively with the object of a person's desire — and ultimately with whether there are sufficiently interesting distinctions to be made between the different objects of desire for these to be the basis for a robust classification of desires — that we are currently concerned. It needs to be pointed out that, in many philosophical quarters, no attempt is made to distinguish between the object of a desire, what will satisfy a desire, and the reason why we desire what we do. Even if they all turn out to be the same, this must be shown.

On the relation of what satisfies a desire to what the person desires, and whether the latter includes the former, I shall have much more to say later. As to how the person's reason for his desire relates to what he desires, it surely suffices to point out that someone can desire something without any reason to do so. That being so, it is hard to see how, when someone does have a reason for his desire, this reason becomes part of the object of his desire, and therefore has to be referred to within its description.

And now, returning to the larger context within which this argument about thing-desires was introduced — that is, whether there are different kinds of desire, or whether there is only one kind of desire – I must point out that, even if all desires that allegedly have things as their objects could be shown not to form, as I have been urging that they do, a kind apart, but to be reducible to another kind, it is not to be assumed that they would turn all to be reducible to one and the same kind, *a fortiori* it is not to be assumed that they would all turn out to be reducible to desires for some state of affairs. It is likely that at least some would be reducible to act-desires.[40] Indeed, in many cases where reduction seems appropriate, that is how things go. The pregnant woman of tradition who says that she desires apricots really desires to eat them: likewise the pearlfisher who says that he desires pearls really desires to bring them to the surface and to find a buyer for them.

I am now ready to conclude that a tripartite classification of desires according to their objects, and along the lines that I have proposed, is robust enough that we do not have to worry about the shaky coalition of the oratio obliqua thesis and its philo- sophical second, the linguistic thesis.

To end this section, I add to the warning against taking too narrow a view of desire, a no less serious reminder of the dangers of taking too broad a view. Desire does not include mere velleities or casual inclinations in so far as these neither arise out of nor engage with our other desires. The acid test by which desires are to be identified is that they, and they alone, are capable of genuine satisfaction, genuine frustration.

These issues, and others, take us directly to the next stage in the history of emotion.

8. (Two) *a desire of ours is satisfied or it is frustrated, or it is in prospect of being one or the other: alternatively, we merely believe one of these things of one of our desires.*

This stage is defined in terms of the twin concepts of satis- faction and frustration of desire. More specifically, it is defined in terms of a certain expansion of these concepts. The expansion raises problems, with which we shall be concerned for much of this lecture, but that the concepts themselves are essential to the concept of desire must be a matter of universal agreement. So, what are satisfaction and frustration of desire?

I start with a widely held view, which I shall call *the semantic view*, because it aims to explicate satisfaction and frustration as they apply to desire in terms of truth and falsehood as these apply to belief. But 'in terms of' is a vague phrase, and it will be no surprise that there are two broad versions of the view, each of which, in explicating satisfaction and frustration, makes such a different use of the notions of truth and falsehood that they need to be kept apart.

The view in its first version holds that a desire is satisfied just when the sentence embedded in its ascription is, or comes, true.

In making this claim, the view makes three assumptions, all of which I shall, in the interests of engaging directly with the view, bracket or leave uncontested.

The first assumption is the oratio obliqua thesis, without which the claim cannot be phrased.

The second assumption, no less indispensable to the formulation of the claim, is that of a sentence's coming true, as opposed to its merely being true. For, if truth appears to resist the idea of truth at a time, satisfaction, with which it is being paired, even more compellingly insists on that of satisfaction at a time. There is extremely little of what we need to say about desire that we could say if we had to hold that all desires are either timelessly satisfied or timelessly frustrated.

The third assumption, which is yet more dubious, is that the view, though appearing to neglect the notion of frustration of desire, can ultimately cope with it. Exactly how is another matter. Satisfaction and frustration are, in the context of desire, generally taken as correlative terms, and therefore it might initially be thought that the semantic view in its present version will come down on the side of holding that a desire is frustrated when the sentence embedded in its ascription comes false. In point of fact, there are two reasons why this solution is untenable.

In the first place, on the assumption of bivalence, it has the totally unwanted consequence that every desire is frustrated from the moment it is formed until it is satisfied. The concept of a frustrated desire, whatever it may be, is clearly not just that of a desire that is unsatisfied.

Secondly, even the most superficial account of what frustration is must show it to include some reference to how long the desire in question has gone unsatisfied, what efforts have been made to satisfy it, and through what agency these efforts have failed. To some ears, this might sound a warning alarm for the semantic view, for, if satisfaction and frustration are not related in the comparatively simple way that truth and falsehood are related – and, in saying this, I am no longer insisting that simplicity requires bivalence – how can frustration be accounted for within the semantic mould?

For the moment I shall go along with the claim that, *somehow or other*, the semantic view in this present version can provide an account of frustration, and I shall confine myself to the adequacy, or otherwise, of what it says about satisfaction.

So, let us start by asking, Is the coming true of the object of a desire either necessary or sufficient for the satisfaction of that desire?

First, Is the coming true of a desire necessary for its satisfaction?

One way of answering this question would be through the anecdotal method, in which an issue is settled by picking on an incident, telling stories about it, and then seeing which side of the issue the stories that are most plausibly told fit with. This method is sometimes fallaciously equated with that of the thought-experiment. 'Fallaciously', because, even at its most declarative, the anecdotal method never presumes to show, of two possible hypotheses, one to be false.[41]

If we adopt the anecdotal method, I believe that we can find stories to tell in which a desire is satisfied, even though what occurs falls short of its coming true. Consider a child who desires to sit up all night. The clock strikes twelve, one, two, three, four, and, when it strikes five, though dawn has not yet broken, the child falls into bed, feeling that there is nothing more that it needs to demonstrate either to itself or to anyone else. Can we not think that the child's desire has been satisfied? Or take the case of a woman who feels that a man, in leaving her, has inflicted upon her irreparable damage. She supremely wants revenge, and she wants him to be financially ruined. She knows how dependent he is upon comfort, and she knows how little he will be able to tolerate the lack of it. She gets news of him. He is not ruined. Financially he is doing well. But the life that he has constructed for himself as an alternative to being with her is, she learns, bleak and dessicated beyond anything that she could have imagined. She has always known that this is something that he would be able to bear even less well than poverty. She feels that her most persistent desire has been satisfied. Can we not find reason to agree with her?

If we find these stories plausible in the telling, a retort on the same level of anecdote would be this: If these really are cases of satisfied desire, then either the desire was incorrectly specified in the first place or, somewhere along the line, there was a change of desire. For it can be inferred from the way the two stories end that, at least by this stage, what the child really desired was to stay up late, very late, and what the woman really desired was that the man should, in some unspecified way, suffer a lot.

Now, without a doubt, for some stories that end as I have indicated, such a redescription would be right. But – this is the crucial question – for all cases? Can I not insist that, for the stories that I tell, about the characters whom I have in mind, on which I am surely the authority, the endings that I recount are the right ones?

This brings us directly up against a methodological problem, which arises whenever we use the anecdotal method to settle philosophical disputes, which we can put by asking, When our critic retells the anecdote that we, in making our point, told him, which of two different things is he doing? Is it that he starts off by trying to tell back to us what we have told him, but then finds, even as the words come out of his lips, that he cannot do so? Is it that the very constraints of language, or of thought, impede him, and oblige him to deviate from the task that he has set himself, with the unintended result that the anecdote that he ends up recounting is a different anecdote from that which we tried, but (if he is right) failed, to tell him? Is it from some such experience that he draws an unfavourable conclusion about the status of the incident behind the anecdote, and with this estimate he expects us, as logical agents, to concur? Or is it that, even before he heard us tell our story, he subscribed to a theory that led him to find unacceptable both the anecdote that we told him and the incident that it allegedly recounts. In consequence, he set out with the intention of translating our anecdote into the least different anecdote about the least different incident of which his theory could purport to make any sense? 'To purport', I say, because he, if not his theory, could make at least enough sense of what we told him for him to try to put it into better words. The point of his telling this different anecdote would then have been at once to reveal his theoretical commitments and to bring, more by dint of example than through explicit argument, ours into line with his. If he uses the anecdotal method in the second of these two ways, he would be more like the missionary who converts the heathen by getting them to say the Lord's Prayer.

The methodological crux is that it is only if our opponent is doing the former that the anecdotal method is being employed suasively. For, if he is doing the latter, then the method is being used illustratively: our opponent is using it to illustrate a theory that he has already arrived at in some as yet undisclosed way. However, for all the importance of this issue, there is highly unlikely to be any neutral point from which to determine it, or to establish which way round the method is being used. Our opponent will say that he is using it in the first way so that it is language, or thought itself, that reshapes his anecdote even as he tries to tell it. Despite his respect for our authorial privilege in the matter of the stories we tell, this privilege, he tells us, cannot ride roughshod over grammar or logic. Our words stick in his throat. We, by contrast, shall say that he is smuggling into his rewritten anecdotes his undefended theoretical convictions, and that he is hiding behind language or thought to pretend that he could not possibly talk otherwise, and thus to secure victory. The truth, as we see it, is that he *chose* not to say what – that is, the very same thing as – we had told him.

However, if the anecdotal method is dialectically inconclusive, it is not without utility. On the contrary, sometimes it can serve a powerful purpose, for sometimes it can, even if only indirectly, let us see what are the theoretical issues at stake. For they are whatever separates the two sets of stories. They are whatever it was that allowed the first side to say what the second side, for one reason or another, cannot bring itself to repeat, alternatively what prevented the second side from retelling what, somehow or other, gave the first side no difficulty.

So let us ask, What could it be that, in the case under consideration, keeps the two sides apart? What allows me to countenance certain anecdotes of satisfied desire, such as that of the child who sits up late, or that of the woman who finds herself revenged, which my philosophical critic refuses to accept, and why am I unconvinced that the emendations upon which he insists are necessary? Certainly the stories that I tell are out of the ordinary, but that is not the issue.

My suggestion is that, in the present dispute, or whether coming true is necessary for satisfaction, what divides the two sides is the thesis that I have been making one of the central themes of this lecture, and will indeed be one of the central themes of the whole book, and that my critic no less clearly rejects: the psychological reality of mental dispositions in general, hence of desires in particular. What is at stake is the repsychologization of the concept of desire.

For, once it is accepted that desires have psychological reality, and it is further accepted that this reality unfolds in psychological histories, then there is always the possibility that there might be a desire that would have a history that, through unexpected causal influences, exhibits the anomalous. What causes desires to wax and wane, and, more to the present point, what leads to their being satisfied or frustrated, might find its explanation, not exclusively where we might at first look for it, or in the relationship of the desire to its object, but in the deeper folds of the person's psyche. In consequence, what will turn out to satisfy, or frustrate, a desire can be an experimental question, and, in the person's own perspective, a matter of trial and error.[42] This is important.

In both life and literature, such cases force themselves upon our attention. The tragedy of King Lear follows from the fact that Lear is devoured by a single desire − the desire to possess, and to know that he possesses, the undivided love of his daughters, in particular of his daughter Cordelia. At the same time, he has no real idea how to satisfy this desire. He has a few thoughts on the subject, whose suitability he seems not to have questioned, and he acts on the worst of them: that love has to live up to, and so can be tested by, the test of loyalty.[43]

If we persist in rejecting an experimental element in determining what will satisfy a certain desire, our error will be comparable to thinking that, when we test an empirical hypothesis, the meaning of the terms in the hypothesis will tell us single-handed what we need to do, for they will give us its observational consequences. Inventiveness, in the one case, or imagination, in the other, are ruled out as completely gratuitous.[44]

Of course, the view that I am propounding is not without its attendant difficulties. The central, and well-rehearsed, difficulty is that, if we abandon the necessary connexion between the coming true of desire and its satisfaction, we have to find a way of avoiding the opposite error, which is that of equating the satisfaction of desire with its mere termination.[45] The answer to this further question must be along the following lines: For a desire to be satisfied, not just terminated, by something that falls short of its coming true, or its object, this thing must be regarded by the person as interchangeable with the object of the desire. There must be a perspective, which is also a perspective in which the person sees the world, in which the object and what substitutes itself for it appear equivalent. And it should most probably be further required that such an equivalence was psychologically implicit in the very formation of the desire. Finally, it must be right to insist that, if a desire can be satisfied without its coming true, it must nearly come true. The notion of nearly coming true lacks, it will be appreciated, exactitude.

I turn now to the next, and far more important, question: Is a desire's coming true a sufficient condition of its satisfaction? In answering this question, I shall again start with the anecdotal method, not expecting that it will determine the question, but hoping that it will elicit the theoretical issues at stake.

So, consider the case of a woman who desires that her country is liberated from the yoke of the oppressor, and it comes true that her country is liberated, but a thousand years after her death. Is her desire satisfied? Or, if death is felt to introduce a special difficulty, consider less extreme cases. A man is deserted by his wife, he desires her to come back to him, and for years he goes on desiring this, and then she returns to him and by now he is old and sick. Is his desire satisfied? In these cases, there is surely room for someone about whom the right answer would be, No.

The critic, who feels confident about meeting anecdote with anecdote, is likely to start by pointing to the fact, on which there will be agreement, that, in the case of some desires, there is a temporal indicator included in the object. For instance, I desire a glass of vodka *now*: the soprano desires to sing at La Scala *before she is twenty-five.* The next step for the critic is to claim that, when it seems to be the case that a desire is not satisfied though it has come true, the desire in question is invariably a desire that contains, if not explicitly, a temporal indicator. So, if it is true that the woman's desire that her country should be liberated was not satisfied even when her country was liberated, and the reason given is that she was long dead, then the explanation is that what she really wanted was that her country should be liberated *in her lifetime.* If it is true that the man's desire that his wife return to him was not satisfied even when his wife returned to him, and the reason given is that he was past passion, then the explanation is that what the man really wanted was that his wife should return to him *while he was still capable of love.*

If we cannot, on the basis of these materials, decide whether philosophy requires that the second set of anecdotes replace the first set, or whether both, retailing, as they do, different incidents, are acceptable, we can once again use the divergences between them to identify what is at stake. If my philosophical critic thinks that one set of anecdotes, my set, is, not just out of the ordinary, but impossible, what principle would he have to concede in order to think them possible? Why does he, faced by the prospect that one of the desires that I posit might come true and yet not be satisfied, feel compelled to redescribe the desire?

I believe that, this time too, what divides us is the psychological reality of desires. For, if we deny the psychological reality of desires, then it becomes altogether natural to insist that the coming true of a desire suffices for its satisfaction. For what else, our critic might say, could satisfaction be? By contrast, if we think of desires as psychologically real, then it is of a piece to expect that, when they are satisfied, this will have some psychological consequence. Most obviously this will include the termination of the desire – even if another closely related desire forms the next moment: the man who has made his first million will instantaneously embark on putting together his next million. But satisfaction might be expected to be marked by some further psychological registration. Indeed it is plausible to think that, when a satisfied desire terminates, it does so in response to this psychological event, or signal. Exactly the form the event might be anticipated to take is another matter, but, concede the principle, and we can see how a desire might come true and yet not be satisfied: the psychological signal does not sound, there is no register of satisfaction.

If the psychological reality of desire is a twofold difficulty for the semantic thesis, at least in this version, the challenge that it presents to the sufficiency, rather than the necessity, of the thesis is the more significant. It is so, because the aspect of the psychological reality of desire from which this challenge derives is deeper. The semantic thesis, in so far as it falls short of necessity, ignores the way desires wax and wane, begin and end: it ignores, we might say, the lives that desires lead. That is serious. But, in failing to attain to sufficiency, the semantic thesis overlooks something far more important: it overlooks the part that desires play in our lives, and how.

To see this, and then to make good the oversight, we must do two things. First, we must make explicit the part that desires do play in our lives. Secondly, we must trace the way this connects with the nature of the satisfaction of desire.

As to the place of desire in our lives, I shall approach this indirectly: by contrasting it with the part played by certain other phenomena in our lives: phenomena with which desire must not be confused.

Let us first imagine that, in circumstances in which we might be expect to form a desire for a certain state of affairs, no such desire formed, and instead we took out a bet on the coming true of the state of affairs. As gamblers, we would undoubtedly have an interest in winning our bet. However, real enough though that interest would be, and gratifying as it might be to win the bet, this interest would not rival that which we currently have in our desires' being satisfied. Our interest in the state of affairs that has won us our bet would be purely instrumental. It brings us in money.

And now imagine a slightly different situation, in which desires continue to form, but, whenever this happens, we additionally take out a bet. We bet that what we desire will come true. Though now the satisfaction of the desire and the experience of winning the bet might be difficult to separate phenomenologically, we can still see no less clearly that the interest that we would take in the two outcomes would be very different. The interest in the bet would be, for instance, mediated by a number of factors, such as what money means to us. There is, in anything like a normal case, no comparable issue about what our desires mean to us, and there is no comparable mediating factor upon which our interest in them depends. That we might have a negative interest in some of our desires, a matter to which I shall return, does not alter the issue.

Or we may imagine a third, yet different, situation, which we certainly can find ourselves in as things are. There is something that we desire not to happen, but which we believe easily might. We want, say, a particular political party to win the forthcoming election, but we fear the power of the opposition, and its control of the press. We anticipate that our desire will be frustrated, but, in order to compensate for the disappointment that this will bring, we take out a bet that the party we do not favour will win. If our party loses, we shall be able to set against the frustration of desire the consolation of money. But the truth is that there is no way of comparing the ache in the heart that, if we really care about the election, the wrong result will bring about with what we shall get out of winning our bet. The two outcomes are not commensurable. If our winnings were large enough, they might obscure this fact by the excitement, and confusion, that they introduce.[46]

I shall refer to the phenomenon upon which each of these cases throws some light, or the particular niche that desire carves out for its object in our sensibility, and which is something beyond the power of a mere bet to induce, as the way in which desire *sensitizes* us to the world. Though registered in psychological minutiae, it is of massive importance in our lives.

And my next point is that, once we have become sensitized by a particular desire, it is totally implausible that this modification of our sensibility should not enter into the moment when the desire and its object meet up: that is, when the desire is in all other respects about to be satisfied. If we are to be serious about the repsychologization of desire, this must commit us to the psychologization of satisfaction of desire.

But is it independently plausible to psychologize the satisfaction of desire?

Arguments in favour of doing so divide into two groups: arguments from the outside, and arguments from the inside.

The crucial external argument is that the psychologization of satisfaction restores symmetry to the overall history of desire. For, on any likely account, desire will originate inside us, or in experience. This being so, it would be incongruous if desire could terminate outside us. But this is exactly what the equation of satisfaction with the coming true, or the nearly coming true, of the desire amounts to.[47]

Internal arguments are those which view the matter in the light of the desirer's own experience, and they depend upon what are, in a broad sense, phenomenological considerations.

Consider, for instance, the contrast between two rather different ways in which desires can terminate. One way is where the desire, which was for something that the person lacked or was without, is satisfied. The other way is where the desire was all along gratuitous, since, unknown to the person, what was desired was already the case: then, at a certain moment, the person becomes aware of this fact. In these latter cases, the desire may be said to resolve itself. Intuitively it seems as though there should go along with this difference another difference, and that would be a difference in how the termination of the desire is experienced. In the second case, all we need expect is that the gratuitousness of the desire will receive cognitive acknowledgment, the person's mind will reconfigure around this information, and then the desire simply evaporates. Resolution is evaporation. However, when the desire terminates in satisfaction, we shall expect something different. At least we shall expect something more. We shall expect something with which the person can reverberate, and, to play such a role, the likeliest candidate is an experience of satisfaction.[48]

At this stage, it might be objected that I have elided two things that need to be kept apart: that of the satisfaction of a desire, and that of the satisfaction of the person who has the desire. From the fact that the latter is something psychological, it cannot be inferred that the former is.

Without a doubt the two concepts are different, for there are situations in which a person's desire is satisfied, but the person not.[49] However the two concepts can differ, and yet the two phenomena have something in common. For instance, they could both be psychological phenomena. Indeed, as we shall see in the next lecture, a common explanation why the two concepts are not invariably co-instantiated, or why we are not always satisfied when a desire of ours is satisfied, is because we have some attitude, some negative attitude, towards the satisfaction of our desire. I shall, in the appropriate place, suggest what this attitude is: it is that we are unable to accept it. But, at this stage, the crucial question to ask is, What is the 'it'? Presumably it is not the mere fact that our desire has been satisfied. That fact we accept. So, if we now need to distinguish between this fact and something further, which is the satisfaction itself, it is surely plausible to think of the latter, or the object of our negative attitude, as a psychological phenomenon.

It will be observed that I have gone beyond talking of satisfaction as a psychological phenomenon. I have deliberately, provocatively, introduced the phrase 'experience of satisfaction'. Provocatively: for there will be many to whom the suggestion that satisfaction of desire could be equated with anything so specific as an experience will seem repugnant, and some of these will all along have suspected that the psychologization of satisfaction of desire was bound to finish here.

I shall now start on the arguments against the notion of an experience of satisfied desire, and I shall try to forestall them, though not, I am sure, in a way that will convince those who are unmoved by the more general considerations that I have raised.

As we normally encounter these arguments, they are likely to be strung together somewhat like this: If there is something that can reasonably be thought of as an experience of satisfied desire, then there are two ways in which it can be identified. It can be identified through a definite description that picks it out by reference to its distinctive content. Or it can be identified indefinitely: that is, as whatever experience is connected with the satisfaction of desire. If it is identified through a definite description, then the question can be raised, What reason is there to believe in what the use of the definite description presupposes: namely, that there is a distinctive experience constantly connected with what we would otherwise think of as satisfied desire? Or, if such a connexion has been observed in the past, what good reason is there to believe that it, being merely contingent, will always hold? And, if it does hold, does not its contingency mean that it has nothing to tell us about the nature of satisfaction? By contrast, if the experience is identified indefinitely, or as whatever experience – that is, whatever experience, *if any* – is connected with satisfied desire, then whether there actually is an experience of satisfied desire, which was begged by the use of the definite description, is left wide open. Those who argue for an experience of satisfaction must, the argument goes, decide which way they intend their reference to the experience to be taken, and, whichever way they opt for, they have hard questions to answer.

What is to be noted about this argument is that, under guise of offering a double-barrelled objection – that is, either a definitely or an indefinitely described experience – it draws upon at least three separate issues, which different authors interweave in different ways.

The first issue is whether there is, connected with the satisfaction of desire, a distinctive type of experience, of which the different tokens are linked by similarity, or whether there are many different kinds of experience: as many, say, as there are kinds of desire, or as there are desires. The second issue is how we are able to identify, or refer to, this experience of satisfaction, and

whether we can do so by invoking its internal or phenomenological character, or whether, to pick it out, we must always rein-
troduce the notion of satisfaction of desire. And the third issue is
how, if we have some reason to believe in the association of satisfaction and an experience, tentatively thought of as an experience of satisfaction, we can be sure that the association will
continue to hold invariably, hence that the experience will merit
its name.

On the first issue, error is to think that there exists across
human psychology a criterion of similarity that can be mechani-
cally applied, and that will decide whether certain experiences
resemble each other sufficiently to be regarded as examples of
the same type of experience. Now, in certain cases, where the
phenomenology of the experience is very simple, like a pain in
the ankle, similarity is something manifest. But we can get led
astray by such cases into thinking of similarity as always similarity in a simple respect. Once we cast our net wide enough, wide
enough, that is, to catch the experience of satisfied desire, we
have to recognize what might be called the diversity of similarity. Similarity is so diverse that, in many cases, the surest index
of sameness of experience is that (one) there exists a concept
that has a psychological application, (two) this concept has an
experiential basis, and (three) we employ the concept with no
difficulty whatsoever. So, in the present case, so long as we have
good reason to think that the concept of satisfaction is grounded
in experience, then the fact that we have mastery of this concept
gives us all the assurance we need for believing in an experience,
a unitary experience, of satisfaction.

Certainly the identity of an experience of satisfaction over very
different instances of desire satisfied must not blind us to the fact
that, each time the experience is brought about, each time a
desire of ours has been satisfied, the experience will turn out to
be something that cannot be separated from thoughts of the
satisfied desire, thoughts about how the desire was satisfied,
thoughts about what satisfaction of this particular desire in this
particular way means to us. A parallel that suggests itself is the
way in which the experience of amusement at a joke – also an
experience common to many very different instances of the same

psychological phenomenon, for many different jokes, and many different kinds of joke, amuse us – cannot, in any given case, be separated from a multiplicity of thoughts about the joke in question, and what is amusing about it, and why it amuses specifically us.

As to the second issue, or the two modes of identification, it is only as the result of a misconstrual of how the two modes are related that there seems to be, within this material, an argument against the experience of satisfied desire, or a dilemma that the notion of such an experience faces. A likely account of the interrelation of the two modes of description, is this: Initially, or when we first begin to entertain the thought that there is an experience linked with satisfaction, we are in no position to refer to it except indefinitely, or as whatever experience accompanies satisfaction of desire. But, given that the thought is correct, then there must in principle be some definite description, perhaps psychological but maybe merely physical, under which the experience can be brought, or through which it can be identified. Whether we shall ever be able to formulate this description, or whether it might not be too complex for human expression, are further epistemic matters. If, for one reason or another, the description continues to elude formulation, then we shall have to go on identifying the experience indefinitely, or through the notion of satisfaction. But that is not of real moment.

And now to the third issue. It is certainly true that the connexion between the rest of satisfaction and the experience of satisfaction is a contingent connexion. Therefore one of the two could – could, that is, in some world or other – occur without the other. That possibility is a direct consequence of their being distinct, and indeed means no more than that. But could this happen in our world? Perhaps: perhaps in our world too. But, if it did, and if I am right in what I have so far said about satisfaction, this would bring about an upheaval such that the concept of satisfaction, the phenomenon of satisfaction, the nature of desire, and what I have referred to as the place of desire in our lives, would all be likely to change out of recognition.

I shall not leave the argument against an experience of satisfaction without pointing out a methodological feature that it shares with a number of current philosophical arguments of a sceptical bent. For there runs through it, but so subtly that it can escape detection, the presumption that there is no such thing as that which is being argued against. This presumption shows itself in what the argument demands before it would be willing to concede defeat. For it to admit the existence of an experience of satisfaction, what it insists on is, not just clarification of the concept of such an experience, but an account of what it would be like to have such an experience. Furthermore it places a very stringent condition upon such an account. The account, to be acceptable, must be so formulated that it would be found intelligible, indeed enlightening, by someone who had never had such an experience, and it imposes this condition as though this were the state that we are all in. It is at this point that, as I see it, the argument presumes against the existence of the experience in dispute.

Imagine that someone expressed some comcern about the experience of colour. He was not denying its existence, he explains. He wants only clarification. But the only clarification that he will accept is an account of colour experience that will inform those who are totally colour-blind what it is like to have such an experience. I am suggesting that we would find such a requirement tendentious.

The most effective defence that we can set up against the sceptic is to remind him, and ultimately ourselves, of the range of experiences to which human nature is exposed. As we start to move away from the simplest cases, of which I have instanced a pain in the ankle, we shall at first continue to find many kinds of experience to which phenomenology, if of ever increasing complexity, is still the best guide: for instance, the experience that we have when we are frightened and that we call butterflies in the stomach, or the oncoming of an epileptic attack, or the imminence of orgasm. But the last example introduces another way that we have of identifying experiences, which at a certain point takes over from the purely phenomenological criterion. It is structural, and it appeals to the place that the experience occupies in some pattern, whether of thought, or of feeling, or of both, that unfolds in our lives. Experiences that can be picked

out in this more contextual way include, in descending order of
specificity, feeling full after a meal, being amused by a joke, appre-
ciating the irony of a situation, sensing that one is wasting one's
time, let alone one's life. To decry these as experiences would
surely be narrow-mindedness, and it is presumably amongst them
that the disputed experience of satisfied desire would take its
place.

A seemingly more intractable, though in fact a shallower,
objection to the link between the satisfaction of desire and an
experience – shallower in that it finds no difficulty in the idea
of such an experience – is that the link would eliminate altogether the possibility that a person's desire could be satisfied after
his death. Such a consequence seems unacceptable, for what of
those who lay down their lives for the satisfaction of one of their
deepest desires? Surely they are not victims of some simple
mistake?

One way of meeting this objection would be to say that a
person's desire is satisfied if it comes true, or nearly so, and the
person would have experienced satisfaction, had he been alive to
do so, and his being alive is, the pursuit of the desire apart, an
empirical possibility. What the proviso 'the pursuit of the desire
apart' takes account of is the case where death is accepted by the
person as a necessary stage towards the attainment of his desire.
On this revised view, the fact that the woman who was devoted
to the liberation of her country could not conceivably have survived one thousand years to witness it gives us reason enough to
think that her desire was not satisfied when it came true.
However, the fact that the hero who dashed into battle in defence
of his ideals thereby made it impossible that he should live to see
their victory that evening is no impediment to our thinking of
what happened that day as the satisfaction of his desire, since
laying down his life was already accepted by him as the price he
would have to pay.

It is important that the experience of satisfied desire is not
misconstrued. Above all, it is important that the contribution that
it makes to the way in which desire motivates us is not misconstrued. For, if such an experience helps to reinforce whatever
motivational force a desire has, as I believe that it does, some-

thing that it most certainly does not do, and something that it would be totally erroneous to look for from it, is to provide us with an independent motive for acting on a desire, independent, that is, from the attraction that the object of the desire has for us. It is not as though we could intelligibly adopt, or assume, a desire for something to which we are indifferent so as to obtain the relevant experience when the desire was satisfied. The experience of satisfied desire is open to us, hence is something that we can look forward to, only in so far as we actually have the desire.[50] Think otherwise, and we are like a medieval king who, to cure himself of depression, hires a jester to tell him jokes, and, though he recognizes that some of the jester's jokes might be good, and some will certainly be bad, he anticipates that, either way round, he will be amused, and the vapours will lift.

The first version of the semantic view of satisfaction of desire, the examination of which is now concluded, is not the only version, and there will be some for whom the view, in this version, does not deserve its name. For of a view so called it might be expected that it should (one) tell us what satisfaction and frustration of desire are, and (two) do so by comparing the way in which satisfaction and frustration stand to desire to the way in which truth and falsehood stand to belief. But, in the present version, the view conspicuously does neither of these things. For (one) it tells us when a desire is satisfied, not what it is for it to be so, and – though I shall certainly make nothing further of this point – on the topic of frustration it is altogether silent. And (two), so far from comparing the way in which satisfaction stands to desire to the way in which truth stands to belief, it claims only that, when a desire is satisfied, truth applies to some component of what is assumed to be the canonical form of the ascription of desire. This seems to take us far short of the conclusion that satisfaction is a semantic category.

A second version of the semantic view aims to make good some of these deficiencies. Though it too skates over frustration of desire, the account that it offers of satisfaction links satisfaction and truth of belief by bringing them both under the broader semantic heading of fit. When and only when a belief is true, there is, it tells us, a fit between the belief and the world:

similarly, when and only when a desire is satisfied, there is a fit between the desire and the world.

One clear advantage that this version of the semantic view has over the previous version, and one which helps to justify its appellation, is that, when a desire is satisfied, the term to the semantic relation is, according to it, the desire itself, and not merely a constituent of the ascription of the desire. And this way of reconceiving the semantic relation and the terms it relates has the further advantage of freeing the view from the oratio obliqua thesis.[51]

But the new version of the theory does not stop here. Having brought truth of belief and satisfaction of desire under the common category of fit, the view now takes it upon itself to distinguish between the two, and this it attempts by introducing the interconnected notions of direction, and difference in direction, of fit. We are told that, when a belief is true, the belief must fit the world, but, when a desire is satisfied, it is the world that must fit the desire.[52]

To this way of making the distinction, there is an obvious objection. It is that fit, if it is to be in a position to do what is asked of it, if, that is, it is to subsume both the truth-relation and the satisfaction-relation, must be a symmetrical relation. But, if it is a symmetrical relation, then the notion of direction of fit is inapplicable. Let us look at this objection.

If fit is to be a relation under which both truth and satisfaction can be subsumed, then it must be a relation arrived at by a process of abstraction from the truth-relation and the satisfaction-relation. The process is a two-stage process, and it goes like this: First, we construct two new relations: one by disjoining 'is true of' and 'is made true by', the other by disjoining 'satisfies' and 'is satisfied by'. Both these new relations are clearly symmetrical. Secondly, from these two relations, we construct a third by disjoining them. This third relation is the relation of fit, and two things about it are obvious: (one) it can subsume both the truth-relation and the satisfaction-relation, and (two) it is symmetrical. Furthermore the two properties that the relation has are connected in that the first property requires the second. In other words, if fit is to subsume the two relations, which is the current way of showing that satisfaction is a semantic relation, then belief and desire cannot be distinguished by which way round, mind to world, or world to mind, the fit holds.

However this does not bring the matter to an end. For it seems that, once we have been introduced to the thought that, though there is something in common between the way in which belief stands to truth, and the way in which desire stands to satisfaction of desire, there is also some deep-seated difference between them, and that this difference requires for its elucidation the ideas of directionality and difference in direction, the preceding objection will not dispel it. What we are now likely to feel is that, if justice is to be done to this thought, what is called for is a change in the context in which fit is discussed. So far we have been discussing direction of fit in a static context, or as that relation which must hold timelessly between a belief, or a desire, and the world if the belief is true, or the desire satisfied. A suggestion is that we should shift the context so that now, while continuing to assume that, for a belief to be true, or a desire to be satisfied, there must be this timeless fit, we now discuss what must be done in time, first, in the case of belief, secondly, in the case of desire, if this fit is to be instantiated.

A first suggestion along these lines is this: If a belief of ours is to have that fit with the world which truth requires, this must be because we have brought it about that it fits the world, whereas, if a desire of ours is to have that fit with the world which satisfaction requires, this must be because we have brought it about that the world fits it. These requirements derive from the nature of, respectively, belief and desire.

The merits of this suggestion, which are real, will have to wait, but, as it stands, it is unacceptable. For it assumes that whether a certain belief of ours is true, or a certain desire of ours is satisfied, is, in each case, dependent upon what steps we have taken to bring this about. But this goes against both the nature of truth and the nature of satisfaction. Truth of belief and satisfaction of desire do not have to come about a certain way.

A new proposal begins by freeing the thesis of direction of fit from any connexion with the nature of belief or the nature of desire. It does so by making the thesis entirely prescriptive.[53] It envisages a situation in which a person has beliefs, some of which he knows not to be true, and desires, some of which are evidently not satisfied, and the person is determined to rectify this situation. He wants to know the best way of doing this, and, at this point, the freshly revised thesis comes to his rescue. It tells him that what he must do, and from the point of view, not just of efficacy, but of something closer to reasonableness, is the following: First of all, he must do something different in the two cases. In the case of his beliefs, he must leave the world exactly as it is, and he must alter his beliefs until they and it fit. But, in the case of his desires, he must leave them exactly as they are, and he must alter the world so that it and they fit.

In an important respect this proposal is a refinement of the previous proposal. For, while it gets rid of its defects, its merits, to which we may now turn, are preserved. For what it does is that it combines the competing intuitions of symmetry and directionality by showing that they are intuitions about different, though closely related, things. Fit between two things is symmetrical, but getting one thing to fit another is not: it is directional. If A fits B, B fits A, but getting A to fit B differs from getting B to fit A. The proposal exploits this fact by suggesting that, in order to bring about a state of affairs, which is itself symmetrical, we are well-advised to follow a strategy, which is non-symmetrical in structure. So, in trying to have true beliefs, we should leave the world alone, and alter the beliefs that we have until they and the world fit. By contrast, in trying to have satisfied desires, we should leave our desires alone, and bend the world as we find it until it and our desires fit. We must not be misled by the fact that if, and when, we are successful, the result can be equally well described by saying that our mind fits the world and by saying that the world fits our mind into thinking that there is no difference, in the run-up to this state of affairs, between a strategy of trying to alter our mind to fit the world – as we are recommended to do in the case of our beliefs – and one of trying to alter the world to fit our mind – as we are recommended to do in the case of our desires.

Given that the new proposal in no way grounds itself in the nature of belief or desire, one way of considering it is as offering us something that philosophy has long promised mankind: *an ethic of belief and desire*. The question arises: Is this an adequate ethic, either in whole or in part?

I start with the ethic of belief, and the proposal that we should always try to bring our beliefs into line with the world. That belief is inherently truth-directed is beyond doubt. But this, as it stands, leaves it open how strenuously a person should, at any particular moment of time, exert himself to see that his beliefs accord with the truth. For, in the first place, we cannot think globally, or of everything, all the time, and, secondly, even when we try to act locally, or to make certain that our beliefs are true in a certain area, and we do so by unearthing evidence so as to match belief against it, the maxim 'Enough is enough' must eventually take over.[54] Indeed we have already encountered one consideration that appears to favour, not just attenuation of, but deviation from, the proposed ethic: that is, the idea that it can be as crucial for us agents to have some beliefs rather than no beliefs as it is to have true beliefs rather than false beliefs.

And how ruthless with ourselves does the truth-directedness of belief require us to be? For are there not moments in the lives of people of the most honourable cast for whom the struggle to bring their beliefs into accord with the world can seem too difficult, or too painful, or too insignificant? In Jens Peter Jacobsen's haunting novel *Niels Lynne*, the hero of that name, the lifelong opponent of religion, who prayed to God when his son died and now cannot forgive himself for his backsliding, is dying from the wounds of battle. An old friend urges upon him the solaces of a pastor. The friend does so without cynicism, and utilitarianism controls the expression rather than the content of what he says. He is concerned only with Lynne's peace of mind. 'Ideas', he says, 'are good only for living; life is where they serve their purpose. Will it help a single human being if you die with one idea instead of another?'[55] Perhaps, when the issue was put thus explicitly to the old freethinker, he had no choice but to turn it down. But might it not have been as well for him if, in making his tortured way to death, he could have slid into illusion?

Finally, it is to be observed that the mechanism, already discussed, that we have inside ourselves that controls the way in which beliefs form and ramify, weaken and vanish, in direct response to the flow of evidence as it reaches us and breaks over us does much to make the very idea of an ethic of belief a superfluity. Human nature does for us, unprompted, most of what such an ethic asks us to do for ourselves.[56]

How adequate, we must next ask, is the proposed ethic for desire, when it requires that we should bring the world into line with our desires?

To this too a host of objections, but coming now from the opposite direction, arise. For, if the ethic is too hard upon belief, it is surely far too indulgent towards desire.

The crucial fact, already rehearsed, is that we all have many desires on which we are not moved to act. These desires, being desires of ours, give us reasons to act, but these are not reasons to which we are inclined to accede. And, in a number of cases, this is so for considerations that anything that could pass as an ethic of desire would have to sanction. Examples of such desires, which are a miscellaneous lot, are desires that are inconsistent with other and far more important desires of ours; desires that we feel should be implemented only if the rest of the society is like-minded; desires whose gratification we enjoy postponing; desires, sometimes quite trivial, sometimes meaning a lot to us, but which we could not abide others' even suspecting that we had; and, finally, in all of us to some measure, truly monstrous desires, which we renounce, but they are none the less still ours.[57] Does the ethic really require that, if a desire is ours, we should pursue it, and that is the end of the matter?

Furthermore, what of the injunction, cherished by many of the Ancients, which blends self-abnegation and self-interest, and suggests that, if we are to know happiness, we should trim our desires to the world?[58]

Such are the objections that may severally be brought against the two ethics. Is there any way of unifying them? I believe so. I believe that a unified criticism of the total ethic would be that, while professing to offer us a comprehensive ethic of belief and a comprehensive ethic of desire, in fact it provides us with, in each case, half an ethic. Furthermore what is missing from one ethic is the converse of what is missing from the other. In the case of belief, the ethic tells us which beliefs we should have, but it does not tell us what this requires of us: in the case of desire, it tells us what the desires we should have require of us, but it does not tell us which desires they are. Whether these defects can be fully remedied, and the broader question whether belief and desire admit of an ethic, let alone one that has this simple architecture, are matters not to be pursued here.

After this detour, I come back to the core of the semantic view itself, and ask whether the view is any more acceptable in the second than in the first version.

I have suggested how the second version avoids certain objections to which the first is susceptible. Nevertheless, in claiming that the satisfaction of desire is exclusively a matter of fit, the second version is as committed as its predecessor to the cardinal philosophical error of the depsychologization of the mental phenomenon it sets out to account for. This error reveals itself in the way that, of the two props on which the concept of desire rests, one being the object of desire, the other satisfaction or frustration of desire, it converts the latter into the mere shadow, positive or negative as the case may be, of the former.

11. I now return to the originating condition of emotion: The condition is met, I have claimed, when *a desire of ours is satisfied or it is frustrated, or it is in prospect of being one or the other: alternatively, we merely believe one or other of these things of it.*

This complex condition is in effect the result of expanding the notions of satisfaction and frustration, and in two distinct ways. First, we add to real cases of satisfaction and frustration cases where we merely believe our desires to have been satisfied or frustrated. Secondly, we add to actual cases of satisfaction and frustration cases where the satisfaction or frustration of our desires is anticipated, or seems to us to be probable. These two ways of expanding the two concepts can overlap. We might, for instance, believe of one of our desires that it will probably be satisfied, and be wrong. This would be a case of satisfaction at once prospective and merely believed-in.

Why do we need to expand the concepts of satisfaction and frustration in these two directions? If there is such a need, it must be because merely believed-in satisfaction and frustration, on the one hand, and anticipated, or prospective, satisfaction or frustration, on the other hand, are also, or can also be, effective in generating emotion: an efficacy that is derivative from, and can be compared to, that of satisfaction or frustration that is at once real and actual.

Is this so? Is there such efficacy? I shall consider in turn the two directions in which such efficacy is to be anticipated, hence in which the two notions are to be expanded.

12. First, then, the expansion of the notions of satisfaction and frustration beyond real satisfaction or frustration to include *merely believed-in satisfaction or frustration*.

On the face of it, the need for this expansion is unproblematic. For, in all contexts, or so it seems, false belief has an efficacy not to be distinguished from that of true belief. (A quite separate question is the efficacy of fictive beliefs, or of beliefs that are, and are held to be, no more than fictionally true, in originating emotion.)

However danger lurks in these seemingly clear waters. For it is tempting (one) to take the truism that false belief about the satisfaction or frustration of desire has the same efficacy in generating emotion as true belief, then (two) to conjoin this truism with what is widely held to be another truism, and is seemingly implicit in the history of emotion that I have given – namely, that real satisfaction or frustration, when it is efficacious, is always believed in – and thus (three) to draw the conclusion that emotion is invariably the effect of belief. Emotion, it would be concluded, is sometimes the effect of true belief and sometimes the effect of false belief: but, in neither case, has the world any direct part to play in its formation. Emotion is solely the product of belief.

To correct this view, I propose a tripartite division of emotions according to their origins. So we would have (one) emotions caused by false beliefs about the satisfaction or frustration of desire, (two) emotions caused by true beliefs about the satisfaction or frustration of desire, and (three) emotions caused by the satisfaction or the frustration itself. How does the third category, which seemingly also requires that the satisfaction or frustration is believed in, justify itself, or in what way does it differ from the second?

What is constitutive of cases where the emotion is caused by the satisfaction or frustration of desire itself is that the person lives through some event that brings it about that the desire is satisfied or frustrated. He lives through the event, with the consequence that the event causes at once the satisfaction or frustration of the desire and the formation of the emotion. However, having partly identified the satisfaction or frustration of a desire with an experience, I must now distinguish that experience, the experience of satisfaction or frustration, from the experience that I am now talking about, which is that of living through the satisfying or frustrating event. Whenever a desire is satisfied or frustrated, the person necessarily has the first kind of experience, but he has an experience of the second kind only sometimes, or in special circumstances. To get the measure of these special circumstances, I shall review three broadly different kinds of desire the satisfaction or frustration of which cannot be lived through. The object of the desire does not allow for it.

In the first place, the desire might be one for which there cannot be an event in which it is satisfied or frustrated. So, if I desire that there should be life after death, and not just for myself, but for humanity, there can be no event in which this desire is either satisfied or frustrated. True, there are certain events that will come about only if the desire is satisfied, such as interventions of the dead in the happenings of this world, and perhaps there are others that are attendant only upon its frustration, but none of these are events that would bring it about that the desire is satisfied or frustrated. What would bring about satisfaction of the desire − *per impossibile*, for I take the desire to be eternally frustrated − is less in the nature of an event, more like a rewriting of the whole human condition.

Secondly, the desire might be one that can be satisfied or frustrated in an event, but the event is not one that can be lived through. Or it is one that can be lived through but not by the person who has the desire. An example of each: If I desire that the ozone layer cease to suffer depletion, then there is an event in which this desire can be satisfied and probably another in which it can be frustrated, but neither event can be lived through. The events would be in the wrong place, and of the wrong dimensions. However, if my desire is that a letter that I send an absent friend for her birthday should come as a surprise, then, though there is an event in which this desire can be satisfied and probably another in which it can be frustrated, and both these events can be lived through, neither can be lived through by me.

Thirdly, though the desire is one that can be satisfied or frustrated in an event, and the event is one that can be lived through by the person who has the desire, the person chances, or perhaps chooses, not to do so. The soprano who satisfied her desire to sing at La Scala before she was twenty-five had also the desire to receive tumultuous acclaim at her first appearance. The audience was in the mood to satisfy this desire, but, as she was about to take her call, she slipped and broke her ankle, and, when news of the ovation was brought to her, she lay in anguish. Alternatively, sudden jealousy of the tenor decided her to keep to her dressing-room, and she depended on hearsay for her knowledge of the audience's response.

When none of these special circumstances hold, and a desire is satisfied or frustrated in an event that the person lives through, I shall say that it has been satisfied or frustrated *by acquaintance*.

If we now ask, Why should satisfaction or frustration by acquaintance, and the emotions that arise out of them, be in any way singled out for special attention?, it cannot be too strongly emphasized that my claim is not that such emotions are more real, more genuine, more authentic, emotions. They are in no sense more emotions than those in the genesis of which belief or imagination pulls more weight. No: the sole justification for picking them out is that they reveal, in a crystalline fashion, something of what all emotions are. When a desire of ours is satisfied or frustrated by acquaintance, the core of what happens is that we experience the impact of the world upon us in a way to which, as I have been putting it, we have been sensitized.

That we experience the impact of the world upon us is, of course, common to all cases where a desire of ours is satisfied or frustrated. For there must always be some experience of the world, some event that we live through, that, without necessarily satisfying or frustrating our desire, tells us of something that has. We read a letter telling us of our good luck: we hear the paper-boy in the street shouting of the outbreak of war. But, when the satisfaction or frustration of our desire is by acquaintance, so that the event through which we learn of its satisfaction or frustration is also that which causes it, then the experience of living through it impacts upon us with a kind of familiarity that is inexplicable without reference back to the desire.

If little can be said directly about the experience in which a desire of ours is satisfied or frustrated by acquaintance, some light can be thrown upon it by contrasting it with two other kinds of situation that we live through. In doing so, I shall concentrate on the case when the desire is *satisfied* by acquaintance. Frustration by acquaintance can be understood *mutatis mutandis*.

In both the contrasting situations, the world changes. In one situation, what I get from the change is that a belief of mine is confirmed: but the belief is not about something in which I take any particular pleasure. For instance, I believe that it is raining, I move my chair, I look out of the window, and I see the rain. I am right. In the other situation, what is distinctive for me about the change is that it gives me pleasure: but the pleasure does not arise because of something that I had antecedently desired. All winter I had forgotten about the sun, for no reason I look out of the window, and a burst of sunlight makes the view a scene of sudden delight. I am lucky.

These two situations with their core experiences flank the experience of satisfaction by acquaintance. One involves confirmation, but without pleasure: the other pleasure, but without confirmation. However error creeps in, error in the form of confusion, if we start to think that the experience of satisfaction by acquaintance can be arrived at by putting together, or blending, the element of confirmation characteristic of one experience with the element of gratification characteristic of the other. Familiarity, which lies at the centre of satisfaction by acquaintance, is not to be understood as the amalgam of elements that do not themselves involve desire. Once again, synthesis cannot do the work of insight.

I have introduced satisfaction and frustration of desire by acquaintance in order to counter the view that emotion invariably arises, not out of the impact of the world upon us, but out of belief about the impact of the world upon us. But does this new notion really counter it? For, when desire is satisfied or frustrated by acquaintance, is not the impact of the world still mediated by a belief of ours?

Let us, for the moment, continue to suppose – a supposition that I shall later have occasion to doubt – that, whenever a desire of ours has been satisfied or frustrated by acquaintance, there is a belief to that effect. Do we have to think that this belief is a link in a causal chain running from the satisfaction or frustration of the desire to the emotion? Might not it, the belief, and the emotion be twin effects of the satisfaction or the frustration? To this there is a parallel in the case of perception. For, when we perceive something, standardly the belief that there is a particular object out there does not mediate between the object perceived and the perceptual experience, thus bringing it about that the latter is of, or has as its object, the former. Rather the belief and the perceptual experience are both caused by the object perceived. From the fact, if it is a fact, that there is no perception without belief it cannot be inferred that perception is dependent upon belief rather than upon the world.[59]

13. Secondly, the expansion of satisfaction and frustration of desire beyond actual satisfaction and frustration to include *prospective*, or *probable, satisfaction, or frustration*.

Why should we believe, as this expansion appears to presuppose, that the promise of satisfaction or the threat of frustration has the same efficacy as the actual thing?

But, first, the removal of a possible source of confusion.

For, if it is a fact that desires can be satisfied or frustrated prospectively as well as actually, it is also a fact, and a further fact, that desires can be for prospective as well as for actual objects, and these two facts interact in ways that can confuse the present issue. Imagine that we know that someone has a desire that is – to put it broadly – directed on to a certain state of affairs, and that this state of affairs has become probable. Initially we might think that such a situation could bring the desire only prospective satisfaction. But this would show that we assumed the desire to be of one out of two possible kinds of desire. We were assuming that the desire, in being directed on to a certain state of affairs, was a desire for its actuality. But the desire could be a desire merely for its probability or likelihood. In that case, that the state of affairs had become probable would, or could, bring actual satisfaction.

A man desires to marry the love of his life. A woman desires to become Governor of California. At a certain moment, all is set for the man to marry: the identifiable barriers, which certainly existed, have been surmounted, and it is not anticipated that there will be others. The woman is, the polls suggest, the front runner: it is hard to see what can stop her now. In both cases, satisfaction of their desires has been brought into prospect. For actual satisfaction of their desires, more is needed: the man's actual marriage, the woman's actual election. The two desires are of the first kind: they are for actualities.

However there could be another man, another woman, for whom this very situation spelt actual satisfaction. For what the man desired was that his marriage to the woman of his choice should be probable, what the woman desired was that her election to office should be likely. Each desire being for something prospective, when the right thing comes into prospect, the desire gains actual satisfaction. Indeed – though we are not asked to suppose this – it might be that actual marriage, actual election, should these things come about, would turn out to satisfy neither the person's desire nor the person. These two desires are of the second kind: they are for something prospective.

To these illustrative examples someone might object, along lines to which we are now averted, that it is only through mis-describing the desires of the persons involved that it can look as though a mere probability could bring a desire actual satisfaction. Had the desires and their objects been properly described, it would have been clear that the second man and woman, just as much as the first man and woman, desired actualities, and therefore only actualities could satisfy their desires. Where the second man and woman differ from the first is in the actualities that they desire. The second man, unlike the first, does not want a wife: the second woman, unlike the first, does not want high office. What each wants is the removal of certain obstacles in the way of a particular goal, and the removal of the disliked obstacle would invariably be an actuality. The man wants that his past, the woman wants that her sex, not be regarded as a barrier to something to which it is felt to be irrelevant. Each desires assurance that such prejudices are not the way of the world.

But, though there certainly could be a third pair of people of whom this would be true, cannot we also believe that, alongside them, there could be people for whom the removal of specific obstacles is not as such important, but for whom the attainment of a probability is? They would be people who had a desire the object of which they envisaged through aiming off from the object of another desire, which they didn't have.

Who is to say that there could not be such people, and such desires?

Before returning to the theoretical divergencies underlying these different sets of anecdotes, I want to acknowledge what is an artificiality in the sharp contrast I have drawn between desires for certain states of affairs and desires that such states of affairs should be probable. The contrast can be validly drawn, but it belongs very much to a philosopher's way of looking at desires, something which has been under continuous criticism throughout these lectures. At the very least, this way of looking at desires needs to be supplemented.

Ordinarily, when we desire a certain state of affairs, our desire sensitizes us to that state of affairs, and this means, amongst other things, that, in the fulness of time, or as the state of affairs reaches its natural term, its coming about seems likelier. Reassurance on this score is not, of course, made necessary by the conditions of satisfaction of the desire. Nevertheless it is integral to the desire, and to what I have called the life of the desire. Desires would certainly play a very different role in our lives if we treated it as a matter for equanimity whether, as the time drew near, the signs were that they would be satisfied, and if satisfaction of a desire regularly arrived like a bolt out of the blue. The former being, I suggest, the mental set in which desire is normally framed, a desire for a certain state of affairs is invariably accompanied by, and therefore cannot be readily contrasted with, the desire that this state of affairs will become probable. Or, if not a desire, then at least a hope, an expectation, along these lines.

Let us, for the time being, think of the contrast that I have introduced as one between desires for states of affairs and desires *merely* for the probability of such states of affairs.

And now I return to the question of the theoretical disagreement between those who think that desires of this second kind are feasible and those who deny this. The disagreement, I believe, concerns the status that objects of desire must have. For one side thinks that objects of desire can include mere probabilities or prospects. The other side thinks that this is out of the question.

In point of fact, it is not relevant to my case to establish the matter either way. For all that I am concerned to show is that, if there are desires for probabilities, which I see no reason to doubt, their actual satisfaction needs to be distinguished from the prospective satisfaction of desires that are for actualities. And this is only a prelude to the question whether prospective satisfaction or frustration should be included in the originating condition of emotion.

So I ask, Why should we think that the mere promise of satisfaction, or the mere threat of frustration, has the same efficacy in generating emotion as the actual thing?[60]

The immediate response is that this is not what we are being asked to think. The rationale for including prospective, alongside actual, satisfaction or frustration in the originating condition of emotion is indeed similar to that for including merely believed-in, alongside real, satisfaction or frustration. Similar, but not the same. For, if a mere belief about satisfaction or frustration invariably has the efficacy of the real thing, all that is claimed on behalf of anticipation is that it can have the same efficacy as the actual thing. For it actually to have this efficacy, more factors must be added.

To see why this should be so, we must first recognize that there are two distinct ways in which anticipation of satisfaction or frustration might precipitate emotion. In only one of these ways can it be held to constitute a special form, or variant, of the originating condition of emotion.

Indisputably anticipation can so completely take us over that we come to believe that our desire has actually been satisfied or frustrated, and, on the basis of this delusion, emotion forms. But, when that happens, it is no more than a special instance of the way in which merely believed-in satisfaction or frustration generates emotion. There is nothing peculiar to anticipation in all this. The way in which emotion forms that is peculiar to anticipation, and therefore gives us reason to expand the originating condition of emotion, works, not through delusion, but through the imagination. What happens is that we anticipate satisfaction or frustration to the point of imagining actual satisfaction or frustration, and imagining actual satisfaction or frustration can – *can*, it must be emphasized – come to generate the emotion that the situation we imagine would induce, were it actual. And, when imagination does this, it does so solely through its special phenomenology, and the causal efficacy that this phenomenology gives it, without any subversion of belief. We continue to be aware that our desire has not been actually satisfied or frustrated.[61]

The efficacy of anticipation rests, as this brief account makes clear, upon manifestly more substantive features of our psychology than does that of false belief, and this may be why it has attracted less philosophical attention.

14. With the argument of the last section before us, we might now clarify its terminology by making explicit a distinction between the prospect, or anticipation, of satisfaction and prospective satisfaction – and *mutatis mutandis* for frustration. The prospect of satisfaction is simply a belief that the person has, as the conditions for this event appear to be drawing near, that one of his desires is about to be satisfied. Sometimes the prospect of satisfaction will, for one reason or another, excite trepidation in the person. But, on other occasions, it will be greeted with pleasure, and, on a certain number of such occasions, the imaginative process described above will be set in train, the prospect of satisfaction will be more or less functionally equivalent to satisfaction, and this I call prospective satisfaction.

Thus described, the prospect of satisfaction and prospective satisfaction, and likewise the prospect of frustration and prospective frustration, require no alteration to fit smoothly into the characteristic history of an emotion. They can take their place in its preliminary stages, which run, (one) desire, (two) satisfaction or frustration of desire, and (three) formation of emotion. They help to constitute the engine that propels the sequence.

But now we must consider another role that specifically the prospect of frustration and prospective frustration can play, which certainly introduces a complexity into the history.

To grasp this complexity, I propose to borrow from a later stage in the history a distinction, which, there applied to the attitude, also holds for the emotions. The distinction is between the *positive* and the *negative* emotions. The positive emotions are those in which our attitude towards their object is favourable, or we look upon it with pleasure, and the negative emotions are those in which our attitude is unfavourable, or we look upon the object of the emotion with unpleasure. Standardly, though not invariably, the positive emotions arise out of satisfied desire, and the negative emotions out of frustrated desire. The negative emotions, which conspicuously outnumber the positive emotions, include hate, anger, loathing, envy, jealousy, resentment, ingratitude, fear, terror, bitterness, scorn, disgust, dislike, indifference, hardness of heart, guilt, shame, regret, remorse, sorrow, melancholy, shyness, indifference, despair, and doubtless others, whereas the positive emotions seem restricted to love, joy, tenderness, gratitude, admiration, compassion, hope, and perhaps pity and pride. It is to be noted that an emotion is none the less positive because, once formed, it may regularly bring in train, largely through the reflexion it induces in the person upon his present condition, unpleasure. For instance, love is a positive emotion, though it may well give rise to despair, and gratitude may induce resentment. There are also emotions that are not necessarily touched by either pleasure or unpleasure, hence are neither positive nor negative, such as amazement, surprise, and confusion.[62]

I take up the role that the prospect of frustration can play in the development of emotion, and I introduce it through a consideration of an initially somewhat puzzling passage in Seneca's *De Ira*.[63]

Seneca has, in line with a tradition of ancient wisdom, been denouncing, first, anger, and then the display of anger, which he regards as reinforcing anger. He then holds up for our admiration two men, whom he treats as equally commendable. In his eyes they display similar self-control in situations of comparable provocation. One, Pastor, a Roman knight, accepted the hospitality of Caligula on the very night that his son, whom the emperor had just condemned to death on the flimsiest of charges, was lying in prison awaiting execution. The other, Priam, King of Troy, venturing into the Greek camp to beg for the dead body of his son Hector, fell to the ground, and, in a gesture that was to be famous across the centuries, embraced the knees of Achilles, who had killed Hector in single combat.

At first sight it might seem that the two cases clearly differ in that Pastor's desire to have his son alive had been only prospectively frustrated, whereas Priam's desire had been actually frustrated. Seneca, who cannot have overlooked this difference, ignores it, and, while it is true that the two cases rival one another in horror, and no-one would choose to be in the situation of one father rather than the other, we might still ask, Why did not Seneca give more weight to the difference?

One explanation is that Seneca, moving somewhat along the lines I have already proposed, reconstructed what went on in Pastor's mind in the following way: Placed in a truly terrible situation, he, while continuing to recognize the fact that his son was still alive, knew that it would be vain to derive any comfort from this fact. Accordingly he allowed his imagination to fill in the gap between the anticipated and the actual frustration of his desire so that, when he came to sit down to dinner with the Emperor, it was for him, in attitude though not in belief, as if he were sitting down with his son's murderer. He was supping, we might say, with *his* Achilles, if not worse.

But there is also another different way in which Seneca might have construed what went on in Pastor's mind.

In the last section, in trying to highlight the idea of prospective satisfaction and frustration, I contrasted two different kinds of desire: desires for certain states of affairs, and desires that these states of affairs should merely be probable. The contrast emerges when we consider the different conditions under which each kind of desire is satisfied. The contrast, it might be said, pairs off each ordinary event-desire with a more exiguous counterpart of that desire. And now I want to construct a new contrast within desire, which has the effect of pairing off each ordinary event-desire with a more exigent counterpart of that desire. The more exigent counterpart is the desire that there should be no chance of this event's not coming about, or that nothing could stop its doing so.

The proposal that I now want to make – and this is what I claim that Seneca perhaps discerned at work in the case of Pastor – is that the prospect of frustration, and further the prospect of the negative emotion that will form in the aftermath of frustration, causes the desire that will be frustrated to give way to its more exigent counterpart. Or, at least, it causes a situation to arise in which it is no longer possible to tell which desire it is that the person has: equally it is no longer possible to say whether the emotion that is about to form will form in response to merely prospective, or to actual, frustration.

If this proposal is applied to the case of Pastor, then, as he was dining with Caligula, the horror that he foresaw forming at his son's death meant that the desire from which he suffered was no longer, as it had once been, the desire, which any father might have, that his son should live: it was now the desire that the shadow of execution should altogether pass from their lives. With this new desire clearly frustrated – and we may believe that it was in order to see the marks of its frustration on Pastor's face that Caligula had asked him to dine, instructing him in particular to come with a smiling face – Pastor was in a state barely to be distinguished from that of Priam.

The claim that subsequent emotion can modify preceding desire, carrying, as it does, some implication of backward causation, is bound to seem puzzling so long as we envisage it as occurring on discrete and comparatively isolated occasions. However enlarge the time frame, and we can then observe a process that, unfolding in successive phases, works its way into our psychology. The phases run like this: First, we form a desire. Then we are led to anticipate its frustration. However, either because the desire seems so likely to be frustrated or because we so dread the negative emotion that we expect to ensue, we, in anticipating the frustration of the desire, find ourselves anticipating the onset of the emotion itself. This is painful to do. So we now form another desire, intended to push the emotion away from us. This the new desire will achieve, if it is satisfied. For the desire is, not merely that what would frustrate the original desire should not happen, but that there should be no chance of this happening. Unfortunately, given that this is what the desire is for, there are two consequences. One is that this desire is likelier to be frustrated than the original desire. The other is that, when it is frustrated, the unwanted emotion will still ensue. What was intended to push the emotion away has only brought it nearer. And so a third desire forms, standing to the second desire as it stands to the original desire, with predictable results.

The overall result of this process, repeated over time, is that our psychology is so modified that, when a desire of the first kind is about to form, its place will be taken by a desire of the second kind, which, in turn, will be overtaken by a desire of the third kind. And so on.

There is at least one emotion, one negative emotion, where this play between emotion and the desires out of which the emotion forms is so enmeshed in our lives that we take it for granted. We leave it unexamined. That emotion is fear, and the factor through which the interaction takes place is danger. For danger lies on the interface between desire and fear. We desire to avoid danger, and, if our efforts are fruitless, and danger is not avoided, fear ensues. However fear, and, for that matter, the prospect of fear, enlarges what we take as danger, and this in turn means that there are more and more things that we desire to avoid.

The mercurial nature that is forced upon danger by the pivotal role that it has to play between desire and emotion is evident as soon as we start to ask, What is danger? When is danger upon us? When have we avoided it? When have we passed through it? What makes these questions so hard to answer are the diversity and flexibility of danger.

Let us look at these two aspects of danger in turn, and I shall illustrate them from danger in times of war.

First, the diversity of danger: A young reservist has just volunteered for a desperate counter-attack against an enemy of superior strength, which is securely dug in. A second man lives in a frontline town, through which the reservists pass on their way up to the start-line. The town has, for the past few weeks, been subjected to continual bombardment, and the man comes out of his shelter to cheer on the reservists. The shelling resumes, and he dives back in. A third man lives in a town a few miles away, the other side of a mountain range, which has so far escaped the ravages of war. But not for much longer, for rumour has it that this is where the enemy will open a new front. All three men could be said to be in danger's way, which they desire to avoid, but each man desires to avoid something different. All three men are susceptible to fear, but, in each case, the fear has a very different object.

As to, secondly, the flexibility of danger, let us narrow our focus, and watch a change as it comes over the young reservist. Initially, as he moved up into the attack, he was in the grip of the heroics of war, and he thought that danger was the moment when the sniper's bullet would crash into his skull. But, gradually, as the battle wears on, his thinking changes, and now he contrasts the danger when he has to charge across open ground, and the comparative safety when he finds cover in the dead ground, or from the line of the hedge. Later, as his companions fall around him, he recognizes that battle is danger, and that he had reason to be frightened as soon as it was joined, and he heard the shells going overhead, and the machine gun fire passing close by. At the end of the attack, as he sits on the objective, he realizes that he was in danger from the very moment that he volunteered. In future, he will know better. He will recognize danger earlier on. There will be more situations that he will desire to avoid.

Montaigne said famously, 'The thing I fear most is fear.'[64] In saying this, he was drawing attention to the way that fear attracts fear. Many, perhaps most, negative emotions serve as magnets for themselves: hate for hate, anger for anger, and fear for fear. Each emotion brings this about in its own way, and the particular interest of fear is that the mechanism by which this happens, or the moving target of danger, is so conspicuous. Under the cloak of fear, the idea of danger ramifies, and so do the aversive desires, the object of each desire standing to that of its predecessor as likelihood to actuality.

15. The phenomenon that we have been considering can, like many others discussed in these lectures, be turned round upon itself to serve a defensive purpose. Instead of there being more and more things that we desire to avoid as we think of more and more things as dangerous, we invert the process. We rigidly refuse to see certain situations as dangerous, because otherwise we should have to think of them as frustrating certain desires that we have. We refuse to think of them in this way so as to be able to deny that we have these desires. We say to ourselves, Here there is nothing to fear, for here there is nothing that we desire.

This theme too resonates with the grandeurs and miseries of war, but, in 'The Beast in the Jungle', Henry James tellingly illustrates it from the vicissitudes of everyday life.[65] John Marcher, the gentle protagonist, self-preoccupied, but with little self-knowledge, has had, from his earliest years, the presentiment that he was being kept for something exceptional that would, sooner or later, befall him. He excused himself alike from the pleasures and from the responsibilities with which other people occupy themselves on the grounds, kept, with one exception, to himself, that he ought to make ready for this event: he should be prepared for what he called 'the beast to jump out'. He could not, for instance, ask a woman to share the life over which this danger hung. His sole confidante is a woman with whom he regularly discusses his predicament. Each time they meet they talk about his fears, but each time he has essentially nothing to add.

Then too late, or after a lifetime spent nursing his fears, he comes to realize that there are other views, other understandings, of what constitutes danger, and, if these views are less dramatic, the dangers to which they would have alerted him were ultimately worse than that which he allowed to engross his life. The one person to whom he confided his great fear, the one person in his life, we might say, dies from a painful disease, declaring her love for him only as she does so. He goes abroad for a year, but the great revelation overtakes him only as, on his return, he goes to the cemetery where she is buried. There, at the neighbouring grave, he sees in the face of a man 'the image of scarred passion'. Graver than losing his life, which is how he mostly thought of his fate, is not to have had a life worth living. By thinking that life contained one supreme danger, that there was really only one thing that he needed to fear, that there was one desire whose frustration was to be avoided at all costs, he was able to put his other desires, supremely the desire for love, to give it, to receive it, out of his mind. This was the desire whose frustration, we must assume, he feared most, and the irony is that the one person who could have satisfied it, he chose to regale with the fear he had substituted for it.

16. I take up a general query raised in the penultimate section.

Putting together the findings of this lecture, we can identify four different occasions on which emotion can form: a desire has been satisfied or frustrated; a desire has been satisfied or frustrated, and the person has lived through the event that has caused the desire to be satisfied or frustrated; a desire has not been satisfied or frustrated, but it is believed to have been; and, finally, a desire is about to be satisfied or frustrated, and its satisfaction or frustration has been fully anticipated. Is it really correct to think, in all these cases, that, as I have been suggesting, the relation in which the person stands to the satisfaction or frustration of his desire is best described as one of belief?

I am prepared to think that standardly the relation is one of belief, but it also seems well within the character of emotion that it should tolerate non-standard cases. In saying this, I am thinking, not merely of the role of imagination, often insisted upon, in the formation of emotion, but also of forms of conviction that fall short of, or are perhaps to one side of, that form of assent which is belief. We take it for granted that our desire has been satisfied: dreading the worst, we assume that our desire has been frustrated: we don't want to know, and our natural optimism, or pessimism, takes over: we fall victim to suggestion.[66]

17. In the next lecture I shall, amongst other things, consider the attempt, ancient and modern, to classify the emotions somewhat

differently: that is, not solely in terms of their origins, but also, like desires, in terms of their objects. This is a more established procedure, about which I shall be led to two conclusions. The first will be that this form of classification is, despite its standing, certainly not more, and is probably less, fundamental. The second will be that there is quite a considerable overlap between the two classifications. So, for instance, it has been proposed that we should distinguish between emotions that are directed towards things that we believe to be the case and emotions that are directed towards things that we do not believe to be the case. If we free this proposal from the assumptions with which it has been encumbered – specifically, the oratio obliqua thesis – it is closely related to the proposal that I have been considering: that we should distinguish between emotions that are generated by actual satisfaction or frustration, and emotions that are generated by anticipated satisfaction or frustration. But neither my proposal nor the proposal that it replaces gives us what anyhow we do not need: a classification that divides the emotions as such rather than their instances.

I mention this to give warning that some of the material that I have been discussing in this lecture will reappear. But some will not: it will be assumed.

LECTURE TWO

AS THE EMOTION FORMS

1. In the first lecture I set out the originating condition of emotion.

This condition, I maintained, is to be understood in terms of the satisfaction or frustration of desire, or, more precisely, of an expansion of these concepts. The expansion consists in including merely believed-in satisfaction or frustration alongside the real thing, and prospective or anticipated satisfaction or frustration alongside the actual thing. The aim of this expansion is to have under a single heading all the vicissitudes of desire that can, in appropriate circumstances, generate emotion.

2. I now continue the history of emotion, as it stretches forward beyond the originating condition.

I take it up at stage (three): *We trace the satisfaction or frustration to some thing or fact that we regard as having precipitated it.*

It is crucial to recognize that the tendency to respond to satisfaction or frustration of desire in this way is deep-seated in our nature. We might not have had such a tendency. But we do. However some of the terms used to characterize this tendency call for comment.

First, *thing or fact*. My reason for using this disjunction rather than some comprehensive term is that it reminds us that we attribute the satisfaction or frustration of our desires sometimes to some thing that is a constituent of a fact, and sometimes to a fact, of which things are constituents. The distinction between the two cases is important for the study of the emotions, and it is arguable that the first case, or one special instance of it − that is, when the thing is a person − enjoys primacy. This is supported by the frequency with which, when we do pick upon a fact as the precipitating factor, we assimilate it to a person. We anthropomorphize the fact. We are grateful to the fact, or resentful of it, though a fact merits neither attitude. To emphasize the significance of persons in the generation of emotion, I shall often use as the appropriate disjunction, not 'thing or fact', but the more specific, less exhaustive, 'figure or fact'.

Secondly, *precipitate*. To regard something as precipitating something else is to make a causal ascription. But 'precipitate' is no synonym of 'cause'. As we have just seen, things can be said to precipitate satisfaction or frustration of desire, even though, strictly speaking, a thing, an individual thing, cannot cause anything. Causation is the prerogative of events, of which things are only parts.[1]

However what crucially singles out the precipitating factor is, over and above its causal role, that it is that to which, under the impact of satisfaction or frustration, our thoughts turn – turn and cling. Our thoughts turn to this factor because of the part we credit it with having played in causing the satisfaction or frustration, and, as to the further question why they cling to it, there will be no single answer. Old patterns of pleasure and sorrow heavily influence what our thoughts adhere to.

To show how we can think, sometimes of things, sometimes of facts, as precipitating the satisfaction or frustration of a desire of ours, let us consider two imaginary examples.

The first example is this: An unattached man, whose life has been rewarding but dull, meets at a party an old love of his, who, some years earlier, had left him for another. In the course of the evening she makes it clear to him that, if he is likely to be interested in her, she is prepared to have her interest in him reawakened. At a stroke an almost forgotten desire of his, the desire that she should think well of him, has been revived and satisfied. Now there are several directions in which his thoughts may go. They may turn to the woman herself, who miraculously, or out of the blue, is once again prepared to return his love: they may turn to the woman's husband, to whom she had been obsessively attached, and who had suddenly and decisively tired of her: or they may turn to the extraordinary coincidence that has brought them together, and at a moment when they are prepared to see each other in a fresh light. The different directions in which the man's thoughts may turn are directions to which they may cling.

The second example is this: A harsh political regime has been instituted in the country of a man, a liberal who fervently desires that none of his fellow-citizens should suffer unnecessarily: he longs for an end to the deliberate infliction of suffering. Rumours are now rife that police squads roam the streets after dark and make random arrests, and then one day he learns that an acquaintance of his has been picked up and savagely tortured. A deep desire of his has been frustrated, and, under the impact of this frustration, his thoughts too may go various ways. They may turn to the torturer, whom, of course, he cannot identify as such: they may turn to the woman, who was, he knows, little interested in politics: or they may turn to the new social reality of his country, which seems to require that, a few hundred yards from where he lives in comfort, innocent people should be maimed by those hired to do so. His thoughts may turn in any one of these directions, and cling.

These two examples have a common structure. Desire having been either, as in the first case, satisfied or, as in the second case, frustrated, there then ensues competition to be the precipitating factor – competition, that is, to secure the person's enduring attention – and, in each example, there are three competing factors: two things, specifically two figures, who are parts of the cause of the satisfaction or the frustration, and a fact, which might be thought to be the cause itself.

The examples make two further points.

The first is that a figure can precipitate the satisfaction or frustration of a desire without necessarily intending to do so: that is, without intending either to satisfy or to frustrate the desire as such, or to do that which, in the circumstances, brings that about. The torturer, who frustrated the old liberal's desire, could not have intended to do just that, since he did not know of the liberal's existence, though he certainly did intend to do that which had this effect: he intended to inflict upon his victims grave and gratuitous suffering. The husband, who suddenly tired of his wife with the result that her old lover's desire could be satisfied, intended, we may be sure, neither the one nor the other.

The second point is that the figure who precipitates an emotion need in no way be responsible for the satisfaction or frustration of the desire from which the emotion flows. In so far as responsibility involves intention plus something else, the imputation of reponsibility seems doubly wrong.

It might be objected that insistence upon the precipitating factor as wholly or partially causal of the satisfaction or frustration of desire sits uneasily with the broad understanding of satisfaction and frustration that was advocated in the last lecture. For, if a desire of ours is not really satisfied or frustrated, but is merely believed to be so, or, if it is not actually satisfied or frustrated, but is only anticipated to be so, is it not implausible to think that, at such junctures, our thoughts will turn in the direction of what caused, in the one case, the merely believed-in, or, in the other case, the prospective satisfaction or frustration? For that would mean that our thoughts will turn, in the first case, to a false belief, or, in the second case, to a prediction. The likelier directions are towards what we falsely believe has caused real satisfaction or frustration or towards what we anticipate will cause actual satisfaction or frustration. When Malvolio falsely believed that his desire for the love of Maria was satisfied, his thoughts turned, not to his delusion nor to those aspects of himself which had induced it, but to whatever feelings he erroneously believed had been aroused in her by his qualities.[2] When Richard II anticipated that his desire for the return of kingly state would soon be frustrated, his thoughts turned, not to his own prescience, which, though so little in evidence throughout his troubled reign, now informed him that it was all but over, but to the fragile fate of kings, in which he saw himself about to be ensnared.[3]

It follows that, in order to employ, across the whole originating condition, a causal notion of the precipitating factor, we must stretch our understanding of causation *pari passu* with our understanding of satisfaction and frustration. In those cases where we falsely believe that our desire has been satisfied or frustrated, cause needs to be expanded to include what we falsely believe to have caused the satisfaction or frustration: in those cases where we anticipate the satisfaction or frustration of our desire, cause needs to be expanded to include what we anticipate will cause its satisfaction or frustration.

And there are further ways in which we must expand or adapt our understanding of cause if, as we cast our net ever wider in order to catch what plays the role of the precipitating factor, we are to go on thinking of what we haul in as causally related to the satisfaction or frustration of our desire.[4] We must, for instance, bring into the causal fold cases where the precipitating factor is something that includes the cause within its intentional content. When Hardy's Farmer Boldwood believed, falsely, that a desire of his to which he had paid very little attention, the desire to be loved, was about to be satisfied, and by someone whom he barely knew, his thoughts turned, not to her, not to the feelings she might or might not have for him, but to the one communication that had passed between them, the unfortunate Valentine, sent by her light-heartedly, which, with its peremptory message, 'Marry me', seemed to tell him all he needed to know.[5] In such a case, the precipitating factor is the message. Then a case beyond this. When Bérénice, after five years of dallying in Rome, waiting for Titus to marry her, learns that his sense of duty as the newly proclaimed Emperor forbids him to marry her, a foreign queen, she vents her fury, not upon Titus, not upon the traditions of Imperial Rome, not upon the decision he makes out of deference to them, but upon her faithful friend, her unhappy suitor, Antiochus. Antiochus attracts her rage only because he had, against all his inclinations, promised Titus that he would carry the message.[6] In this case, the precipitating factor is the messenger, who brings her the message, which imparts to her what causes the frustration of her desire. If the message is at one causal remove, the messenger is at two, from what in fact satisfies or frustrates the desire. But the mind, in pursuing the precipitating factor, readily leaps over these stages.

The direction in which a person's thoughts will, under satisfaction or frustration, turn and cling cannot be prized apart from what specific emotion it is that forms. This link holds both ways round. Not only will the direction in which the thoughts turn influence the emotion that forms, but the emotion as it forms will reinforce the direction in which the thoughts cling.

An example: A man is left by a woman with whom he has been living for some time. His friends are worried on his behalf. What, they wonder, will happen to him? Schematically we can predict the emotional outcome thus: If the man's thoughts turn predominantly towards the woman who has gone away, his emotion will be despair; if his thoughts turn predominantly towards the man for whom she has left him, he will be jealous; if his thoughts circle round and round the many preoccupations, and responsibilities, and forms of indolence or self-indulgence, that, over the years, gradually, surely, separated them, he will feel regret, or remorse, or sadness. Conversely, as despair creeps over the man, he will think more and more about the woman who has left him: as jealousy dominates him, the man who has replaced him will be seldom out of his thoughts: and, if he gives way to regret, he will torture himself with the question what it was in him, in her, that so inevitably drove them apart.

In all this, what we must not lose sight of is that what we are discussing are different emotions, which have different natures, which follow different histories, and which take different objects. Error is to think that there is one undifferentiated thing, which is emotion itself, and which we call by different names depending on the particular circumstances in which it arises, or on the particular cause of which it is the effect, or on the particular object on which it is focussed, even though these varying circumstances, and causes, and objects, might leave no other mark on the emotion.

3. Now to the next stage in the history of an emotion: (four) *An attitude develops*. Here we approach the core of the emotion.

It has been a welcome development in recent years that philosophers have come to recognize the place of an attitude or orientation within emotion.[7] An attitude is to be distinguished at once from a belief, and from a desire. But, without recognition of the developmental dimension to this attitude, the nature of emotion is still not properly apprehended.

A broad claim that I shall advance is that the attitude in emotion is fundamentally a variation upon, or a transform of, the original experience of satisfaction or frustration of desire. It is for this reason that the emotion, in its primary role of colouring the world or some part of it, also memorializes the past in which it originates. It does not escape its origins.

The transformation of the experience of satisfaction or frustration into an attitude admits of grades, or levels, of complexity. I shall identify three different grades, and, starting with the first, or least complex, shall ascend through them.

At its least complex, the transformation of experience is abridged, and what forms in its wake falls short of an attitude, hence of an emotion. What forms is a mere disposition to repeat or to revive the experience of satisfaction or frustration. The revived experience retains the original tone of pleasure or un-pleasure, and also the original agglomeration of thoughts that satisfaction or frustration of a desire can be expected to induce. These would include thoughts about the desire, thoughts about what the desire was for, thoughts about satisfaction or frustration, thoughts about what satisfaction or frustration of this particular desire means to the person, and thoughts about the figure or fact that precipitated it. Indeed how, without some of the original toning, without some of the original body of thought, could we think of the revived experience as just that? Or, better, how could that be what it was?

However, even in these truncated cases, there are two ways in which the revived experience departs from the original experience. In the first place, it lacks the original element of surprise. Secondly, it is permeant. The new experience permeates or infiltrates adjacent or resembling mental states so that they take on something of what the original experience was like.

So: The man whose desire for an old love was miraculously satisfied through a chance encounter starts to think, for no good reason, of an absent friend, and, as he does so, the revived experience of satisfaction spreads outwards, and he feels pleased that he has such a friend. He reaches for the telephone. The liberal whose desire for reconciliation in his country was frustrated by the introduction of torture goes for a walk along the city walls, a place long associated for him with the beauty of something ancient, and straightaway the experience of frustration recurs like an ache, and the walk, which he used to enjoy, he no longer does. The brambles, the cartons thrown into the river, the detritus of picnics and surreptitious love-making, scar a place he had known and loved since a child. In each case, as the experience is recreated, the satisfaction, the frustration, spills out of the mental state and, in the one case, creates a glow around an old friend, and, in the other, spoils a familiar pleasure. Meanwhile, thoughts of the life that is about to dawn, thoughts of the new regime of terror, are never far away.

If none of this quite adds up to an attitude, the central reason is that the colouring of adjacent experiences, which where the revived experience comes closest to an attitude, is too arbitrary and too transient. It would be different if there were a better reason why certain parts of the world had been selected to be coloured, and if the colouring were more enduring.

It is on this first level, where there is mere repetition, that we find many instances of joy, rage, and sadness: though this is not to suggest that any specific emotion occurs on just one level of complexity. What occurs on the first level is close to a mood, though moods, of which amusement and boredom are examples, are at once less transient and more permeant. Someone who is truly bored is likely to be bored by everything to which his attention turns. Someone truly amused finds the world an amusing place. It is here that we should locate the so-called objectless emotions.[8]

I move up to the second grade of complexity.

It is here that something that is fully an attitude develops, and an emotion proper forms. Now the original experience of satisfaction or frustration undergoes, not repetition, but a transformation. There is a turning outward, a turning inside out, of the experience. The experience is, in the original sense of that term, extroverted. And let us not forget that, when the experience is extroverted, the experience remains inseparable from the thoughts about the desire and the satisfaction of the desire. This is the memorialization of desire in emotion.

To this extroversion there are several aspects.

In the first place, extroversion does something, it achieves something, for the person. It moves the person on from a state in which he is basically immured in a prior experience to one in which he increasingly concentrates upon what brought about that experience.

However the person's thoughts about the precipitating factor need not remain stable. They may turn, first in one direction, then in another, though no longer in arbitrary directions. They may, for instance, become more specific, more particular. They may zero in on just what aspect of the circumstances it was that brought the person to where he now is. Or they may become more general. Or, a third possibility, they might start to reach back in time, trying to see if, and, if so, why, there was a moment when the fate of the originating desire was sealed. And there will be other times when the precipitating factor is revealed, not slowly, but instantaneously and indubitably. Our desire for safety is frustrated, we shudder with fear, and there, to account for the experience, is the snake in our path.

From all this it follows that there is no one way of connecting the originating condition of the emotion with its precipitating factor.

Secondly, as the experience of satisfaction or frustration is extroverted, so the precipitating factor, or what can, with increasing justice, be thought of as the object,[9] comes to be perceived a certain way. And it is how the object is perceived or imagined – rather than how it is thought of or evaluated, which are the aspects that modern philosophers have emphasized – that is crucial to the formation of an emotion.

The most general thing to be said about how, as the attitude develops, we are led to perceive the object is that we come to perceive it as the cause, or as some part of the cause, of the satisfaction or frustration of our desire.

If this sounds mysterious, let us first distinguish the present claim, which is that we can experience a thing or a fact as the cause, or as part of the cause, of something that has happened to us, from the different and incoherent claim that we can experience the causal relation itself.[10] Confusion between the two claims can lead to the wrongful dismissal of that which I am advancing.

My claim makes use of a notion of which, I believe, any overall account of the emotions has need. The notion is that of *correspondence*, and there are at least four places where our understanding of the emotions depends upon it.[11] Correspondence occurs in connexion with the expressive perception of nature, such as when we see an estuary as melancholy, or an Alpine landscape as happy. Correspondence occurs in connexion with the expressiveness of art, such as when a painting by Watteau is said to be melancholy, or a Bach cantata jubilant. Correspondence occurs in connexion with the physiognomic expression of emotion, such as when a scowl reveals anger, or a drawn face sorrow. And the fourth place where correspondence occurs is in the present context. In the first three cases, something corresponds to an existent emotion, whether it be some part of nature, or a work of art, or the lie of the face or body. In the present case, the suggested correspondence is between two things, neither of which is an emotion. One is the satisfaction or frustration of desire, the other is that which is thought to have caused or helped to caused it, and it is because of the correspondence, or, more precisely, because of our perception of this correspondence, that an attitude, hence an emotion, forms. As far as the nature of emotion is concerned, this fourth context is the most fundamental, though not necessarily the most important, context in which correspondence figures.

I can see no sure way either of getting someone to grasp the notion of correspondence who has not experienced correspondence, or of getting someone who has not experienced correspondence to do so. And someone might experience correspondence without recognizing it, and might continue not to recognize it even after this fact has been pointed out. In the face of correspondence, there is ineliminable room for obduracy, philosophical piled upon psychological.

As a relation, correspondence has certain properties that can be specified. Consideration of these properties will help to distinguish correspondence, which is a subjective phenomenon, from fit, as it was discussed in the last lecture, which is an objective phenomenon. In the first place, the relation is non-symmetrical. If one term corresponds to another, it does not follow that that term corresponds to it: though it may. Because correspondence is non-symmetrical, though not asymmetrical, correspondence has direction, and we may therefore distinguish between (one) the corresponding term, or the term that provides correspondence, and (two) the term that is corresponded to, or that finds correspondence. Secondly, the relation is non-transitive. If one term corresponds to another, and it in turn corresponds to a third, it does not follow that the first corresponds to the third: though it may. Correspondence is non-transitive, but it is not intransitive. Thirdly, the relation is sensory. We are aware of its holding in virtue of what we perceive, and, once we are aware of its holding, that in turn affects how we perceive further, similar things. But the relation is weakly sensory in that, when we are aware of its holding, it is not necessary that we do so through perceiving the two terms to the relation and the relation between them. Indeed it is not necessary that both terms to the relation should be perceptible: sometimes only one is, and that is generally the corresponding term. (This is the basis of the expressive power of art: coloured shapes may correspond to an emotion.) And, when both terms are perceptible, it is not necessary that both should be so within the same sense-modality. A colour may correspond to a smell, or a smell to sounds. Fourthly, the relation is grounded in trains of association, and it is these associations that function as the background against which correspondence is perceived. It is a fact that some associations are much deeper or more firmly rooted in the psyche than others, and most often the associations on which correspondence depends are very deep. In all four respects, correspondence differs from fit.

To resume: As the experience of satisfaction or frustration is extroverted, as the attitude develops, the person comes to experience a correspondence between, on the one hand, the satisfaction or frustration of a desire of his and, on the other hand, what he identifies as the precipitating factor. He sees the figure or the fact to which his thoughts have attached themselves as having it in him, or in it, to produce such an outcome. And, once this correspondence has been experienced, the person will be disposed to go on looking upon the precipitating factor, and things appropriately similar to it, in the light of this correspondence. Now he sees the precipitating factor as what he in fact takes it to be: the cause of what it precipitates. 'Takes', as we saw at the end of the last lecture, is certainly not the same as 'rationally believes'.

In his essay *De l'amour*, Stendhal writes of a process he calls 'crystallization',[12] which, though he is concerned with it exclusively as the source of love, can be generalized so as to find a place in the explanation of emotion generally. Indeed it answers to the first two aspects of the formation of an attitude: the concentration upon an outer object rather than an inner state, and the perception of that object as having it in it to produce the inner state. The term 'crystallization' Stendhal adopted after a visit to the much-frequented salt-mines at Hallein, near Salzburg. There, in the winter months, the miners would throw a leafless branch of a tree into the disused workings, and when, later on in the year, they pulled it out to give away as a curio to the summer sightseers, the action of the salt water had covered the branch, down to the smallest twig, with a very fine deposit of shining, scintillating crystals. Stendhal compared the process by which the wood was transformed into a spray of diamonds to the way in which a woman is so transformed in her lover's eyes that she comes to possess every perfection.

By talking of every perfection, Stendhal does not mean that the young man converts his mistress into a paragon of all the objectively admirable qualities. What he means is that the man invests her with just those qualities which are likeliest to have made him, specifically him, fall in love with her. Stendhal, believing that such susceptibility is influenced by culture, speculates that, if the lover is German, he will see the woman he loves as tender and kind, if he is English, he will find her aristocratic and ladylike. In each case, the qualities come from correspondence.

True love involves, according to Stendhal, two successive crystallizations. The first crystallization is succeeded, after a moment of doubt, by a second crystallization, which is dominated by the involuntary thought, 'Now she loves me'. But why this thought? What is its place in the growth of love? It is not Stendhal's suggestion that, as the man recovers from doubt, he forms a new desire, which is that the woman should reciprocate his love, and that the second crystallization develops when he believes that this desire has been satisfied. For Stendhal, there is no such desire, and the lover, in crediting his mistress with love for him, is conferring upon her another, the ultimate, perfection, or the quality that could supremely account for, and so corresponds to, the love that she has aroused in him for her.

A crucial point in common between my account of the growth of an attitude and what Stendhal talks of as crystallization is that, it will be observed, both are ultimately activities of the imagination. Crystallization is, Stendhal says, '*une certaine fièvre d'imagination*',[13] 'a certain fever of the imagination, which makes something that is often quite ordinary unrecognizable'. Stendhal cites how the lover will, in thought, transport the object of his love into a variety of unfamiliar situations, fabricated out of chance materials, but each chosen to emphasize the correspondence between her and the experience of satisfied desire that she has brought on. So, a lover has only to hear a traveller talking of the orange groves along the sea at Genoa, and the cool that they offer against the summer heat, for him to think, 'Oh, to share that with *her*!' A friend has gone hunting, he breaks his arm, and straightway the lover imagines, 'And then I would be looked after by the woman I love.'[14]

The third aspect of the transformation of the experience of satisfaction or of frustration into an attitude is a shift from passivity to activity. As emotion forms, it finds us passive and it leaves us active, and, in so doing, it fulfils a deep need in our nature.[15]

However there are various ways of misunderstanding this last claim, ways which in turn lead to further misunderstandings of the nature of emotion.[16]

In the first place, the claim does not mean that the formation of an emotion is an action of ours, or that it is something that we do, or even – though this is weaker yet – that we can inhibit it, should we want to.[17]

Secondly, the claim does not mean that, once an emotion of ours has formed, it is then under our control.[18] On the contrary, in certain familiar circumstances, our emotion can pull us, now in this direction, now in that. In other, no less familiar circumstances, it can completely immobilize us. Love tormented Phèdre: guilt, vicarious guilt, becalmed Hamlet.

Thirdly, the claim does not assert any direct link between emotion, once formed, and action. Emotion is not a motivating force. Motivation is the prerogative of desire, and any connexion of action with emotion is invariably indirect as we saw from the characteristic history of emotion. Generally emotion will lead us to form desires, and these desires, conjoined with appropriate instrumental beliefs, may cause us to act.

What then is the content of the claim that emotion involves a shift from passivity to activity? It is, I believe, this: When we respond to something towards which we have not formed an emotion, our response can readily be wayward. We are hostages to the moment. However, once we have formed an emotion, our response is something that arises out of us, even if, for reasons connected with imperfect self-knowledge, it does not strike us like this. Our response now derives from how we are, and from how we perceive the world, and ultimately from the history that we have led. It is this kind of stability, or non-waywardness, that justifies the claim before us.

I now pass on to the third, or most complex, level on which emotion forms.

What distinguishes the process on this level is its starting-point. The originating condition having been met, and a desire having been either satisfied or frustrated, the person is then unable to tolerate the subsequent experience of satisfaction or frustration. Instead, anxiety is experienced, a defence is activated, in consequence of which the situation is perceived afresh, an attitude appropriate to this fresh perception arises, and an emotion that could never have been anticipated on the basis of the originating condition now forms, or, we might say, malforms.

There are a number of broadly discriminable situations in which this inability, mentioned briefly in the last lecture, might manifest itself, and, if I initially characterize them in a purely descriptive, hence superficial, way, I do so solely to isolate the phenomenon.

First, then, the fault may lie with the object of the desire, and how it is thought of. Guilt or anxiety may attach to its attainment. Secondly, the fault may lie with how the person stands to the desire itself: he may be too committed to it to tolerate his being denied it, or too little committed to it to tolerate his being granted it. Thirdly, the fault may lie with the pleasure that follows upon satisfaction of the desire, or the unpleasure that follows upon its frustration. For these may be envisaged in such an extreme fashion that the person dreads their oncoming. They threaten to excite him beyond endurance or to reduce him to a state of total inactivity, to enflame him or to suffocate or stifle him. And a final possibility is that what is at fault is a certain history that the person cannot avoid ascribing to the pleasure or unpleasure he experiences. The pleasure that comes with satisfaction, he finds himself thinking, has been robbed or filched from another, whose anger has thereby been provoked, and cannot be deflected. The unpleasure that comes with frustration is experienced as punishment: punishment that leaves an indelible brand, and is meted out for some long forgotten transgression.

In philosophy, we appear to hear little about malformed emotion, but it is a fact, which has escaped notice, that one of the most detailed discussions of the emotions to be found in the twentieth-century literature, Jean-Paul Sartre's *Sketch of a Theory of the Emotions*,[19] confines its attention to this third level on which emotion forms. Sartre talks only about malformed emotion, and malformed emotion he too in effect traces to the person's inability to tolerate satisfaction or frustration.

However both these points need to be vindicated against other interpretations of what Sartre says, and that is because of three idiosyncrasies of his approach. First, he never concedes, even in the most roundabout way, that his essay has as its subject-matter anything other than the standard process by which the emotions form. Secondly, and as a direct consequence of the first, he calls the emotions whose formation he traces, not by the names they merit, but by the names of those emotions which they displace, or which would have formed, had satisfaction or frustration been tolerated. And, thirdly, Sartre assumes that all emotions are formed in this deviant way.

Sartre develops his theory around a few key examples of emotion, which occur in situations that he asks us to imagine.

First, there is a situation of danger, in which what Sartre calls fear arises.[20] The second is a situation of loss, in which what Sartre calls sorrow arises.[21] The third situation is one of good luck, or, more precisely, of anticipated good luck, in which what Sartre calls joy arises.[22] Sartre illustrates this third situation by two examples, one of a man who is about to receive a fortune, the other of a man (I simplify Sartre's example a little) who is about to meet someone whom he loves but whom he has not seen for a long time. In the first two of these three situations, those of danger and loss, the man's desire is frustrated, actually frustrated. In the third situation, the man's desire is satisfied, though, in both examples, only prospectively.

Sartre does not explicitly say of any of the three situations that the person finds the satisfaction or the frustration of his desire intolerable, or that this is how the emotion arises. How he puts it is that the emotion arises because the world becomes 'difficult',[23] unbearably difficult, for the person. Sartre's lack of explicitness might encourage the view that he has an alternative way, or a way other than that which I might seem to foist upon him, of explaining how, in these cases, emotion arises. It might be thought that Sartre, in saying that the world becomes difficult for the man, is referring to facts of a simpler order. He is referring, in the first two situations, those of danger and loss, to the fact that the man's desire has been frustrated, rather than to his inability to tolerate the frustration, and, in the third situation, that of anticipated good luck, he is referring to the fact that a desire so important for the man is only prospectively satisfied, rather than to the man's inability to tolerate any form of satisfaction.

These alternative accounts of what Sartre is saying are closer to commonsense, and the alternative explanations they supply would account perfectly well for what many people situated similarly to those whom Sartre asks us to consider would do. But they do not, I believe, hold for *them*, for Sartre's *dramatis personae*. *They* react otherwise, and this, I believe, is what Sartre is telling us.

To justify my interpretation, I shall look closely at one of Sartre's examples, and, since they are all said to have a common structure, I shall choose that about which he has more to say: the man who is about to be reunited with a friend long absent.[24]

The fundamental fact about this man is, we are told, that one of his deepest desires will soon be satisfied. He starts to reflect upon his position, and, as he does so, he comes up with various thoughts. First, he thinks that he has a further period of waiting in store for him, and that is something that he cannot bear. Then he thinks that, when that period of waiting is over, he will have to behave so as to bring himself and the woman he loves closer. He will have to try to please her, to make himself deserving of her love, to make her love him in return – and that is more of what he cannot bear. But what he can bear least of all is the thought that, when at last the moment of possession arrives, when at last she is his, then, through the very nature of human love, his possession of her can never be exclusive, or total, or sealed and delivered in a single moment of time.

It is at this stage that the world becomes difficult for the lover, and it is in direct response to this difficulty that he turns away from his situation, and seeks to transform the world as he knows it, and to replace it with another world so pictured that whatever has proved difficult for him in this world is now negated. There the impossible becomes possible. In this new world, the lover's possession of his mistress is 'an instantaneous totality'.[25]

There are two elements in this account, both of which are echoed in Sartre's other examples, that support my claim that the emotion that he tells us of is emotion that is (one) malformed and (two) the product of a failure to tolerate satisfaction or frustration.

In the first place, take the thoughts that the man rehearses as he waits for his desire to come true. Are they the thoughts of someone who has a simple commitment to his desire and its satisfaction? Satisfaction has been postponed, and that makes it natural for him to look into the future. But, when he does, what he sees in store for him is not pleasure, not some state of the world to which his desire has sensitized him, but the travail of surviving what he wants when he gets it. Sartre being the sort of thinker that he is, he proposes metaphysical in preference to psychological reasons for the lover's inability to tolerate the satisfaction, the still merely prospective satisfaction, of his desire, but it is this inability that is the fundamental reason why the world turns out to be so difficult for him to live in, and why he flees the woman, and love, and ultimately the world itself. It is why he replaces the world as it is with another world that he wishes into existence.

And this brings us to the second element in Sartre's story that supports my interpretation: the so-called transformation of the world,[26] which is for him the core of emotion.

Of the transformation of the world Sartre says that it is a 'magical' act, and the term 'magic'[27] covers various aspects of the act. First, it captures how the person's picture of the world is changed: it is changed through the will, which is, in turn, a piece of thinking to which the person, even as he engages in it, attributes powers that mere mental activity couldn't have. What the person resorts to is more familiar to us through Freud's term, or the term he appropriated from a patient: 'omnipotent thinking'.[28] Secondly, 'magic' conveys how the person stands to this change, once it is effected: he does not merely believe that it has occurred, he lives it. He cannot stand outside it. And, thirdly, the term implies that the transformation is global. It is not a mere alteration of the world at the empirical margin so that the person gets rid of things that he doesn't like, replacing them with things more to his liking, while leaving all the general conditions of human desire and its pursuit – the adaptation of means to ends, the reliance upon trial and error, the need for causal knowledge – intact. The person who invokes magic to escape the difficulty of the world wills to transform the world out of all recognition.

It is supremely the global nature of the changes that the person seeks that reveals his attitude to the satisfaction or frustration of desire. For someone who can accept satisfaction or frustration – though, all the while, as a human being must, preferring satisfaction to frustration, and satisfaction sooner to satisfaction later

– will be someone who continues to act in, and to act upon, the world as he finds it, whereas someone who wills to abolish the world he inhabits, and to substitute for it one in which gratification is immediate and total, is someone to whom both satisfaction and frustration are alike intolerable. There is, in other words, no plausible story that runs forwards from the acceptance of satisfaction or frustration to the global transformation of the world, or that runs backwards from the invocation of a magical solution of life's difficulties to anything except the inability to tolerate satisfaction or frustration.

And let me reiterate something raised in the last lecture: that is, that, in talking of the inability to tolerate satisfaction or frustration, I am talking, not of the inability to tolerate the fact that a desire has been satisfied, or the fact that a desire has been frustrated, but of something quite different, which is the inability to tolerate the corresponding experience. (There are many situations in which it is a sign of our humanity that we cannot tolerate the fact that a desire of ours, possibly an altruistic desire of ours, has been frustrated.) Indeed I regard the phenomenon that Sartre implies as an indirect argument for the existence of the kind of experience that I argued for in the first lecture.

It might now be objected that, if I have shown that Sartre's account of emotion does indeed trace it to the failure to tolerate satisfaction or frustration, and hence is exclusively an account of, *in my sense of that phrase*, malformed emotion, I have not shown this for a more neutral sense of the phrase. I dispute this objection. For surely the most neutral, the most basic, way of understanding malformed emotion is as emotion that is an oblique, or an inapposite, response to the circumstances in which the person is, or believes himself to be. If that is so, then any emotion the history of which appeals to an adjusted perception of the world, let alone a wilfully adjusted perception of the world, must qualify as malformed.

There is one deceptive element in Sartre's account of emotion which might prevent the unwary reader from recognizing how starkly emotion, as Sartre conceives it, opposes itself to an appropriate response to the world. We must go back a little to see what this element is.

Sartre, as we have seen, places at the centre of emotion the transformation of the world, which is fundamentally a change of consciousness. This change is induced through the will.

So a question to ask is, How does the will bring this about? What is the means – if we may use a term that so clearly belongs to a more instrumental conception of acting upon the world – that the will employs? Sartre's answer is that the will employs behaviour: behaviour, which, like the will itself, now has magical powers attributed to it.[29] As the world becomes difficult for us, so we engage in behaviour that Sartre calls 'incantatory':[30] it is incantatory of the world, wooing it to submit to the transformation willed upon it. He talks of 'the making use of our bodies as insrtuments of incantation'.[31] The next question is, How, in the case of each emotion, is the behaviour selected? Or, What pairs behaviour to the emotion it introduces?

Without explicitly answering this general question, Sartre in effect pairs each emotion with the specific behaviour that, not only is standardly associated with it, but owes this association to a rational link generally thought to hold between the two. Sartre, of course, rejects the rationality of the link, but he continues to assert the link itself. And this he justifies by claiming that, in each case, the behaviour, in some primitive symbolic fashion, denies that aspect of the world which the person finds difficult. And this is the element I have called deceptive.

The case of fear will illustrate my point. Sartre acknowledges the familiar association of fear, or rather what he thinks of as one kind of fear, which he calls active fear, with flight. To the obvious objection that this goes against the view of emotion as a form of magic, Sartre's reply is that the profound error in ordinary thinking is to believe that the primary aim of the fleeing person is to put as much distance between himself and the danger as possible.[32] He suggests that, to grasp the real nature of the link between fear and associated behaviour, we should start, not with active fear, but with the other kind of fear, passive fear, and the behaviour with which it is associated: fainting. When a person faints in a situation of danger, he is doing two things. He is trying, first, to negate or annihilate the difficult character that the world has taken on, and, secondly, to induce, to induce magically, incantatorily, another, a different kind of, world. Once we have understood this, we can then turn back to the person who, in the grip of active fear, flees. For the two people are doing exactly the same thing, to which what the person who is gripped by passive fear does provides the clue. Flight is, in Sartre's words, 'fainting away in action'.[33] By running away, the person who flees is at once denying that danger exists and conjuring into existence a world, alternative to the present world, from which danger has been purged.

In claiming that Sartre implicitly offers us an account of malformed emotion, furthermore an account that gives malformed emotion an origin similar to that which I propose, I am not implying that Sartre gives us a full, or accurate, picture of how such emotion comes about. He does not. For the rest of this section, I shall offer the outlines of an adequate account, using where possible, and refining as necessary, the materials that Sartre provides.

In the first place, an adequate account must explicitly identify the originating condition of malformed emotion. This, I have contended, is the inability to tolerate satisfaction or frustration of desire. Sartre specifies the condition only implicitly, and he confuses the issue by thinking of it as a metaphysical, not a psychological, condition.

Secondly, a mechanism of defence needs to be inserted between the failure of the person to tolerate satisfaction or frustration and how he then comes to perceive the world in a transformed way. Examples of these mechanisms are projection, introjection, splitting, and projective identification. It is such a mechanism, initially triggered by anxiety, and not, as Sartre would have it, the will, embodied in incantatory behaviour, that brings about the next stage in the development of the emotion.

Thirdly, this next stage, which Sartre calls 'the transformation of the world', is better thought of as the formation of a phantasy, of which more later. In the case of a malformed emotion, phantasy takes the place that is occupied, in the case of normally formed emotions, by an attitude. And, as to Sartre's insistence that the transformation is total, this is an exaggeration. All that it is necessary to maintain is that the phantasy tends to occlude any aspect of the world that might falsify the phantasy.

Fourthly, the account must say more about the content of this phantasy. We might begin by learning from the account posited for emotion standardly formed. For, just as that account proposes as the object of the attitude whatever is believed to have precipitated the satisfaction or frustration of the relevant desire, so, in the case of malformed emotion, we might think that the content of the phantasy is whatever is believed to have made the experience of satisfaction or frustration intolerable.

Fifthly, once the function that Sartre attributes to behaviour is delegated to a mechanism of defence, the role that behaviour actually plays needs to be reconsidered. My suggestion is that much of the behaviour ordinarily associated with emotion is best thought of either as an expression of the emotion or as an acting-out of the core phantasy. I shall return to these ideas.

Finally, a revised account needs to correct the systematically misleading way in which Sartre bestows upon the malformed emotions the names of those quite different emotions for which they substitute themselves. Sartre, as we have seen, talks of fear, sorrow, and joy, when he would have done better to have talked of mania, melancolia, and envy. Better, but still not well. The truth is that malformed emotions necessarily resist a clear taxonomy, and that is because, in any given instance, the malformed emotion owes its content or character, partly to the situation to which the person now perceives himself to be responding, but partly to the mechanism of defence that accounts for the misperception. Malformed emotion is, in Freudian terminology, a 'compromise-formation'.[34] It is a compromise between the old, or defended against, emotion and the defence, which introduces the new emotion.

At one point in his essay, Sartre makes a revealing admission.[35] There is probably no work of literature that illustrates more succinctly what happens to our emotions when we repudiate our desires than Aesop's fable of the Fox and the Grapes. The fox cannot get what he wants because nature has put it out of his reach. Unable to accept frustration of his desire, he is led off on a path that, starting from denial of his desire, leads him, through scorn of its object, to envy.

And Sartre tells us that this fable delivers to us the essence of emotion.

4. The last discussion prompts the question whether there are any emotions that are invariably malformed, or that, in all cases, arise from the person's inability to tolerate satisfaction or frustration of desire. The answer, I believe, is Yes. Envy, as it has come to be refined within contemporary psychoanalytic theory, is such an emotion. In substantiating this claim, which involves identifying the originating condition of envy, I shall draw on the work of Melanie Klein, and in particular her essay *Envy and Gratitude*.[36] While leaving the content of her findings intact, I shall reorganize them so as to fit them into the structure I have been proposing.

Klein's account of envy too starts from the satisfaction or frustration of desire. Indeed, within the life-history of the person, envy first appears as a response on the part of the child to the earliest version of satisfaction or frustration to which we are exposed: to that brought about by the primal object, or the mother's breast. And, since envy, like all emotions, but more so, never outgrows its origins, later instances of the emotion reviving earlier instances, I shall, in reconstructing the nature of envy, not move far away from the infantile edition.

However, for Klein, envy is not merely a response to satisfaction or frustration. It is – and, in this respect, it continues to resemble a malformed emotion – a mediated response. If envy is to arise, something, something psychological in nature, has to interpose itself after the desire has been satisfied or frustrated, and the satisfaction or the frustration has been either experienced or fully anticipated. However, if the resemblance is to be close enough for envy to be a malformed emotion, not just like a malformed emotion, this something must include, or amount to, the inability to tolerate satisfaction or frustration.

In the Kleinian account, the interposing factor is phantasy. Phantasy is the bridge between the experience or anticipated experience of satisfaction or frustration and the onset of envy. At this stage I need to draw upon what I shall have to say later about what phantasy is only to the extent of pointing out that (one) phantasy occurs both on the level of disposition and on the level of mental state, that (two) phantasy on the level of mental state, or occurent phantasy, is like a daydream, except that, phantasy never becoming wholly conscious, its content cannot be spelt out in full, but (three) of the phantasy that ushers in envy, we can reconstruct it sufficiently to say this: that, shaped partly by constitutional factors, partly by the infant's actual situation, it represents the breast as something wholly external to, or independent of, the infant's body, and, at the same time, the source of everything good.

If we want to determine the nature of Kleinian envy, and specifically whether it is, as I suggest, a malformed emotion, what we need to grasp is what the mental states are like in which the phantasy of the breast manifests itself when the child's desire is, on the one hand, satisfied, on the other hand, frustrated.

In the case of satisfaction, the answer is not hard to find. As the child is fed, as sustenance is taken in, as satisfaction is experienced, the phantasy erupts, and floods the child's mind with an ever-heightened sense of its dependency upon something that it cannot control. The associated feelings are best described as those of humiliation, and of fear: humiliation, because the source of goodness is external, and fear, because, the source being external, the goodness might dry up.[37]

In the case of frustration, the answer is more complex. As the child fails to get fed, as the sustenance is not forthcoming, as frustration is experienced, so the underlying phantasy again erupts, and again floods the child's mind with a sense of dependency, but now intensifed by pangs of hunger. The associated feelings are humiliation and, this time, deprivation. But there is more. For now, and only now, a part of the phantasy that has been in reserve, since it is irrelevant to satisfaction, manifests itself. The phantasy represents the breast when it is ungiving as denying the child something. The breast withholds the sustenance, the goodness, that it does not give the child for one or other of two purposes. Either it retains it for its own enjoyment or, more ominously, for another whom it wishes to pleasure. (In Klein's revised chronology of early development, this moment when the child ceases to be exclusively preoccupied with its own frustration at the breast, and finds its thoughts turning to the satisfaction that another will receive at its expense, inaugurates that triadic conflict, child–mother–father, which Freud, with a much later dating, christened the Oedipus complex.)

However both occurent phantasies, that inspired by satisfaction of desire and the more phantasmagoric part inspired by frustration of desire, since they concur in emphasizing the externality of goodness, and the depths of infantile dependence, ultimately trigger anxiety. Fear, in the one case, deprivation, in the other, make this a certainty. Anxiety induces a reaction, and this reaction leads, in both cases, to the formation of the same hostile attitude. The awareness of an external source of goodness, in supplying the child with this new attitude, also supplies the attitude with a target. The new attitude is envy, and its target is the breast. Envy, which is hostility directed at goodness because it is goodness, is, in its original form, envy of the breast.

A check that may be run on any account of what Klein has to say about envy is provided by a somewhat puzzling remark that she makes early on in *Envy and Gratitude*, when, having observed that envy forms in response both to satisfied and to frustrated desire, she says that envy is 'more understandable'[38] as a response to satisfied desire. Envy being a negative emotion, the expectation would be that it calls for more, not less, explanation when it forms in response to satisfaction. Accordingly, to the degree to which any reconstruction of Klein's account of envy makes her remark fully intelligible, to that degree the reconstruction is confirmed as in accord with her views. And, along the way, some of the finer grain of just how envy arises is likely to be brought out.

The two crucial factors that shape the formation of infantile envy are (one) the association of the breast with goodness, and (two) the phantasy of total dependence. Let us now consider how these two factors are activated in the mind, first, of the satisfied child, then, of the frustrated child. Does this occur in a more roundabout way in the one case than in the other?

First, then, the association of the breast with goodness. The route by which this comes before the mind of the satisfied child is very straightforward. What makes the satisfied child associate the breast with goodness is identical with what makes it satisfied. By contrast, the frustrated child perceives the breast as good through the piecing together, and the merging, of different experiences of the breast. The frustrated child must combine recalling what it received in the past, sensing what it is deprived of in the present, and resenting what others will receive in the future.

Secondly, the phantasy of total dependence. Once again, it is clear how, and to what effect, this factor is activated in the case of the satisfied child. Satisfaction exemplifies dependence, and dependence converts the pleasure of satisfaction into pain. By contrast, it might initially seem that the phantasy of dependence has nothing to add to the pain of frustration. In fact it does have something to add, but that is only because, in the wake of frustration, the more phantasmagoric parts of the phantasy, or the parts further removed from reality, are invoked and deployed.

It is, I believe, by reflecting upon these materials that we can come to how Klein's account of envy, as I have reconstructed it, does indeed make envy 'more understandable' in the case of satisfied, than in the case of frustrated, desire. To that extent, my reconstruction is vindicated.

That being so, let us next ask whether this account does indeed make envy a malformed emotion. I believe that the answer is Yes. First, the account shows envy forming in response to some experience that the child is unable to endure either in actuality or in full anticipation. Secondly, since the account also tells us that envy forms in the wake of desire satisfied or desire frustrated, we know what the experience is. Envy – and this is the total view – originates in the inability to tolerate satisfaction or frustration, where this is understood, not as a cognitive inability, or the inability to accept a fact, but as an affective inability, or the inability to accept an experience.

In fact the Kleinian account, in showing us the envious child, or – for this is the moment when we may generalize the account – the envious person, as unable to tolerate the experience of satisfaction or frustration, also shows us more about what this inability involves. It shows us its inner structure, which, we learn, has two parts to it. There is something that doesn't happen, as a result of which something else does happen. The satisfied person cannot feel gratitude, the frustrated person is powerless to turn away and seek satisfaction along some other route. However the awareness of goodness, either of goodness given and devoured or of goodness retained and resented, survives. But it survives transformed, transformed into the hostility that is at the core of envy. The awareness of goodness is transformed into hostility of a special kind: hostility that is against goodness, and is against goodness because of its goodness.

5. I return, after this lengthy detour, to the narrative of the emotion. Stage (e) gives us that broad division of the emotions, already considered, based on whether the attitude is tinged with pleasure or with unpleasure. If the desire has been satisfied, the attitude will be tinged with pleasure, and the emotion will be positive: if the desire has been frustrated, the attitude will be tinged with unpleasure, and the emotion will be negative – at least in the standard cases. As to the abnormal cases, the review of malformed emotion has given us some understanding of when and how they develop.

6. So to stage (f): *the attitude persists.* If the development of the attitude is central to the formation of an emotion, the persistence of the attitude, once developed, is central to the emotion itself. Now the emotion has come to be: it really exists.

The centrality of the attitude within emotion urges upon us further questions about it, which may be organized into two broad groups: those concerning the object, and those concerning the content, of the attitude.

7. First, then, the object of the attitude.

So far, when not critical of the very idea on the grounds that it can make the emotion seem more rigid, less fluid, than it is, I have considered the object exclusively in a developmental light, or as providing the principal strand in the early history of an emotion. In the aftermath of the satisfaction or frustration of desire, our thoughts turn to what we think precipitated it, this being either a fact or a thing, and, if a thing, often a figure. In time, this precipitating factor acquires the status of the object of an attitude, and then, as the attitude becomes the core of the emotion, the object of the attitude is set to become the object of the nascent emotion.

Such an approach is fundamentally correct. It prepares us for two features of the object of an emotion that philosophy cannot overlook, though it has great difficulty in reconciling them: first, the internality of the object to the emotion, and, secondly, the fact that there can be occasions — that is, those when the satisfaction or frustration is merely believed-in, and perhaps some of those when it is anticipated — on which there is nothing in the world that corresponds to the object.[39] Other approaches, linguistic or logical, which hold sway, may tell us how, in particular cases, to pick out the object of an emotion, but they do not tell us what it is that we are picking out, and why.[40]

However I shall temporarily bracket the developmental approach. Having arrived at that point in the narrative when the emotion is fully formed, I shall abandon questions of history, and shall ask whether there are constraints, arising from the nature of the attitude itself, upon what can serve as the object of emotion.

This is the approach favoured by most contemporary philosophers. Disregarding developmental considerations, they find in the nature of the attitude various general requirements upon the object of emotion, no matter the emotion.[41] A different topic is whether there is specific to each emotion a range of objects to which that emotion is confined. Medieval philosophers referred to this topic as that of the proper or formal objects of an emotion.[42]

A commonly asserted requirement, which runs counter to what I have been assuming, is that the object of an emotion cannot be a figure, it must be a fact. This claim, which is the analogue of a claim we have considered in the context of desire, and is certainly less plausible in the context of emotion, is sometimes similarly expressed. Emotions, it is said, are propositional attitudes.[43]

However, once philosophers descend to detail, they have difficulty in denying that there are some emotions that do take figures as their objects, and indeed that there are some that seem debarred from taking facts.[44] It would be a poor theory of the emotions that started off by ignoring the claims of love, hate, admiration, and pity.[45] Accordingly, the claim that emotions are propositional attitudes needs to be cut down to size, and to be qualified in the following way: that emotions that can be directed both on to figures and on to facts are primarily, or more fundamentally, or really directed on to facts.

In what I shall now find to say, I shall simply assume this qualification, and I shall not necessarily repeat it. Furthermore, in line with how I have proceeded so far, I shall treat the claim as a claim about the nature of the emotions, and not about the logical form of statements about the emotions.

In favour of the claim, there are two principal arguments.

The first argument is this: Let us imagine a person whom we would initially describe by saying that he is saddened by, or is angry with, some figure. It would then be natural to think of this figure as the object of the person's emotion. However in any such case it can be asked, Why does the figure sadden or anger him? The answer, it is presumed, takes the form of citing some fact about the figure. We are told what it is about the figure that saddens the person, or that makes him angry. That being so, the argument claims that it is surely more accurate to think that the object of the person's sadness, or his anger, is not the figure, but is a fact about the figure. Generalize this substitution, and the effect is to show that, within the restrictions of the argument, any emotion that initially appears to be directed on to a figure is in reality directed on to a fact.

This argument has two steps. The first step is from an emotion to the nature of a reason for it: it concludes that the reason for an emotion is always a fact. The second step is from the nature of the reason for an emotion to the true nature of the object of that emotion: it concludes that an emotion that can have a fact as its object always has a fact as its object. For present purposes, I have no need to contest the first step, even though its presupposition – that there is a reason for every emotion – seems untenable. I shall concentrate on the second step.

If it were true that the reason for an emotion is always a fact, would it follow that the object of the emotion is likewise a fact?

First, we must recognize that, within the argument, this step is subject to a constraint. What we certainly cannot do is to infer the object of a person's emotion from just any reason that might be given for it, nor even from just any reason that the person might be inclined to give for it. The only reasons that will do as premisses of such an inference are those which state something about the thing or the figure that the person would initially identify – not totally correctly, the argument will go on to claim, but with some measure of truthfulness – as the object of his emotion. If the reason states a fact about some different thing or figure, it cannot be used in such an inference.

An example: I am writing a book, and a dog barks throughout the day, and I get angry. Asked why I am angry, I reply truthfully, Because the dog barks all day. Does this answer show that what I am angry about, or the object of my anger, is the fact that the dog barks all day? It does so only on one condition. And that is that, were someone to have asked me what, or whom, I was angry with, the truthful answer would have been, The dog. Had I answered, as might have been, in some circumstances, the truthful thing for me to have done, The dog's owner, or My neighbour, then it would not have followed that what I was angry about, or that the object of my anger, was the fact that the dog barked all day. In such circumstances, the dog's barking would have been no more than the occasion of my anger, leaving its owner, whose inability to control her dog is typical of her as a neighbour, as its object.[46]

Suppose then that the argument is so understood as to respect this constraint, is it still acceptable?

The argument still faces two broad difficulties. I shall ignore any lesser difficulties.

First, the argument has to presuppose what it ultimately refutes. For, not only does it concede that people often think of an emotion that they have as directed on to a thing, but it must insist that, when they do, a distinction can be drawn between totally incorrect ways of doing so and ways that are less incorrect, or ways that I have been calling truthful, though still not true. In the original version of the last example, to the question, Who, or what, are you angry with? the answer, The dog, was correct in a way that the answer, The dog's owner, would not have been, even if, ultimately, the argument tells us that neither is correct. What notion of correctness is here in use?

Secondly, no argument has been presented for thinking that, when a person is asked to give his reason why he has a certain emotion, and he cites a fact, he (one) is not doing what he thinks he is doing – that is, giving his reason for his emotion – but (two) is instead doing what the argument asserts he is doing – that is, revising its object. The argument cannot assume that the first collapses into the second.

I turn to the second of the two arguments for the claim that emotions that can have both figures and facts as their objects are fundamentally directed on to facts. The crucial consideration here is something briefly considered in the last lecture in connexion with desires. If emotions are to interact with other mental dispositions, and, in particular, with beliefs and desires, so as to produce new dispositions, there must be a common element, which serves as a junction-box through which the interaction occurs. A natural suggestion is that this common element should be some propositional content. If this suggestion is correct, then the implication is that all emotions are directed on to facts.

But, as we saw in the context of desire, there is an alternative, and less intellectualistic, view of the matter, which, instead of trying to reconstruct every interaction between mental dispositions as an inference, stresses the role, and the power, of imagination.

Let us suppose that I am saddened by the thought that the subsidies voted to prevent the decline of Venice into the lagoon have been, and will continue to be, embezzled by criminal types. Then, one summer, I conceive the overwhelming desire to move to Venice for my remaining years: it will solve all my problems at a stroke. Sadness suddenly turns to bitter anger at these layabouts, who sit around on the Lido, squandering money pointlessly, while the Salute, and the great convent church of San

Giorgio Maggiore, and the modest house that I could get, all slowly keel over into the polluted waters of the lagoon. Or imagine the case of Elizabeth von R., Freud's patient, who had nursed a secret love for her brother-in-law, of which she dared not breathe a word, even to herself. Her sister falls ill. She arrives after a long sleepless journey by train, and finds that her sister is dead. Suddenly, like, we are told, a flash of lightening, the unwanted thought, 'Now he is free again and I can be his wife' shoots into her mind, and will not be dislodged.[47] In one case, an emotion is changed by a desire into another emotion: in the other case, a belief intensifies an emotion beyond the point at which it can be contained. These interactions are regulated, not by inference, but by the imagination.

However the shared assumption so far has been that there is a real difference between emotions that are directed towards a figure and emotions that are directed towards a fact. By a 'real difference', I mean a difference that is rooted in the nature of the emotions, and that does not automatically follow from the ontological difference between figures and facts. I mean a psychological difference. Is this assumption correct? I believe that it is, and that there are many cases that the subsequent distinction illuminates.[48]

Legend has it that Plato, upset by what one of his slaves had done, excused himself from thrashing him on grounds that he was angry, and asked his nephew, Speusippus, to do so instead.[49] How are we to make sense of Plato's behaviour, which, over the ages, has been held up for general admiration? Surely, if what the slave had done was, in Plato's eyes, grave enough to merit a thrashing, it was also grave enough to make Plato angry? Or did Plato find offence in what his slaves did only when he was unmoved by it? If we introduce the distinction at issue, we can, I believe, make Plato's thinking fully intelligible. For, though he might very well expect to be angry when his slave had done something that he, Plato, thought deserved a thrashing, he was not prepared to carry out the punishment himself when he was, not merely angry *that* the slave had done what he had done, but angry *with* the slave for doing it. The form that his anger took would give him, he felt, an unhealthy interest in the matter.

Montaigne, who retells the story about Plato, tells another story, in which we can, I believe, discern similar thinking, based on the same distinction, but taken one step further. Charillus the Spartan says to a helot, who was insolent, 'By the gods, if I were not angry, I would have you put to death right now.' Charillus exceeded Plato in self-distrust, for he would seem to have believed that his being angry with the helot affected, not just whether he should administer the punishment, but whether he should sentence the man. Once again we must believe that he would not have thought that his being angry that the man had done this or that would have similarly disenabled him.[50]

My interest in these two stories extends only to their dependence upon the distinction at issue. But what does the distinction itself depend on?

I suggest that there are two broad differences between the two kinds of emotion. One difference has to do with the origins and – a closely connected issue – the later manifestations of the emotion. The other has to do with the decay or termination of the emotion. These differences do not necessarily coincide with the idiomatic ways in which we refer to emotions.

First: Emotions that have a figure as their object – say, I am frightened of my friend – are likelier to originate in, and then to manifest themselves on the occasion of, some experience of the figure. (Here, as elsewhere, imagination in absence can have the causal efficacy of experience, or presence.) By contrast, emotions that have some fact, generally some fact about a figure, as their object – say, I am frightened that my friend will betray me – are just as likely to originate in, and then to manifest themselves on the occasion of, reflexion upon that figure, or upon some fact about that figure.

In the previous lecture, we saw how sometimes, when a person's desire is satisfied or frustrated, he may – though he need not – live through the event that satisfies or frustrates it. When he does, the desire is said to be satisfied or frustrated in acquaintance. There is a structural similarity, and perhaps more than that, between this way in which a desire may terminate and the way in which an emotion directed on to a figure is likely to originate. Emotions directed on to figures characteristically form, and subsequently manifest themselves, in acquaintance.

Secondly: When emotions directed on to a figure wane, this requires that, under the impact of some fact, real or merely believed-in, our overall view of the figure changes. No matter how minute or trivial the consideration may be, its effect must spread itself over the whole figure for it to modify the emotion. And it is crucial to recognize that sometimes, and with some emotions, love being an example, it is unclear, independently of the specific emotion, and who has it towards whom, why the consideration that makes such a difference should have any special impact. Why, in the clear light of Rome, did Mr Casaubon's scholarly interests, which had originally earned him Dorothea's love, suddenly make him seem so crabbed and unlovable?[51] Furthermore some emotions are in their nature more persistent, more conservative, than others. Other things being equal, which they not often are, anger has greater staying-power than gratitude, envy than sincere admiration. Gratitude and admiration often wear themselves out. By contrast, with emotions directed on to some fact, something relevant either to that fact or to its significance for us is required to loosen their hold.

If, as I have been claiming in this section, not all emotions are directed on to facts, some certainly are, and some of these are very important, and so are the various classifications that have been proposed for them. A traditional classification of emotions that have some facts as their object divides them into those directed on to a past or present fact and those directed on to a future fact.[52]

To this classification two objections have been raised, and out of them an alternative classification has been proposed.[53]

In the first place, the temporal classification fails to divide the emotions as such. The line it draws runs, not between type-emotions, but only between token-emotions. For reflexion shows that any emotion that is standardly directed on to either a past or a present fact can, in certain circumstances, be directed on to a future fact: and vice versa. So remorse is standardly directed on to either the past or the present, and hope is standardly directed on to the future. Yet, knowing that I shall soon be confronted by a temptation that I shall not be able to resist, I could already feel remorse about what I shall do. In the dark about your past behaviour, I could hope that, when you had the chance to betray my confidence, you did not do so.

Secondly, the division that the temporal classification can effect between token-emotions can, in the light of these observations, come to seem superficial, and to derive whatever interest it has from another underlying classification, which the new proposal attempts to articulate.

It does so by dividing the emotions into those directed on to facts about which we are certain, which are called *factive emotions*, and those directed on to facts about which we are not certain, which are called *epistemic emotions*. (More precisely, though for reasons that need not concern us, epistemic emotions are emotions that are directed on to facts (one) about which we are not certain, and (two) where the uncertainty is not of a sort that can be resolved by some action on our part, and factive emotions are the rest.) Factive emotions, which are by far the more numerous, include amazement, anger, disappointment, disgust, gratitude, horror, indignation, pride, resentment, joy, sadness, surprise, sorrow, shame, guilt, and regret. Epistemic emotions are fear, terror, worry, and hope.

The new, or cognitive, classification claims superiority over the old, or temporal, classification on three counts. In the first place, it divides the emotions themselves, not just their tokens. Secondly, it does so by invoking a characteristic that it holds to be intrinsic to the emotion as such: that is, its relationship to certainty. And, thirdly, it can account for the appeal exerted by the classification that it displaces. For, the claim goes, it is because we standardly have certainty about the present or the past, but not about the future, and are standardly uncertain about the future, but not about the present or the past, that the idea of trying to classify the emotions temporally ever seemed attractive.

However, at the outset, the new classification presents us with a problem of interpretation. For, if factive emotions are to be identified in terms of the presence of certainty, and epistemic emotions in terms of the absence of certainty, what is certainty?

Is it knowledge, or is it belief? Furthermore, is it the same in both cases?

Before answering this question, we should be aware that the new classification at once differs from, and presupposes, another distinction within emotions, which parallels that applied, at the end of the last lecture, to desires. For, just as there is a difference between desires for actual things, such as the desire of a man to be married to a certain woman, or the desire of a woman to be elected to high office, and desires for the likelihood of certain things, such as the desire of another man that it should be on the cards that he should be married to the woman of his choice, or the desire of another woman that there should be nothing to stop her being elected Governor, so emotions directed on to actual facts differ from emotions directed on to likelihoods. An example of the first would be one woman's happiness at her pregnancy, and, of the second, another woman's happiness that, after undergoing an operation, she now could become pregnant, or that childbearing was open to her. The second woman might feel happy at this prospect, because the prospect made her feel better, or more in control of her life, or, as some might put it, more complete in herself, even though she had no foreseeable desire to become a mother.

That this distinction within emotions differs from the factive versus epistemic distinction can be seen from the very last case. For the object of this woman's happiness is a likelihood: a likelihood of which, her surgeon's confidence tells her, there is certainty. If the operation had gone less well, he could not have given her this assurance, and her emotion would have been formed out of uncertainty about a likelihood. This example, in showing that the two distinctions are different, also shows that one distinction, that between the factive and the epistemic emotions, can be applied only after the other is in place.

So back to the interpretation of the new distinction, and how certainty is to be understood. I shall ask, first, whether factive, secondly, whether epistemic, emotions are to be identified in terms of knowledge or in terms of belief. I shall contend that the best understanding of factive emotions is as entailing at most the presence of belief (rather than that of knowledge), and the best understanding of epistemic emotions is as requiring at most the absence of knowledge (rather than that of belief).[54] My proposed interpretation is therefore, in both regards, what might be thought of as on the weak side.

I start with factive emotions, of which I claim that they require no more than the presence of belief: belief, that is, about the object of the emotion.

Indeed that there are emotions − type-emotions, that is − that require the presence of knowledge seems unsustainable. Let us, for a moment, think schematically of knowledge as having two components, a *certainty-component* and a *truth-component*. Then we have to recognize that, for any given type-emotion, there could be, because of the conditions under which emotion forms, a token that fell short of knowledge on one or other, if not both, of these two counts.

For, in the first place, when an emotion forms, or the attitude that is central to it crystallizes, this does not necessarily occur under the influence of the beliefs, let alone the considered beliefs, of the person. Imagination, or senseless conviction, could be in the ascendancy. In such cases, the certainty-component will most likely not be satisfied. Secondly, when the attitude forms under the influence of the person's beliefs, even his most considered beliefs, some of these beliefs may, for all the care that the person has taken in exposing them to the best evidence, be false. When this happens, the truth-component will most likely not be satisfied.

I cannot see how any type-emotion could be proof against either, let alone both, of these shortcomings.

Take, for instance, the case of my anger with my neighbour over the barking dog. Initially I might be angry that my neighbour incites her dog to bark when I am trying to finish this very book. However, someone points out to me that I should be more reasonable: that no-one can control when a collie barks, that my neighbour has no idea of my habits of work, and that she doesn't know that I am writing a book. So, in a chastened frame of mind, I try to limit my anger to that for which I have evidence that she has evidence. Now I am angry only that she got a collie instead of the silent greyhound that she had been offered. But I am still wrong. She was never offered a greyhound, and she took the collie to prevent its being sacrificed in some unnecessary experiment.

If our opponent refuses, as he always can, to be swayed by imaginary examples, and he stands his ground, and accepts, indeed welcomes, the conclusion that, since anger is factive, hence requires knowledge, neither of these cases is a case of anger, he is faced with a real problem. What has he to say about these cases, except what they are not? If they are not cases of anger, because of the absence of knowledge, since, in all other ways – that is, in all psychological ways – they resemble anger, what are they? The absence of knowledge has been tied to what we *call* these emotions, but it has not been connected, in any comprehensible way, with what they actually *are*. The requirement of knowledge seems stipulative, and not to be intrinsic to the emotion.[55]

I turn next to epistemic emotions, of which I claim that they require no more than the absence of knowledge. I shall approach this claim through the stronger claim that epistemic emotions preclude belief as well as knowledge, for which there are two arguments.[56]

The first argument bases itself on the role of epistemic emotions in our lives. Epistemic emotions, it claims, often act, for the person who has them, as beliefs. They act as, or instead of, beliefs: beliefs, which the person therefore doesn't have. An example: Two farmers both want their crops not to be ruined by the threatened drought. Both are uncertain, and equally uncertain, whether the drought will be averted by rain. However one farmer puts out irrigation hoses, and the other doesn't. How can this be, since the two farmers concur, not only in their desires, but in their beliefs? According to the present argument, the factor that explains why each does what he does, and why they do different things, is the difference in the emotions that they have. The first farmer is afraid that it won't rain: the other is hopeful that it will. And what happens (the argument continues) is that, in each case, the emotion, fear or hope, substitutes itself for a belief of which the farmer stands in need, hence for a belief that he does not have.

The structure of the foregoing argument is presumably this: The two farmers, evidently under the influence of a common desire, act differently. How are we to explain how each acts, let alone why they act differently? The obvious answer – obvious since action requires for its causation desire plus belief – would be that they differ in their beliefs. But they do not differ in their beliefs. Accordingly there must be something, and something different in the two cases, that substitutes for the belief that the farmer does not have. The candidate for this role is an emotion. For each farmer has an emotion, and a different emotion, that is relevant to the issue. So (the argument goes) the first farmer has substituted for the belief that he needs his fear that it won't rain, and the second farmer has substituted for the belief that he needs his hope that it will rain. This done, it is clear why the two farmers act in the different ways they do.

But the argument, as it stands, is broken-backed.

For the beliefs that the two farmers need, if, given their common desire, we are to explain their different actions, are instrumental beliefs: beliefs, that is, that indicate certain actions as, in the circumstances as they see them, best adapted to the realization of their desires. So, in the case of the farmer who puts out his hoses, the belief that he needs is the belief that putting out hoses would, in the apparent circumstances, be the best way of preserving his crops. In the case of the farmer who doesn't put out his hoses, the belief that he needs is the belief that, in the apparent circumstances, putting out his hoses would make no contribution to preserving his crops, and would in fact be a serious waste of his resources. Could the emotions that the farmers have substitute themselves for these beliefs, which they do not have? Surely not. For the only belief for which an emotion can credibly substitute itself is a belief about the same thing. What the argument appears to disregard is that the instrumental belief that the first farmer requires does not share an object with his fear, and the instrumental belief that the second farmer requires does not share an object with his hope.

Let us then uncouple the argument from any issue of how action is explained, and simply start from the not implausible claim that, in certain circumstances, for whatever reasons, to whatever effect, the emotions known as epistemic emotions can substitute themselves for beliefs having the same object. So fearing that it won't rain can substitute itself for the belief that it won't rain, and hoping that it will rain can substitute itself for the belief that it will rain. What follows? Specifically does it follow that these emotions require the absence of such beliefs? It seems not. Of course, in those cases where the substitution *actually* occurs, the belief must – because this is what the word 'substitution' implies – be absent. There is no reason to conclude that, whenever such an emotion is present, the corresponding belief must be absent. For there is no reason to think that, in those cases where the belief is absent, and hence the substitution can occur, the absence of the belief is due to the presence of the emotion. To think otherwise would be like arguing that, since we can use a bottle of wine to fill a glass, wherever there is a bottle of wine, the glasses around it are empty.

The second argument for the claim that epistemic emotions preclude beliefs about their objects takes as its premiss the nature of the reasons, or of the kinds of reason, that can be given for them. For factive emotions only one kind of reason, or what is called an attitudinal reason, can be given. However there are two kinds of reason, epistemic as well as attitudinal, that can be given for epistemic emotions. The following examples illustrate the point, and the terminology: If someone says that he is frightened that he will step on a pinecone (an epistemic emotion), and we ask Why? he can say one or other of two things. He can say either, 'Because it will bring me bad luck' (an attitudinal reason), or 'Because my eyesight is bad' (an epistemic reason). However, if had he said that he was angry that his mother had arrived to stay (a factive emotion), and we ask Why? only an answer of the first sort is appropriate.

Now, from the fact that epistemic reasons can be given for epistemic emotions, it is concluded that epistemic emotions preclude the relevant kind of belief.

At first sight, this argument might seem back to front. For, if epistemic emotions can be supported by epistemic reasons, does this not suggest that epistemic emotions, so far from precluding belief, entail belief? For what else could the function of epistemic reasons be but to support some belief-component to the emotion?

But this objection is based on a misunderstanding of what the relevant kind of belief is. The argument concedes, indeed it claims, that epistemic emotions entail beliefs, and that epistemic reasons for them support such beliefs. What the argument denies is that the belief that an epistemic emotion entails is a belief in its object. What it claims is that the belief entailed is the belief that the object of the emotion is a probability or likelihood. So, when someone who is frightened that he will step on a pinecone gives the state of his eyesight as the epistemic reason why he is frightened, this reason supports, not the belief that he will step on a pinecone, but the belief that he easily could.

What seems correct is a weaker contention: namely, that epistemic reasons given for epistemic emotions sometimes function in this way. That epistemic reasons invariably function in this way seems unwarranted. Consider the following case: A man is frightened that his wife will leave him if he tells her that he is homosexual. He gives as his reason, his epistemic reason, the strength of his wife's religious views. Now it is undeniable that, in certain situations, these views of hers might have given him reason to believe no more than that, if he told her what she somehow must already suspect, she might very well leave him. But not so on this occasion. Our man is certain that, if he unburdens himself, she will go. Her views will require her to leave him, and it is because of this certainty that he is frightened. Otherwise he would not be.

With both arguments in, the truth of the matter is that, not only is there no overwhelming case against the concomitance of an epistemic emotion and a belief in its object, but we find cases where an epistemic emotion concords, not just with belief in, but with knowledge about, its object.

Let us consider the last hours on earth of Faustus, as Christopher Marlowe describes them. As Faustus waits in his study for the Devil to arrive and carry him off in fulfillment of the pact made between them, two mental dispositions dominate his mind. One is his fear that he will go to Hell. The other is his certainty that God has irrevocably damned him: it is this certainty that makes him impatient with the consolations of the German scholars, companions of his student days, who come to visit him and advise hope. Faustus knows that he will be in Hell on the last stroke of midnight, and this is what terrifies him.[57]

At this late stage someone might yet try to defend the factive versus epistemic distinction. The distinction has, he will claim, ordinary language on its side. For no-one would ever say both that Faustus was frightened that he would go to Hell, and that Faustus knew that he would go to Hell.

But, as a defence of the distinction, this is a fatal move to make. It draws attention to the limitation inherent in the distinction. For it has only to be pointed out that there is no similar objection to saying both that Faustus knew that he would go to Hell and any of the following: that Faustus was frightened of going to Hell, that Faustus was frightened about going to Hell, or that going to Hell frightened Faustus. From this, three very important conclusions follow. One is that the alleged incompatibility of certainty and, say, fear is not grounded, as the argument would have it, in the nature of the emotion. The other is that the incompatibility is an artifact of the oratio obliqua construction. And so, for that matter, is the factive versus epistemic distinction itself.[58]

It would, as I have indicated, be a different matter if either we could discern a serious psychological difference to which the distinction corresponded, or we were independently convinced that the oratio obliqua construction was itself a way of revealing the structure of the emotions. But we have found no reason to believe either thing. Indeed, as to the second, what now appears to be the insubstantiality of the factive versus epistemic distinction provides another reason to distrust any linguistic fundamentalism.

So far we have discussed the factive versus epistemic distinction solely as a distinction within emotions directed on to facts. But most of the emotions that are classified as epistemic emotions can also be directed on to figures, and then presumably would also count as epistemic. If they do, then upholders of the distinction are likely to uphold the natural extension of the original claim: namely, that, when the emotion is directed on to a figure, it precludes certainty about the existence of that figure.

But this seems unfounded. Faustus was not only frightened that he would go to Hell, he was also frightened of the Devil. But he was as certain of the existence of the latter as he was of the truth of the former.

8. Behind the factive versus epistemic distinction, giving it much of its appeal, there lies another, more intuitive project, age-old, which is, I believe, strongly deserving of our sympathy. That philosophy can contribute little to it does not mean that it cannot learn a lot from it. The project is to rank the emotions into a hierarchy, starting with evidently central cases of emotion, and then arranging the others in a descending order of whatever property it is that ensures the central cases their centrality. But what could this property be?

Certainly the task of finding central, or preeminent, cases of emotion is less daunting than that of divining their rationale. Such emotions arise in circumstances in which we are profoundly affected. We are so by something that our senses tell us, as clearly as they can, is part of external reality: powerful feeling wells up in us: marked physiognomic expression, which it is difficult to bring under control, stamps itself over the body: our concentration is disturbed, and our sense of what is important changes, even if momentarily: much of our lives seems bound up in this moment, for which we nevertheless seem totally unprepared. It has, over the centuries, been one of the ambitions of the poets to capture moments of such intensity.

Two famous passages from the poetry of antiquity illustrate how the world, impinging upon our already sensitized nature, can produce states of heightened perception that are paradigmatic of the onset of powerful emotion. In one, a man is overwhelmed by the sight of a woman's beauty, and he tries to give voice to his astonishment. In the other, a man is frozen with terror at some uncanny sight of nature.

In Book I of the *Aeneid*, Virgil describes how Aeneas, after many adventures, many hardships, anchors his fleet off the coast of Libya, and, with a companion, comes ashore. He enjoys a night of peaceful sleep, and he rises early next morning to explore the terrain. Crossing a forest path, he suddenly sees a young woman, of great beauty, her hair hanging loose, carrying a bow, her skirt looped up above the knees. He starts to ask her a question, when he is ravished by her looks. Admiration overcomes him, and, wondering who she can be, he expresses his sexual enthralment in the language that comes naturally to a lover: that of religious adoration. '*O dea, certe*', he exclaims, 'Goddess, beyond a doubt.'[59]

The second passage comes from Homer, and the emotion that he tries to capture is embedded in a simile. For the first time, the forces of the Trojans ride out to confront the army of the Greeks on the open plain outside Troy. Paris, in the vanguard of his soldiers, catches sight of his enemy, the ferocious Menelaus, husband of Helen, as he descends from his chariot to engage in combat. Terrified, Paris seeks refuge in the ranks of his own warriors. Homer compares him to a man in the grip of universal, primordial terror. Paris, he tells us, is like a man who, wandering in a mountain valley, startles back on seeing a snake across his path: he recoils, he shivers, he starts to run away, his cheeks are filled with a green pallor.[60]

But, if these are central cases of emotion, once we start to move away from them, and to try to account for other cases, which deviate from immediacy, and to order them on a scale, we run into difficulties. On the idea of a system of the emotions, three deflationary observations can be made.

In the first place, such a project is likelier to finish up with a classification of token-emotions rather than type-emotions. Secondly, the classification is likelier to take the form of laying the emotions out on a spectrum rather than bringing them under a binary categorization. And, thirdly, there is no reason to believe that a single spectrum will do justice to the many varied ways in which we can think of some emotions as more immediate, more direct, than others. It is highly unlikely that any proposed system will have the properties of transitivity or connectedness.

9. I turn now to questions about the connexion between the attitude, hence the emotion, and *evaluation*. Recently philosophers, going back to an earlier tradition, have asserted the connexion to be identity. The attitude *is* evaluation.[61]

But, first, the terms to the connexion in which we are interested. The connexion I take to hold between a person's emotion and an evaluation that that person himself sets upon the object of his emotion. I am not concerned, as some philosophers have been with the connexion between the ascription of an emotion and an evaluation that the person who makes the ascription sets upon the object of the emotion. According to these philosophers, if I say of someone 'He is ashamed of not having repaid the money', then I must myself hold that person at fault for not having discharged his debt, or, if I say 'She was embarrassed by her nephew's behaviour', then this entails that I assess the nephew's behaviour unfavourably. On this view, it is not further required that the evaluation is shared by the person to whom the emotion is ascribed.[62]

I shall ignore this second connexion because it reveals something, not about the nature of the emotions, but only about the assertibility of those speech-acts by means of which the emotions are referred to.

As to the first connexion, the central claim is that someone's emotion forms in response to – amongst other things perhaps – an evaluation on that person's part. However there are two versions of the claim, and they differ in the kind of evaluation they postulate. On the first version, the value appealed to is one that is logically prior to the emotion: that is, it is possible to identify the value without reference to the emotion, though not vice versa. On the second version, the value that is appealed to is one that is logically posterior to the emotion: that is, it is impossible to identify the value without reference to the emotion, though not vice versa.

To illustrate the claim in its first version, the examples of emotion must be very carefully chosen. One would be indignation, which presupposes injustice, another envy, which presupposes goodness. Within these prescribed limits, the claim has two distinct parts to it. First, it asserts that, when I am indignant over something done to someone, another or myself, I must think that this involves, not just harm, but injustice, and that this thought of mine partly accounts for the emotion. Secondly, the claim asserts that indignation cannot be understood without reference to injustice, though injustice can be understood without reference to indignation. Similarly with envy. The claim is that, for me to be envious of someone or something, I must hold that this someone or something is good, and this must partly account for my envy, and furthermore envy cannot be understood without reference to goodness, though goodness can certainly be understood without reference to envy.

However, if some emotions are thus connected with independently identifiable values, this is clearly not so for all emotions. Anger, scorn, love: what are the independently identifiable values in response to which these emotions arise?

At this point, in the attempt to secure universality for the connexion between emotion and evaluation, the claim modulates into its second version, and now it takes its examples from across the whole range of the emotions. And that is because, for any emotion, we can find a value that is logically posterior to it, or that can be understood only through understanding it. This is guaranteed through the wide availability of prefixes like 'worthy of' or 'deserving of', and of suffixes like '-able' and '-ible', where these are appropriately understood. Examples of emotion and value connected in this way, are – and the examples are necessarily taken at random – anger, and deserving of anger; scorn, and being despicable; love, and being worthy of love; hatred, and being hateful.

But, as the claim in its first version showed, this is only one part of what has to be established. What the claim must additionally establish is two things. First, that, when we are angry with someone, we find that person worthy of anger, and, secondly, that our doing so is partly why we are angry with him. Similarly it must be that, when we despise someone, we find him despicable, and that is partly why we despise him, and that, when we are in love with someone, we find that person lovable, and fall in love accordingly. In other words, any token of an emotion presupposes an associated evaluation, to which it owes its existence. Is this right?

The truth of human nature seems to be that we can be angry with someone, or despise someone, or love someone, without finding the person deserving of that emotion. A man can despise a woman for what he regards as her virtue, and a woman can love a man just for his worthlessness. Balzac's Baron and Baronne Hulot settle, it would seem, into just such a mould.[63] Perhaps, if we are to think of some emotion of ours as altogether rational, we must think of its object as deserving it. But that is neither the norm that our emotions follow, nor one to which we think they should comply. In our emotional life, we do not always feel ourselves to have right on our side.

And now I must distance myself from those for whom it will seem good enough to object that, if a universal connexion is asserted between forming an emotion and making some dependent evaluation, this can be done only by trivializing the evaluation – that is, by reducing it to the mere formation of the emotion. The argument goes that, if we think that a politician who despises his rival must find him despicable, then *for us* finding someone despicable cannot mean anything over and above despising him: or, if we think that a lover necessarily finds his mistress worthy of love, then *for us* finding someone worthy of love is the same as loving her. But, as I have argued earlier, in anticipating critics of an experience of satisfaction, this kind of objection is far too hasty. To universalize can be to trivialize, but it need not be. Before we claim that a certain universalization legislates out of existence a fact of life, or legislates into existence something that is not to be found on this earth, we should first determine what is the case. It so happens that the present universalization attempts to bulldoze our experience.

In the next lecture, I shall return to other forms of connexion there might be between emotion and value.[64]

10. The history of emotion resumes: *As the emotion persists, it will manifest itself. It will certainly manifest itself internally, and, if the conditions are congenial, it will manifest itself externally.*

Let us start with the *internal manifestations*.

Emotions manifest themselves internally in *occurrent thoughts*, *feelings*, *wishes*, and *phantasies*. For these to manifest the emotion, they must be caused by the emotion, and generally they will be directed on to, or will circle around, what, once the precipitating factor, is now the object of the emotion. These different kinds of manifestation are not independent of one another. For instance, the thoughts, feelings, and wishes may be directed on to the object as it is believed to be or as it occurs in some phantasy that the emotion induces. Or the wishes may be intensified by the feelings, or the feelings by the thoughts.

Of these internal manifestations of emotion, wishes and phantasies are the most complex. They account for the deeper, or more buried, side of emotion, and they will receive separate, if still rather perfunctory, treatment at the end of this lecture. Something has already been said descriptively about phantasy, and, for the present, it is enough to add that phantasy, unlike belief, is not something that is tested against reality.

As to thoughts, in this context three things must be borne in mind. (One) the thoughts need not be complete thoughts: they do not have to be propositional in character. (Two) the relevant thoughts will be mostly about the object of the emotion, and only to some lesser degree to the effect that the person has the emotion. (Three) we must include, not only thoughts that we think, or thoughts that we use to work something out, but also thoughts that float into the mind unbidden, as in a daydream, or when we associate to some event or figure. This is a further reflexion of the fact that emotion is connected at least as closely with imagination as with belief.

In contemporary philosophy, there is a tendency to go beyond the view that emotion manifests itself in thought, and to claim that emotion *is* thought: there is nothing, or very little, to emotion but thought.[65] A special version of this claim, to which things said in the last section are relevant, is the view that emotion *is* evaluation, or that there is nothing, or very little, to emotion but a thought that ascribes to something a certain value. The currency given to the phrase, a 'cognitive theory of the emotions', and the corresponding thesis that emotions have a cognitive content, have done a great deal to confuse the present view, or that emotion is thought, with the very different view, already considered, that emotions are invariably directed on to facts.

If the claim that emotion is thought is evident hyperbole, it meets, from the side of popular thinking, the complementary exaggeration that emotion is nothing but feeling, and, though neither view is of interest for what it asserts, each view deserves attention for the confidence with which it denies any place in emotion to what the other view accords a monopoly. For, in each case, what is denied is first traduced through a gross but explicable misconception.

When thought is denied a place in emotion, this is for the reason that to allow it in would be to intellectualize emotion in an unacceptable fashion.

But this argument erroneously assumes that, inside emotion, thought will operate in the same way as it does inside, say, inquiry, and it overlooks the fact, considered in the first lecture, that thought is a merely instrumental disposition. Thought takes on an end from the outside. So, when thinking is made to serve inquiry, it serves the end that inquiry pursues: it aids in the construction, or purification, of some truth-oriented picture of the world. Equally, when thinking is recruited into the service of emotion, it helps to strengthen, or elaborate upon, some attitude that we have towards something in, or held to be in, the world. It follows that, if thinking intellectualizes belief, there is no reason to conclude that it will intellectualize emotion. When Othello entertains the thought that Cassio possesses the handkerchief spotted with strawberries, and, under the tutelage of Iago, turns it over and over in his mind, he does not intellectualize his jealousy. He plunges deeper and deeper into the jungle of his imagination, as he is the first to realize.[66]

A common role that thought plays within emotion is to cement those identifications or mergings of one figure with another, and of one fact with another, which give the life of the emotions their chaotic, overgrown, vegetal character. It is plausible that the intersubstitutivity of objects of desire, which is what allows desires to be satisfied without coming true, is to be explained in terms of the intersubstitutivity of objects of emotion. For the likelihood is that those desires which exhibit this fluidity in the most florid form are those which derive from emotion.

When feeling is denied any place in emotion, this is because feeling is thought to be inadequate to two demands that emotion would need to make of it.[67] In the first place, feeling is held to lack the intentionality that emotion possesses. Secondly, feeling cannot be thought of as reasonable or justified in a way that emotions regularly are.[68]

Both arguments are flawed. The first contains an error about feeling. For some feelings have considerable intentionality, as when our fingers register a particular kind of silk, or we experience in our shoulder blades the oncoming of snow, or we experience anger in the softest-spoken words.[69] The second contains an error about emotion. For, contrary to much contemporary philosophy of mind,[70] many emotions are not susceptible to rational adjudication. However, these objections apart, the best that these arguments could establish is that emotion is not exclusively feeling. Neither argument shows that feeling has no place within emotion.

But there is a third and more powerful argument. It is that there is no way of exhibiting feeling as integrated with emotion. Feeling must stand outside emotion, and remain a mere appendage to it, and an account of emotion that includes it must degenerate into a mere inventory. This cautionary consideration needs to be kept in our minds at all times when we turn, as I now do, to the proper place of feeling within emotion.

11. A natural starting-point for any such inquiry is William James's discussion of feeling and emotion. However, for James's views to prove serviceable, we must rescue them at once from James's critics and from James himself.

The disservice that James did to his own views lies in the way he viewed the ontology of emotion. For James, as was briefly noted in the first lecture, failed to recognize the dispositional nature of emotion. He equated emotions with mental states, and this he showed in the way he used the terms 'emotion' and 'emotional reaction' interchangeably: for the latter term clearly refers to a transient mental event.[71] In consequence, for James, the crucial step in the analysis of emotion was to isolate the special kind of mental state with which emotion could be identified, and for this role he selected feeling, or, more accurately, feeling as he saw it.

Rescuing James's views from James is then a matter of two things: first, restoring to emotion its dispositional status, and, secondly, seeing how far James's view of feeling has to be revised so that feeling, now no longer identified with emotion, can stand to emotion as a mental state does to the disposition it serves. If feeling is to serve emotion, it has to be able to do three things, and the philosophical task is to show how this is possible. Feeling has to be able (one) to initiate emotion, (two) to manifest emotion appropriately, and (three), in manifesting emotion, to inform the person of, or to provide him with evidence for, the specific character of the emotion. Of these three requirements, the first two come from the general nature of dispositions, and how dispositions relate to mental states, whereas the third is specific to the nature of emotion. The mental states that are connected with emotion play a large part in impressing upon us what our emotions are.

Clearly, if these requirements are to be met, feeling must emerge as more than an item in an inventory: it must be more than correlated with emotion.

But, first, let us take stock of the fact often overlooked – and now the obstacle is no longer James himself but his critics – that James too set feeling within a dispositional structure. Only James, having called feeling emotion, now calls this structure, not emotion, but instinct. In consequence, in order to understand James, we need to read, alongside the famous Chapter XXV in *The Principles of Psychology* on the Emotions, the preceding chapter, which is entitled Instinct.[72]

For James, instinct operates in the following way: A person, or non-human animal, becomes aware of an object. The object may be external or internal: it may be present, absent, or merely believed-in. However, because of the person's instinctual endowment, this object triggers an impulse. This impulse, as it diffuses itself through the body, finds expression successively in physiological excitation, bodily expression, and, finally, voluntary muscular action.

And now the stage is set for what James calls emotion. For, as the various bodily changes occur, the person experiences them, and emotion is the feelings that the person has of that gamut of bodily changes which follow upon the awareness of an object that excites an instinct.[73]

The first question to ask is, Can the account that James offers of what he calls emotion be taken out of this context, and reused as an account of the element of feeling within the structure of emotion, properly so called? Or is his account too influenced by the context in which he introduced it to be exported? If the answer is that his account can be salvaged, then how is this to be done?

If James's account is to be re-used, it is on one point in need of revision, on another of clarification.

First, revision: James, in linking feeling and bodily change, thinking of one as the inner lining of the other, takes what is, from the perspective of emotion, undoubtedly an excessively broad view of bodily change. He should not have grouped together glandular secretions and acts that we do intentionally, as well as everything that lies in between, as though all of them could be thought of as direct responses to the perception of an exciting object. It is this broad understanding of bodily change, and the consequent broad understanding of feeling of bodily change, just as much as the subsequent identification of emotion with such feeling, that makes James's better known formulations of his theory seem to some 'preposterous'.[74] If, instead of saying, as he notoriously did, 'We are frightened *because we run away* [i.e., an intentional action]', or 'We feel sorry *because we cry* [i.e., a bodily expression]',[75] he had limited himself strictly to saying things like 'We are disgusted *because of the acidity in our stomach* [i.e., a visceral change]', he would still have have been wrong, but not preposterously so.

Accordingly, if we are to have an account of feeling that can be fitted into the structure of emotion, we need to revise James's view so that (one) the only bodily changes it recognizes are changes that occur beneath the skin, and (two) it correspondingly restricts the relevant feelings to feelings of just such changes.

And now for clarification: For James's view of feeling is still not fully utilizable until we clarify what it is for a feeling to be a feeling *of* a bodily change? Clearly the relationship of bodily change to feeling is causal, but is the cause of the feeling registered in its subjectivity? On this matter there are four possible views. Which did James adopt, and how does this ultimately effect the accommodation of Jamesian feeling within emotion?

One view is that the feeling has a certain quality, like a smell, or a taste, which enables us, once we have learnt that this quality is causally connected with a certain bodily change, to develop a habit of inferring from the feeling to the bodily change. A second view is that the feeling not only is an effect, it is a perception, of the bodily change so that we do not have to rely upon an inference to know what the bodily change is. Once our sensibilities have been sharpened, we are directly aware of it. A third view assigns to the feeling an enlarged informational content. For it maintains that, in perceiving the bodily change, we can also be aware of it as having been brought about by a certain, or by a certain sort of, object. The fourth view retains the idea of the feeling as having a distinctive quality, it allows that this distinctive quality can inform us about the cause of the bodily change, but what it now plays down is the role of the feeling as giving us either direct, i.e. perceptual, or indirect, i.e. inferential, information about the character of the bodily change. The feeling is of the bodily change to the extent that it is caused by, and makes us cognizant of what caused, the bodily change.

If James leans towards all four views in turn, it is the third and fourth for which textual support is strongest, and it is they – and, more particularly, the fourth, which is anyhow more plausible than the third – that provide the most congenial interpretation of feeling if feeling is to be transposed into the orbit of emotion, and there discharge the three tasks required of it.

As to the first two tasks, it is highly plausible that a feeling of bodily change, as determined by either of these last two views, should occur both when emotion is initiated and when it manifests itself. For it is plausible that specific bodily changes should occur at both such moments. But the question is, How, and why, do we come to think of such feelings as intrinsic to, rather than merely correlated with, the emotion?

Consider the case of the boy who wakes up in damp grass, finds a frog sitting on his chest, and develops a fear of frogs. On seeing the frog, the boy will have an experience, which he calls, and later finds that others call, butterflies in the stomach. What is the difference between the way this experience stands to the oncoming emotion and the way a hiccough would have, had the boy happened to hiccough when he saw the frog on his chest? And what accounts for this difference?

The ultimate explanation is complex, but there are two kinds of experience that play a large part in bonding feeling with emotion to produce the effect of which we are all aware.

The first kind of experience occurs both when the emotion forms and when it later manifests itself. As we have already seen, it is part of the attitude constitutive of any emotion that, as it forms, we start to experience its object as having it in it, or as having the causal power, to bring about either the satisfaction or the frustration of the originatory desire. But this is not the whole story: it needs to be amplified. For, when feelings of bodily change are also aroused, the object is further experienced as having it in it to bring about them too. So, in our example, the boy will perceive the frog as cause at once of the frustration of his desire for tranquillity and of the butterflies in his stomach. And note two things: (one) the boy will perceive the frog this way, he will not simply believe that the frog has this causal power, and (two) the causal power is not limited to a single bout of butterflies in the stomach, it extends to the feeling as a kind. Here is one way in which the feeling works itself into the emotion.

The second kind of experience occurs when, the emotion once formed, it manifests itself. For our present purposes, such occasions may be divided into two. First, there are those occasions when – to stay with our example – there is, or is believed to be, a frog, and the same bodily changes and the same feelings occur as on the original occasion, and, in effect, fear is freshly experienced. Secondly, there are those occasions when there is no frog, but the frog in its primary awfulness is either recalled or imagined. On these latter occasions, which are significant for the further integration of feeling and emotion, it is not to be expected that the original bodily changes, or the corresponding feelings, will recur, but what will occur are recollections, or imaginings, of those feelings. The boy will recall, or imagine, butterflies in the stomach.

Why are these occasions, or what I have called *secondary occurrences* of feeling,[76] so significant?

Contrast them with the occasions on which an emotion manifests itself in response to the world, or stimulated by its object: the boy's fear is aroused by seeing a frog again. On such occasions, there is nothing in the structure of the experience to indicate whether the feeling is part of the emotion, or a mere accompaniment. However, when the feeling occurs secondarily, or in response to an act of recall or imagination directed on to an emotion, the fact that the feeling responds to this summons strongly suggests that it belongs with the emotion, or is part of it. What we find ourselves remembering or imagining when we set ourselves to remember or to imagine something internal, or a psychological phenomenon, is an index of the scope or limits of that phenomenon, or of how it is individuated.[77]

I turn now to the third task that feeling must fulfil if it is to be integrated with emotion, and ask whether, as revised, it can be expected to give us information about the emotion that it manifests.

There are certainly occasions when the occurrence of feeling seems to teach us that an old emotion is still extant, or that a new emotion has silently formed, or that a familar emotion is again in evidence: that we are still in love, or now jealous, or angry again. And, if sometimes we can feel something, and not know what emotion manifests itself, this is no objection. It shows only that, when feeling does tell us something about emotion, it does so, not unaided, but against the background of ancillary or contextual belief. This being so, we might expect, in the absence of such belief, to be ignorant of what the emotion is, or, for that matter, what the feeling is like.

To this view of feeling, and its evidential role, there are three putative objections. The first two come from philosophy, and the third from experimental psychology, and, between them, they seem to cover the field. The first objection challenges the very concept of feeling that the view employs. The second concedes feeling existence, but denies it any evidential role. The third claims that, when feeling functions evidentially, the role of ancillary or contextual belief is very much larger than I have allowed for. Of necessity I shall present the objections, and their rebuttals, perfunctorily.

The first objection is that feeling, as I have introduced it, can only be a 'private object', and therefore cannot be appealed to in any public discussion of the nature of, or our knowledge about, the emotions. Its presence, or absence, must leave any situation unaltered.

But this objection exemplifies a common error. For Wittgenstein, to whom we owe this argument and its terminology,[78] makes it totally clear that his target is, initially, a particular theory of language – that is, one which allows certain words to cut loose from the general web of public discourse and its constraints, and yet apply to the mind – and then, derivatively, any fragment of language, of which this theory is true, or which necessitates its acceptance. It is therefore only if what I have been saying about feeling offends in this way that I fall victim to the objection. Now, strictly speaking, to talk in this offending way is, by the standards of the argument, conceptually impossible, and so the charge would have to be that I have suggested that my words need to be taken in a way that requires the nonsensical theory. Evidently any such charge would be a very complex matter, but I see no way in which it could be levelled against my account of feeling, and what it tells us.

The second objection comes from a different philosophical direction. It starts from the premiss that the states of feeling that characteristically manifest a certain emotion – say, fright manifesting fear, or rage manifesting anger – are nothing more than the consciousness of these emotions. Accordingly, to contemplate the hypothesis that one of these mental states could occur and we remain ignorant of the underlying disposition is to entertain the conceptually impossible. There being no way in which doubt or ignorance can get between the mental state, once it has occurred, and the mental disposition, it follows that there is no way in which the mental state can serve as evidence for the mental disposition.[79]

To this objection, there are two responses. First, it depsychologizes a familiar kind of mental state, at least to the extent of interpreting it as a purely informational state. If there were psychological states of this order, it needs to be explained how the information is encoded. But then, secondly, the process of depsychologization is carried further forward when the state is treated as incorrigible, or (the same thing) its informational content is said to be beyond dispute. For surely any way in which the information about the emotion is encoded must allow for the possibility that we might make a mistake in grasping, or decoding, the information. Furthermore the information itself might be erroneous.

The third objection contends that my mistake lies, not in overlooking the incorrigibility of states of feeling, but in seriously underestimating the influence of contextual belief upon such states. For this objection, I draw upon a well-known experiment by the psychologists Stanley Schachter and Jerome Singer, which is credited with showing that feeling is, to some large degree, a function of contextual belief.[80] Since ambiguity surrounds this experiment, I shall offer a rather pared-down description of it, but which is, I hope, free of controversy.

A set of subjects are injected with adrenalin, under the guise of a vitamin supplement. Some, or the 'informed', are told of the side-effects of the drug, and others, the 'ignorant', are not. The two groups are then distributed between two environments, which, by the painfully crude standards of the experimenters, are regarded as conducive, one to rage, the other to euphoria. Each environment is manipulated by a 'stooge', who has assigned to him a repertoire of behaviour thought appropriate to the feeling associated with that environment. So, in the rage room, a questionnaire is passed round to the subjects, and, when it has been conscientiously filled in, the stooge tears it up. In the euphoria room, the stooge flies paper aeroplanes. At the end of the experiment, the subjects are asked two things: first, whether they felt angry or happy, and, secondly, to what degree. The answers given turn out to correlate with the environment in which the subjects had been placed, though the 'informed', in virtue of having another explanation of the state they found themselves in, give themselves a lower emotional rating than the 'ignorant'.

However, if we ask what this experiment shows about the dependence of feeling upon contextual belief, the question cannot be answered independently of what view we take of the nature of feeling.

If we take the view that I have been assuming, or a corrected Jamesianism, what the experiment appears to show is something like, but considerably less than, what the experimenters themselves claim for it. It shows that, in some cases, perhaps in many, though it provides no reason to think in all, belief influences feeling. But note that it shows this only if it can be assumed that certain conditions have been satisfied. As the experiment is actually set up, their satisfaction is not ensured.

The first condition is that the subjects answered the very questions that they were asked. In other words, they set out to report what they felt rather than what they thought they should be feeling, or what they were expected to feel. For, unless this is what they did, the experiment could not possibly show that what they felt – as opposed to what, out of deference to the experimenters, they said that they felt – was influenced by contextual belief. The experiment, as it was set up, did not obviously encourage the subjects to make these distinctions.

The second condition is that the answers that the subjects gave were, not merely relevant to the question that they were asked, but were truthful. Once again there is room for scepticism. For (one) the subjects' reports were elicited from them by questioning, rather than volunteered, and (two) the questions were put to them in circumstances that so little resembled those in which anger, or happiness, or indeed any other human emotion, normally arises that their replies might seem undermotivated.

The third condition is that the experimenters had to have a way of distinguishing between the subjects' feelings' being influenced by beliefs about the environment, which is what the experiment claims to find, and their being influenced directly by the environment itself, which is, of course, what we should expect of feelings. Again, there is no reason to believe that the experiment was set up in such a way as to make this discrimination.

The fourth condition, which is closely connected with the third, is that, before the subjects experienced any influence coming from beliefs about the environment, there was something else that they felt. Or at least this: that there was something else that they would have felt, had their feelings not been subjected to experimental pressure. Otherwise the beliefs might be totally idle: there would be nothing that they could be said to have influenced. Once again, there is nothing to suggest that there was anything in the conduct of the experiment to ensure that this condition was met.

However at this stage it needs to be pointed out that there is another view that can be taken of the nature of feeling, and that would very much alter what we might think that the experiment shows. It is, oddly enough, the view explicitly taken by the experimenters. In fact, they treat the view, not so much as an assumption of the experiment, as something that the experiment further establishes. I say 'oddly enough', because the view is incompatible with what they think that the experiment otherwise establishes, or that feeling is influenced, indeed strongly influenced, by belief.

This second view of feeling is, broadly speaking, that (one) every feeling has, as a common core, an indeterminate experience of arousal, and (two) what further distinguishes the various specific states of feeling, such as rage as opposed to terror, or euphoria as opposed to jealousy, is, in each case, a matter of contextual or ancillary beliefs.

Now, on such a view, feeling, constituted of arousal plus belief, evidently lacks the required apartness from belief for the conclusion that belief strongly influences feeling to be fully intelligible. If feeling is partly constituted by belief, as Schachter and Singer appear to think, then to say that feeling is influenced by belief is like saying that a poem is influenced by the words it uses, or a car by the engine that drives it.

If some of the inappositeness of the experiment to its conclusion is not always totally evident, this is partly because of the preference the experimenters show for the scientistic term 'to label' as the word for what the subjects do to their feelings when they say what they feel. The aim of the experiment is then said to be that of finding out how the subjects label their feelings.

Now, if the subjects really were doing something best thought of as labelling, then they would be following a practice with very much its own rules. It would be a practice that required them, first, to dissociate certain words from the meaning that they ordinarily possess, and then to apply them to their feelings in a way that attached importance solely to consistency of usage. It would be crucial for them to avoid applying either the same word or 'label' to different feelings, or different words or 'labels' to the same feeling. That being the paramount aim, a promising strategy might be to classify feelings, not at all according to how they are experienced, which is irrelevant to this project, but by reference to the outward circumstances in which they are manifested. If that strategy were followed by the subjects, then it would be a matter of no surprise that 'feelings', or how people's feelings were labelled, would be heavily influenced by contextual, or ancillary, beliefs. But note that this way of classifying feelings has very little to do with the ordinary practice of describing them, and, in consequence, a study of how it would be carried out has virtually nothing of psychological interest to tell us.

12. I turn now to *the external manifestations of emotion*, or how emotion relates to behaviour.

Here my fundamental claim is that emotion is not directly motivational. Emotion does not, either unaided or in conjunction with some ancillary psychological factor, cause the person to act in some particular way, for which it then provides the reason. Judged by the standards set for motivational force by desire and appropriately paired belief, that of emotion is woefully inadequate.

In claiming that emotion lacks *direct* motivational force, I am not denying the indirect influence that emotion can have upon behaviour through the desires that it generates. For these desires, combining with instrumental beliefs, may then cause actions. This will be the topic of the next section.

There are four interrelated considerations that support my present negative claim.

The first starts from the role of emotion. The role of emotion is to be understood in terms of a certain end that emotion has: that end being, as we know, to supply the person with an attitude. In including an end, the role of emotion resembles that of belief, or that of desire, and is in contrast to that of a purely instrumental disposition, like thinking or imagination. But as important as the fact that belief, desire, and emotion have ends is the fact the ends associated with these different kinds of emotion differ amongst themselves. For, desire, having supplied the person with a target, then supplies the person with the further end of aiming at the target. There is nothing comparable that belief does when it has supplied the person with a picture of the world: belief does not supply the person with a further end vis-à-vis this picture. And, in this respect, emotion resembles belief rather than desire. Emotion, having supplied the person with an attitude towards the world, does not supply him with a further end towards this attitude.

Some will object that this cannot be right. Wrong about desire, it cannot be depended upon to give us, through the contrast between emotion and desire, a trustworthy conclusion about emotion. If desire were as it is claimed to be, it would be caught up in an infinite regress. Having supplied the person with the end of aiming at the target, it would then have to supply the person with some further end, such as that of girding himself to aim at the target, and so on, and so on.

But this objection misunderstands the structure of the claim about desire. That desire, in supplying the person with one end, supplies him with a second end is not based on the general nature of an end. If it were, that would indeed give rise to some form of regress. Rather the claim is based on the specific nature of the first end that desire provides: this end specifically requires a second end, which does not itself require a further, or third, end. The claim is based, it might be said, on the intrinsic nature of a target, or the intrinsic difference between a target and, say, an attitude.

To bring this difference into focus, let us look closer at what happens when an attitude forms. First, suppose that my emotion is positive, with the implication that a desire of mine has been satisfied, then it will be intrinsic to my attitude that I shall find the world, or that part of it which has been altered as the result of the satisfaction of my desire, a better place. Next, suppose that my emotion is negative, now with the implication that a desire of mine has been frustrated, then it will be intrinsic to my attitude that I shall find the world, in some respect at least, a worse place for me. But, in each case, it would be a further step, a step beyond what the attitude intrinsically requires, were I to want to do something about this: say, to repay the world, or to take steps to see that it stays as it is, alternatively, to take revenge upon the world, or to make it revert to what it was before. An attitude is not inherently directive, whereas this is precisely what a target is. I cannot be held to take something as a target unless I recognize its directive character, and recognizing its directive character is giving myself – if I am the appropriate person – the end of taking aim at it.

The second consideration follows close upon the first, and it involves recognizing how, in the aftermath of satisfied or frustrated desire, the mere formation of the emotion can, in certain circumstances, establish a kind of equilibrium. That it can sometimes do this shows us something about the nature of emotion. When Aristotle and other ancient thinkers defined anger as a desire for revenge, they might have reflected that anger itself can be a form of revenge. Nietzsche, writing of Schopenhauer, said that his anger against his enemies – Hegel, women, sensuality – was 'his balm, his refreshment, his reward, his specific against disgust, his *happiness*'.[81] A once well known woman novelist said in my presence, 'Some people, when others do foolish things, try to get their own back. Margaret and I just bear malice.' Malice I take to be an emotion.

The third consideration is grounded in a further contrast between emotion and desire. Desire can terminate in a variety of ways. Desire may be given up or abandoned, willingly, or under duress, or in error, or for some less clear motivation. Or it may wither away. Or it may be defended against. *Or* it may be satisfied. In the first lecture, I argued against any mechanical inference from the object of a desire to what will satisfy it. Nevertheless I insisted that what will satisfy a desire is still internal to the desire: in so far as it does not derive from the object of the desire, it derives from its formation. In contrast to satisfaction, the other ways desire may come to an end are external.

I now claim that there is nothing comparable to satisfaction in the case of emotion. There may be, particularly with emotions directed on to facts, events that are likely to bring them to an end. If I am angry that you insulted me, or am frightened that you will attack me in a drunken rage, and you apologize, or stop drinking, my anger, or my fear, might well change. But, not only is it possible to visualize situations in which it would not, but bringing an emotion to an end is not comparable to its satisfaction. It is not the consummation of the emotion. Nor is anything else.

The final consideration is structural. If, contrary to what I have been contending, emotion were motivational, and were, in this way, like desire, then there would have to be some further factor with which emotion could combine, as desire does with instrumental belief, so as to channel its motivational force in an appropriate direction. The serviceability of belief to desire derives from the structure of desire. But, again, there is nothing similar in the structure of emotion. Belief can supply desire with means only because desire is directive.

Against the view that emotion lacks direct motivational force, it may be countered that there are clear cases where, asked why someone did something, we cite an emotion. But, to assess this response, we must first note that these cases fall into two rather different classes. Neither class justifies our thinking that emotion is motivational.

First, there are those trivial cases where, since a particular emotion regularly gives rise to the same desire, the emotion-term gets stretched so that it comes to cover the conjunction of the emotion and the subsequent desire. When this happens, the explanatory, or semi-explanatory, force of the emotion-term as far as action is concerned is unproblematic. (I say 'semi-explanatory', for, of course, the action is not fully explained until the instrumental belief that had combined itself with the encapsulated desire is retrieved.) So, for instance, in our unheroic culture, 'fear', which is generally used to refer at once to the emotion fear and to the desire to run away, which the emotion is expected to excite, can be used to explain a range of cowardly actions. Then, as cultural habits and social anticipations change, the use of the emotion-term may shrink, and peel back, so as now to pick out only the emotion, and, when this happens, the previous extended usage is revealed as a cultural artifact, or as the imposition of culture upon the emotions. If it now seems quaint that the term 'anger' should ever have included the desire for revenge, this is because we have lost that sense of honour which makes insults left unavenged impossible to bear, but which finds many adverse situations supportable so long as one's good name is not impugned.

The second class of cases is more interesting. Such cases arise when, in the first place, the action to be explained is in some way exceptional — it was especially reckless, or especially noble, or especially ignoble — and, secondly, though the desire that motivated the action is manifest, it is hard to understand either how the person came by such a desire or why, having come by it, he should have thought of acting on it. If we ask, Why did Regulus return to Carthage? Why did the widowed Princesse de Clèves renounce the duc de Nemours? Why did Steerforth abandon little Emily? Why on earth did Oscar Wilde sue Lord Queensberry?, and, if we are told, quite accurately, Because he wanted to keep his word, Because she desired to follow the path of modesty, Because he craved to be on his own, Because he loved showing off, we can accept that, in each case, we have been given the proximate cause of the action, but we have not been told enough to understand why it was done. Keeping one's word, the love of modesty, the preservation of one's independence, the cult of the fine gesture: these are familiar, and in general comprehensible, aims to set oneself. But to pursue them in the face of certain death, or to the total sacrifice of love and happiness, or in the knowledge that an innocent life would be broken, or in the certainty of disgrace and ruin? That is another matter, we might think, and then what we need to do is to go behind the desire, and try to grasp what the emotion was out of which the desire, which in itself explains so little, was generated. Brought face-to-face with the great emotional intransigencies of manic pride, or unfathomable guilt, or the fear of goodness, or parricidal omnipotence, we start to find what initially seems an improbable act something that is only too human in some deep, indisputable way.

I turn now to the indirect motivational force of emotion.

13. *The emotion generates desires.*

The word 'generate' must be understood with caution. For, though, when emotion gives rise to desire, this is a step beyond the mere formation of emotion, this is not a step that we necessarily, or generally, take intentionally. Nor, when the step is taken, is there any simple, or straight, or even any well-trodden, path, running from the emotion to the desire, on which we set foot.

In his essay *De la peur*, Montaigne considers the variety of ways in which man can react to fear. Some have hanged themselves, some have drowned themselves, some have leaped to their death. The Emperor Theophilus, defeated by the Agarenes, could not flee, but fell into a deep stupor. And ten thousand Roman infantrymen, terrified by Hannibal's army, panicked, and, throwing themselves upon the main body of the enemy, brought about what would, in other circumstances, have been reckoned a glorious victory.[82]

Some order can be introduced into this matter by bringing under a few headings the different ways in which a desire can stand to the emotion that generates it. If we take care to pay equal attention to positive and to negative emotions, we can observe that the desire may be directed (one) towards the object of the emotion, advancing or retarding it, (two) towards the consequences of the object of the emotion, maximizing or minimizing them,[83] or (three) towards the emotion itself, reinforcing or attenuating it. Examples: Someone who admires a woman will want her to be happy. Someone who admires a poem will want it widely read. Someone who admires a politician may want not to learn too much about his early life. Or again: Someone frightened of a rattlesnake by the kitchen door will want the snake shot. Someone who is frightened of an earthquake, but knows that he can do nothing to stop it, will want his house proof against the worst ravages. Someone frightened of heights, or of being touched, or of picking up the telephone when it rings after dark, will want to master this fear, and with this aim will struggle to understand it.[84]

Of course, within each of the three broad ways in which a desire can relate to the emotion that generates it, there will be a variety of specific desires open to the person, so that which desire actually forms will be dependent upon a multiplicity of factors other than the nature of the emotion. So consider the emotion of hope, and contrast those who hope to enjoy life in heaven, and those who hope for union with a lover on this earth. In both cases, a desire of the first kind, or one that might broadly be thought of as a desire for the furtherance of the hoped-for object, will form. But note that those who hope for life eternal will not, a few fanatics apart, desire to bring it any closer. However those who hope to be rejoined with a lover will, even if they relish a mild postponement, desire that it come soon. Indeed, as with Orpheus returning with Eurydice from the underworld, it is comprehensible to rate immediacy of gratification over enduring satisfaction.

Sometimes in the wake of a strong or unmanageable emotion, a desire forms that is a defence against it. Irked by a life in which indolence alternated with irresistible physical passion, the poet Alfieri tells how he instructed his valet to tie him to a chair in front of a window opposite his mistress's house, from where he could watch her every movement. The cords, concealed under the copious sleeves of the habit he wore, left one hand free, so that he could write when he had attained the necessary calm, and he had himself released only when, as far as he could see, the fury of love had burnt itself out.[85] But this is a simple case. On other occasions, the desire that is a defence against the emotion, conceals itself in the heart of the emotion. A middle-aged man, who looks to women to satisfy his every need, endlessly falls for women much younger than himself, brisk, organized, quick to laugh at the weaknesses of others, and with no evident softness of temperament. Ought we to be surprised? Only so long as we fail to observe that, each time he finds his ideal partner, what he hopes for from her is, not that she will love him as he wants to be loved, but that he will be able to get rid of his inconsolability, and those needs of his out of which it springs, and bury them inside her and her seductive self-sufficiency. Each time she puts her own needs above his, he has the momentary delusion of success.

One factor likely to mediate between a person's emotion and the desires that will form under its aegis is the person's values.

Humanity mostly prevents us from even thinking of destroying those who have caused us moderate grief: attachment to money, from rewarding adequately those to whom we owe a great deal. When philosophers talk of emotion as appropriate to its object, there is, in addition to the error of thinking that, for every emotion, there is such a norm, the further error of thinking that such a norm, when it exists, is a single thing, capable of comparatively simple application. In reality, in so far as appropriateness is a notion we need in considering emotion, it marks the intersection of many warring values.

That value filters emotion in this way is surely one reason why emotion itself is thought by some – incorrectly, I have argued – to be intrinsically value-laden. Specifically it helps to explain why emotion is thought to be value-laden by those who conceptually merge emotion, desire, and the propensity to act into one whole, which they call emotion.

That value mediates between emotion and desire, and thus between emotion and action, further explains why the influence of emotion upon action should be, not only indirect, but unpredictable. For our values, and our commitment to our values, and our preparedness to act upon this commitment – three totally separate things, let it be noted[86] – are all inherently fluid, and we in relation to them are often lazy, neglectful, or cowardly. The vaunted stability that values give our lives they give, at least in the first instance, to our inner life, or how we see the world, rather than to our outer life, or how we act upon the world. As to the outer life, our values have too many powerful rivals, as well as too many internal disagreements, for their impact to be predictable.

One of the most significant factors in the generation of desire by emotion is the state of restlessness into which emotion in general, and some emotions in particular, can throw the person. Fear, love, hate, jealousy, remorse, are such emotions. There are two reasons why restlessness encourages the formation of desires. First, the desires that form might lead to action that would, without necessarily terminating the emotion, terminate the restlessness. Many an unhappy man has pointlessly challenged his rival in love to a duel. Secondly, the mere formation of desire, even without being acted upon, can serve as a steadying influence upon the tumult that the emotion causes. We may be sure that many a challenge, fully formed in the mind, was never delivered.[87]

I have already said that, for all their conceptual independence, it is difficult to conceive of the formation of desire of any seriousness except against the background of emotion. And now I suggest the converse: that in actuality it is hard to envisage emotion of any seriousness that does not give rise to desire. But this latter point should not lead us to conclude, indeed it should provide us with the antidote against thinking, that emotion entails desire.

However, if emotion is connected only indirectly with action, there is another, and a direct, relation that emotion has with behaviour. Emotion can express itself in behaviour.

14. What is the relation of '*expressing itself in*'?

This is a relation that holds between a mental phenomenon and something else.[88] Mental phenomena other than emotions can find expression. Desire can, and so can anxiety, and so can uncertainty. But emotions do so famously. What the something else is in which mental phenomena find expression is generally something that, even if not wholly external, is partly external: a frown, a cry of pain, the broken syntax of speech. But it can be something altogether internal: for instance, a state of confusion. (Artistic, or aesthetic, expression, which is achieved intentionally, and through something completely external, is a different issue.)

Some cases of expression are very simple, some are very complex, there are intervening cases, and, with the expression of emotion, the full spectrum of possibilities is employed. A simple case is when a man who is happy smiles, or one who is angry scowls. More complex cases would be where a woman, disappointed with a man, meets him at a party, and cannot bring herself to talk to him: she cannot bring herself, even when she is sitting next to him at dinner, to acknowledge his existence. Yet more complex is the kind of case where a young man hopes against hope that the woman with whom he is infatuated will extricate herself from the supper party after a concert to which she has committed herself, and come and visit him. Meanwhile he does not settle down to work. He writes a few sentences, he gets up from his desk, he walks around the room, he pretends, not to anyone else but to himself, that he is studying a print, which hangs on his wall, and which he has looked at a hundred times. He counts the windows in the house opposite, and on a pad of paper he writes her name over and over again. In all this he expresses his hope that the woman will excuse herself, and come to him.

In considering expression, I shall, on grounds that are not purely stipulative, exclude two kinds of case: on the one hand, those cases where the person does absolutely nothing, and natural processes, over which he has no control, completely take over, as when a blush is said to express embarrassment, and, on the other hand, those cases where the person does something intentionally so as to communicate his emotion, as when an angry driver is said to express his anger by cutting in front of the car next to him on the freeway.[89]

If this is the extension of the concept expression, what actually is expression?

We can enumerate some characteristics of expression. In the first place, expression is a causal relation. Secondly, it is a causal relation that appears to be unconstrained by initial conditions. Expression erupts. Or if, on some level, it is constrained, that is not how it strikes us. Thirdly, expression has no obvious practical role to play vis-à-vis emotion. This may be obscured by the fact that certain crude phantasies, of which we cannot rid ourselves, may ascribe an instrumentality to expression: so crying is phantasized as purging us of sorrow, losing our temper as ridding us of what might otherwise fester within us. But, if such phantasies, and the yet deeper phantasies from which they spring, depicting the mind as a sort of container, come to influence how we see the emotions, they are not straightforwardly descriptive of their nature. Fourthly, as a generalization of the last point, expression is not justified by emotion, instrumentally, or any other way. Fifthly, it is possible to inhibit expression of emotion. Expression, without being something that we do intentionally – it does not derive from appropriately paired belief and desire – is something that we can, on occasion, intentionally stop ourselves from doing. Sixthly, there must be some causal mechanism on which expression is dependent, though we are in the dark what that is. And, finally, most modes of expression have an evolutionary pedigree. If they do not have an instrumental role vis-à-vis the emotions, it certainly does not follow that they never had one, or that they don't still have an instrumental role within the broader life of the person.[90]

However this still leaves the core of expression, or expression itself, unspecified. Something has been left out, and a start on identifying it may be made along the following, familiar lines: As things currently stand, joy and smiling are expressively linked, and so are anger and scowling. Now what would it take, over and above the uncoupling of the existing conjunctions and their reassemblage, for scowling to express joy, and for smiling to express anger? Or could that never be done? How much deeper than constant conjunction is the expressive link?[91]

Let us note that there is a hidden complexity to this seemingly obvious issue. When we think of joy and smiling as expressively linked, the link has two aspects, neither of which has priority over the other. We link joy at once with the smile on the face, which we know from the outside, and with the activity of smiling, which we know from the inside. However these two aspects of the link – and there is the same twofold pattern with every expressive link – are themselves linked. For the bodily activity of smiling is partly identified as the process that issues in the facial configuration of the smile. Conversely, the facial configuration of the smile cannot be fully identified except as the product that issues from the bodily activity of smiling. The baby with wind does not have a smile on its face. And all this goes for scowling too.[92]

This gives us the scale of the changes required if the prevailing expressive links are to reconfigure. But what would these changes be?

What would surely be needed is large and reciprocal changes in, on the one hand, our perception of others when they express their emotions and, on the other hand, our proprioception, or our perception of ourselves, when we express our emotions, and the only way open to us of describing the required changes is to say that they must converge upon our being universally able to perceive, or experience, joy in the scowl – that is, in the scowl itself and in scowling – and anger in the smile – that is, in the smile itself and in smiling. Note that this account is not circular in that it explains a change in the way emotions express themselves in terms of a change in the way we perceive or experience emotions expressed.

And, if we now ask for an account of what it is to perceive or experience an emotion in what expresses it, whether this be the bodily expression, or the bodily activity of expressing it, I again invoke the notion of correspondence. In other words, I suggest that, when we experience joy in a smile, or in smiling, and anger in a scowl, or in scowling, we respond to a match between the smile, or smiling, and joy, alternatively between the scowl, or scowling, and anger. Recycling the notion of correspondence is based on the conviction that the process whereby we come to see a certain lie of the face or a certain bodily activity as linked to – which, in this context, means as 'expressive of' – an emotion parallels the process whereby we come to see a figure or a fact as linked to – which, in that context, means as 'having it in it to bring about' – the satisfaction or the frustration of some desire of ours.

If this gives us some insight into what would be involved in any expressive transformation such as a scowl and scowling coming to express joy, is there a coherent way of applying this insight as we shift from the simpler, to the more complex, emotions, such as disappointment, or hope, or indignation? I think that, as we make the shift, we can retain the notion of correspondence, but only if we modify the terms of the correspondence. For, with the more complex emotions, the correspondence is no longer between the expression of the emotion and how the emotion seems to us, which is how I have implicitly been taking the matter, but between the expression of the emotion and how the world, or the relevant fragment of it, seems to us when we are under the influence of the emotion. The restless behaviour of the infatuated young man in his study corresponds to the unstable, flickering vision of the world around him that hoping against hope has induced in him.[93]

15. We have now reached the final constituent of emotion, or that which gives emotion its depth: that is to say, phantasy, and its cognate, the wish.

Phantasy,[94] like emotion itself, occurs on both sides of that great divide running across our mental life, on which these lectures opened. For phantasy can be instantiated as mental state, and as mental disposition. We can at a particular moment episodically phantasize someone doing some particular thing, and we can be disposed, over a period of time, to phantasize a certain figure, now doing this, now doing that. Sometimes our phantasies will be about real-life characters, but sometimes they are solely about 'internal figures', or figures that do not exist outside phantasy. How such figures come into being will concern us.

Of its two realizations, as mental state and as mental disposition, it is as mental state that phantasy is most readily grasped. For we may, as I suggested earlier, think of states of phantasy on the model of states of imagination, or, more specifically, daydreams, with this proviso: that they are invariably unconscious, and, in consequence, their content can never be fully, or explicitly, captured in conscious terms. And this inability is not just a local inability, or one that springs from the peculiarly compressed, or peculiarly unstable, content of this or that phantasy. It is an inability inherent in the nature of phantasy.

However, if phantasy is most easily understood as mental state, it is its existence in the mind as disposition that assures it the significance that it has in our lives.

To consider dispositional phantasy, we should, as with any disposition, start from the notion of role. In the case of phantasy, we need to think of its roles, and these roles can be arranged in a hierarchy.

On the bottom level, phantasy serves as the internal representation of desire. It represents desire by bringing before the mind in a particularly vivid form the object of desire. However, in doing so, phantasy can fall victim to error. Dominated by an infantile mode of mental functioning, it can engender a confusion between the representation of the object of desire and the object itself. In consequence, when this happens, there is an illusory sense of satisfaction, and desire desists, only to return once the illusion has passed. Freud called this condition 'hallucination'.[95]

On the second level, what is malfunctioning on the first level is exploited. For now we phantasize the object of our desire so that, through the confusion between phantasy and reality, we can obtain, however briefly, the experience of satisfied desire. This phenomenon, which is not intentional, is teleological, in that it serves an end: it rests on a mechanism that would not survive if it did not continue to serve this end. For this, Freud used the term 'wish-fulfilment'.[96]

On the third level, phantasy provides the vehicle for the various defence-mechanisms, which are designed to ward off anxiety. The content of the phantasy varies with each defence-mechanism, but the underlying mode of operation, or the way in which phantasy brings about its end, is essentially the same in all cases. What happens is that, spurred on by anxiety, we episodically phantasize a state of affairs from which the occasion of anxiety has been removed, and this phantasy is so powerful that we are now disposed to phantasize the world this way. So, for instance, we fear, or fear for, something outside us: we phantasize our taking this thing into ourselves, where it will either do, or come to, no harm: and this sets up the disposition to phantasize it as existing inside us. This is introjection. Alternatively, we fear, or fear for, something inside us: we then phantasize our expelling this thing into the outer world, where it will be safe, or we safe from it: and this sets up the disposition to phantasize it as existing outside us. This is projection.

Phantasy, on the next or fourth level, concerns itself solely with figures, internal figures. Internal figures are those figures which, in the aftermath of introjection, we are disposed to phantasize as existing inside us. These figures are, up to a point, controlled by individual repertoires, which provide them with ways of thinking, feeling, acting. However, once the figures are inserted into phantasies, their repertoires can be overridden by the exigencies of the narrative, which correspond to, or mediate, our desires, wishes, and emotions. Later on, in the wake of further anxiety, we may need to project these internal figures back into the external world they come from. However, even after they have been reprojected, and thus come to be phantasized as outside us, there are a number of ways in which they are still thought about as, and thus remain, parts of ourselves.

On the final level to be considered here, though doubtless further levels could be inserted, phantasy provides us with the internal representation of emotion. This it does basically by depicting a cast of figures in a world of facts, acting, and being acted upon, in ways that accord with the attitude that lies at the core of the emotion. The stage will be centrally occupied by the object of the emotion.

At all levels, the efficacy of phantasy, or its aptness to the various roles it assumes, takes advantage of the close association between phantasy and narrative. But it is on the last level, or with the representation of emotion, that this association is most heavily utilised. The flexibility of emotion, or the way it responds to pressures, external and internal, and the twists and turns of narrative seem tailored to one another. Narrative can capture the fluctuations to which most emotions are subject.

Finally, a word on the wish.[97] The wish is the reiteration of a thought, or belief, so as to make the thought, or belief, come true. There is, this time, no question of the confusion of the thought, or belief, with what it is of. The thought, or belief, is recognized as what it is, but it occurs under the aegis of a phantasy, according to which it and what it is of are linked as cause to effect.

16. A parallel that I have already invoked is between a phantasy and a daydream. A crucial difference lies in the essentially unconscious nature of phantasy. Another parallel is between a phantasy and a true dream, a nocturnal dream. The advantage of this parallel is that the true dream is essentially connected with the unconscious. However the dream is essentially connected with the unconscious only in virtue of its latent content. The dream's manifest content, which is what we directly experience when asleep, and what we report on when we wake is by no means unconscious. Should we think of the phantasy in the same layered way that we have learnt to think of the dream?

It seems not. There is no sustainable reason to attribute to phantasy either something so accessible as the manifest content of the dream or something so heavily disguised as its latent content. Rather it seems as though the phantasy, as we directly experience it, and the unconscious mental phenomena that it represents interpenetrate, and that the form of disguise that the phantasy offers these mental phenomena is largely that of rearrangement. In addition to condensation, or compression, of which the dream makes lavish use, the principal means of concealment available to phantasy are devices that derive directly from what is its principal vehicle of expression: narrative.

I single out two ways in which narrative helps to dissemble phantasy. One is that the narrative distributes over stretches of time elements of the phantasy that, in their significance, belong together. The other is that the point of view from which the narrative presents the phantasy shifts or becomes ambiguous. I shall consider one example of each mode of disguise.[98]

The first example comes from Freud's famous case-history of the Rat Man, and the phantasy that I shall look at encapsulates the salient aspects of the Rat Man's relations with 'his lady'. Since this phantasy was 'acted out', we have a way of partially reconstructing its content.

What the Rat Man actually did was this: One day, when his lady was due to go to the country, he took a walk, in the course of which his foot knocked against a stone. He kicked the stone out of the way, because, he reflected, his lady might shortly pass along this road, and, if she did, and if the wheel of her carriage struck the stone, she might come to grief. Twenty minutes or so later, the Rat Man thought what he had done absurd, and he walked over to the stone, picked it up, and replaced it in the middle of the road.[99]

Now, if we were to be guided solely by what Freud's patient actually did on his walk, if, that is, we were to assume that the phantasy was enacted *en clair*, we would have to conclude that the motivations that dominated the Rat Man's relations with his lady were profound solicitude, and the need for rationality when his solicitude was carried to excessive lengths. However, once we start to suspect the element of disguise, a different view of what was involved emerges.

The stripping bare of the phantasy, the peeling away of the disguise, falls into three stages.

First, we abstract the chronological aspect. We start to think of the two actions that make up the Rat Man's overall behaviour – the kicking away, then the putting back, of the stone – as really one action, and thus as representing, not two motivations, but two aspects of one motivation. The phantasy expresses one, if one highly complex, attitude. Secondly, having disputed the separateness of the second action, we discount the reasoning that is supposed to have led the Rat Man, not just to doubt the reasonableness of kicking away the stone, but to replace the stone physically, as rationalization. Once we have done this, the second action looks less like a return to reason, more like hostility. It looks most like a hostile lining to an action that we are still ready to think of as solicitude. Then, thirdly, we recognize that, in acting out his phantasy, the Rat Man probably acted out only part of it, and that the two phases that saw the light of day were excerpted from a continuing cycle that played on in the Rat Man's head. In this cycle, not merely was the stone that he replaced the stone that he had removed, but the stone that he removed was a stone that he had put there in the first place. Now, if the first action still represents solicitude, it represents the Rat Man's solicitude in response to a hostile action that he himself had taken. It is the solicitude of remorse.

Once Freud had peeled away these various deceptions of narrative, and thus revealed the underlying phantasy, he had no difficulty in assigning to it the ambivalence that, by this time, he had ample evidence to believe lay at the centre of his patient's two great attachments: one with his father, the other with his lady.

In my next example, disguise is achieved through the exploitation of another feature of narrative: point of view. The example comes from an essay of Freud's in which he examines a widespread, or generic, phantasy, which many patients of his, often with reluctance or embarrassment, confess to having indulged in from some early age. The phantasy itself they generally describe perfunctorily. 'A child is being beaten', they say, and Freud reuses this as the title of his essay.[100]

Freud soon realized that he would not be able to identify, in sufficient detail, the underlying desires, emotions, and wishes to which individual patients were giving expression through this phantasy until he had answers to a number of questions, which their telling of the phantasy passed over. He needed, in each case, to know,

> Who was the child that was being beaten? The one who was himself producing the phantasy or another? Was it always the same child or as often as not a different one? Who was it that was beating the child? A grown-up person? And if so, who? Or did the child imagine that he himself was beating another one?[101]

When, Freud, through the alliance with the patient, got his answers, and perspective was restored or corrected, it became apparent how what was, on one level, the same phantasy turned out to represent a number of different emotional constellations. Each constellation was characteristic of a different stage of psychosexual development. Freud identified three separate editions of the phantasy.

So: In the earliest version, according to which the child being beaten is not the child producing the phantasy, but is another child, who, at least for the duration of the phantasy, is disliked, and the person beating is almost certainly the father, the phantasy represents, in a triumphant form, the child's jealousy of other children who are rivals for its father's love. They are suffering for it.

In the next version of the phantasy, the child producing the phantasy has become the child being beaten, the person beating is certainly the father, and an aura of intense pleasure surrounds the event. The phantasy has moved on, and is in keeping with the child's more complex emotional condition. By now, its incestuous love for the father has partially, though not totally, succumbed to guilt, and its sexual aims have regressed. The beating that the child receives, and clearly enjoys, is, at once, a representation of the only kind of sexual intercourse it permits itself to desire and a punishment for having desired it.

It was the final version of the phantasy that turned out to be the hardest to decipher. The patients' wording gave no clear indication who plays which role. The giveaway was that, according to all reports, the pleasure experienced from the phantasy, which was intense, was of an unambiguously masochistic kind. With this clue, the phantasy in this third version is brought close, perspectivally that is, to the second version. Freud felt able to assume that the child being beaten *is* the child phantasizing, that the person beating *is* the father, and that it was just the intensity of the desires that caused the point of view to shift from vagueness to dissimulation.

The examination of these ways in which phantasy seeks concealment allows us to retrieve and reassemble the true phenomenology of phantasy. But note the word 'phenomenology'. Phenomenology I defined as the fusion, or amalgam, of subjectivity and intentionality. I now wish to emphasize the point that, though phantasy is fully at home in a pre-verbal stage of a person's life, probably dominating it, that must not be taken to imply either that phantasy is without intentionality or that its intentionality can somehow be equated with its subjectivity. Even if, amongst the pre-verbal, subjectivity is somehow the essential ingredient out of which thought-content is concocted, there is no identity between the two. With language-users and non-language-users alike, thought *is* thought.

17. There is a question that I have been postponing: Can the originating condition of emotion deviate from that which I have been insisting on?

I believe the answer to be Yes. There are, in fact, two deviations that should be considered, and both can be accommodated within the general scope of the account that these lectures offer.

Emotions can arise in two sets of conditions, one of which displays, by the standards that I have been setting, a shortfall in sufficiency, the other a shortfall in necessity. In both cases, the shortfall can be made good in the same way. It can be made good by the introduction of imagination: but not the sort of imagination that we have so far been considering. What is called for is imagination where this is something that I set myself to do.

The two sets of conditions are these: First, there is the case that falls short of sufficiency, where I have certain desires, and these desires have not been satisfied or frustrated, even in the most extended sense that I have been giving to these notions, but I set myself to imagine their satisfaction or frustration. Secondly, there is the case that falls short of necessity, where I find myself in circumstances where certain desires would be satisfied or frustrated, but I do not have these desires: however these desires are close in content to desires that I do have, and I then set myself to imagine my having one or more of them.

In both cases, it is two things – the way in which the desires that we have sensitize us to them and to their close neighbours, and the power of imagination – that extend the originating condition beyond the limits traced in these last two lectures.

Further out there is another unanswered question, and that is whether some emotions do not arise completely outside the orbit of desire. This question will lie at the centre of the next lecture.

LECTURE THREE

ON THE SO-CALLED MORAL EMOTIONS

1. In this lecture I shall consider a special group of emotions. The group includes shame, guilt, remorse, and regret. These emotions are generally regarded as having something in common in that they all bear upon morality. It is therefore conventional to call them *the moral emotions*. The title of this lecture comments on this practice, though it is only later that I shall consider what there is to be said against it. I shall concentrate upon *shame* and *guilt*.

In the first lecture, I claimed that an emotion possesses two very general features. The first, which is shared by all dispositions, and distinguishes emotion from other kinds of mental disposition, just as it distinguishes each of these other kinds from the rest, is its *role*, or the part that it plays within the psychology of the person. The role of a disposition may, as with belief, include an end, or, as with thought, or imagination, the role may be purely instrumental, in which case the disposition will borrow an end from the further project that it serves. Projects that instrumental dispositions may serve range from inquiry to idle amusement. Secondly, and perhaps peculiar to emotion, there is its *characteristic history*.

Specifically I claimed, first, that the role of emotion is to provide the person with an attitude or orientation, where this is contrasted with a picture of the world, which belief supplies, and with a target, which desire provides, and, secondly, that the characteristic history of an emotion is that it arises out of desire satisfied or desire frustrated: that is, satisfied or frustrated (one) really and actually, or (two) in mere belief, or (three) prospectively.

Let us see how these claims stand to the emotions to be discussed in this lecture.

2. The role of the moral emotions, as of the non-moral emotions, is to provide the person with an attitude, or orientation. What is distinctive of the moral emotions is that the attitude is reflexive. It is an attitude that the person, specifically and of necessity, has towards himself: himself as a person. However it is in their characteristic histories that the moral emotions differ most strikingly from the other emotions. Indeed, as we shall see, in line with what is true of the emotions hitherto considered, what is distinctive about the attitude that they enshrine, or that it is reflexive, is to be, in large part, explained by what is distinctive about their history.

But, first, a note on the phrase 'the history of an emotion'. Thus far, in talking of the history of an emotion, I have been talking about the way in which a particular instance, or token, of an emotion develops within a person. For instance, I am frightened of bats: my daughter loves dogs. So the history that I have had in mind is a matter of how, for example, my fear of bats, or her love of dogs, began, and waxed, and maybe waned – as mental dispositions do, but none more so than emotions – and might, within our lifetimes, come to an end.

However it is arguable that an inquiry into shame and guilt requires us to consider history, the history of these emotions, in some further sense. We need to take account of how they, the emotions themselves – say, guilt, or remorse – and not just their instances – say, my guilt about having deceived a friend, or my friend's remorse at having insulted an annoying stranger – mature across a single life. Crude and primitive in the early stages of life, our emotions gradually, and not without constant danger of regression to an earlier condition, become subtler, more refined, perhaps less urgent. As they do so, their later instances shed the rawness that marks the earlier instances, which never altogether lose the characteristics of that phase in personal development at which they originate. Of no emotions is this truer than of shame and guilt. Accordingly, if philosophy here follows its normal practice with psychological phenomena, and pays exclusive attention to our adult experience of them, we shall be misled. We shall fail to grasp why shame and guilt have the importance or power in our lives that they do. In this lecture, I shall indicate a developmental account of these emotions, which, though initially it may seem, at least in detail, implausible to some, is, I believe, explanatorily promising.

But there is a further sense in which the emotions can be historically studied, and, according to some, should be. This would be to study them across the history of the species, or across the diversity of human culture. Once again a special case can be made for thinking that this project, enlightening in all cases, is crucial in the case of the emotions to be studied in this lecture. Shame in the world of the Ancient Greeks is, it will be said, not the shame that Dmitri Karamazov experienced when, about to be arraigned on what was for the Greeks the most shameful of crimes, parricide, looked down at his feet, and observed the coarse, flat, crooked nail on his big toe, which, in a moment, all would see,[1] nor is it the shame that a young girl of today might feel when it is disclosed to her peers that she is still a virgin at the age of seventeen. I am ready to believe that there are some such differences – though whether this is the best way to describe them is another matter – and I am prepared to be convinced that such a study would be worthwhile. But I am unqualified to undertake it. And I am greatly discouraged by recent work in this tradition.[2]

3. I turn now to the characteristic history of the moral emotions.

Particular instances of the moral emotions originate, not, like particular instances of those emotions hitherto considered, or the non-moral emotions, in the vicissitudes of desire, but in a change in something more fundamental: something more fundamental in that it underlies the very formation of desire, as well as much else in our psychology. I call this something the person's *sense of self*. My claim is that the moral emotions are attitudes that arise in response to changes – or, more narrowly, since the moral emotions, or those which I shall consider, are negative emotions, to falls – in the sense that the person has of himself.

However the term 'sense of self' covers a variety of ways in which a person can relate to himself. It can cover what the person takes himself to be, or his knowledge of himself: it can derive

from introspection. It can cover his self-esteem, or the particular worth that he sets upon himself: it can derive from self-
assessment. Or it can cover his self-respect, or what he thinks is
due to him as a person, and what he will most probably try to
exact from others: it can derive from his scale of values, and not
take his particularity into account. Without wishing to claim that
any of this is irrelevant to the moral emotions, I claim that what
is more directly involved is that awareness which a person, any
person, has of himself, and which allows him to think of himself
as an ongoing person: influenced by his past, living in the present,
and concerned for his future.[3] The moral emotions that constitute the topic of this lecture are triggered by something that the
person experiences as a disturbance of, or as a threat to, this sense
of himself. There is a fall in his sense of security, and this gives
rise to anxiety.[4]

However, if shame and guilt originate in a fall in the person's
sense of his own security, they do not originate in just any fall.
Guilt and shame are responses to such falls only when these are
in turn caused by falls in the regard in which the person is held.
It is a regard that is singularly important to, and has a special
authority over, the person. Nor are the two falls merely externally related. One fall causes the other, and additionally the
feeling of insecurity is experienced as in direct response to a loss
of regard. That we are regarded less well is felt to be dangerous,
and the danger is experienced as due solely to this drop in regard.

But the originating condition of the moral emotions is still
insufficiently defined. For we need to know, Held in less regard
by whom? In whose regard do we have to fall for the subsequent
sense of insecurity to give rise to shame or guilt?

A natural answer, attractive because it ensures the autonomy
that many feel to be crucial to the moral emotions, is, In our
own regard. It is, on one, and one widely held, view, only falls
in the regard in which we hold ourselves, or in our self-esteem,
that, detonating a fall in the sense of self, can provide the originating condition of shame and guilt.[5]

But I do not accept this answer. It does not properly record
the origins of these emotions. It is neither phenomenologically
correct, nor even fully coherent, and it has been devised to

protect something that we have no good reason to think exists. Perhaps in maturity – and this is not a strictly chronological notion – we feel shame or guilt only when we concur with the low view of ourselves that induces the emotion. But this autonomy of the moral emotions – and it is, as we shall see in a moment, only a very limited notion of autonomy – is an achievement, due to much psychological work on our part, and is not originary. Certainly it is nothing like the dawning of a conceptual truth. In their beginnings the moral emotions are not responses to changes in the regard in which we hold ourselves, and our adult experience of these emotions is replete with vestiges of their early condition.

The fact of the matter is that a person can feel shame over what he has become or guilt over what he has done, and yet any one of the following conditions, indeed the lot, may hold: In the first place, the person may totally disagree with the lower opinion in which he is held. Secondly, he may in no way agree or sympathize with the reasons that appear to account for the lesser opinion in which he is held, and he might be bewildered by thinking that there are, or even could be, such reasons. Thirdly, he may be convinced that what occasions the shame or guilt that he feels was not something that he could have avoided. It was outside his control.[6] And, finally, and the relevance of this will emerge later, there invariably seems to be packed into the person's experience of shame or guilt more in the way of structure or narrative, more in the way of reference to others, and how they relate to him, and what he can do about this, than his merely coming to think less well of himself can plausibly call for. If this setting is omitted, there is the chance that we may account for something resembling in certain respects shame and guilt, but not for these emotions themselves. Later I shall introduce theoretical considerations to support the inherent liability of shame and guilt to heteronomy.

However the terms 'autonomy' and 'heteronomy' are used in various ways, and the view that I am urging attributes, not mere heteronomy, but a radical heteronomy, to early instances of shame and guilt.

To grasp this distinction between two kinds of heteronomy, consider a familiar way of distinguishing between shame and guilt. Shame is said to be heteronomous whereas guilt is not, and this is so because shame necessarily appeals to the standards of one's peers in the culture. An act that is shameful is one that causes one to lose face in their eyes. Homeric warriors who live to avoid shame live by the codes of other warriors. Without the external existence of some such code, there could not be shame: or so it is claimed. However, if this makes shame heteronomous, it does so only in a weak sense, in that heteronomy is solely a matter of the source, or origin, of the standards that regulate shame: these standards must originate outside the person. But not merely is it consistent with this view of heteronomy that the person should find himself in full accord with these standards, the view could insist that, for shame to be truly experienced, the person must make the standards invoked his own.[7] By contrast, the radical heteronomy for which I claim that room must be made in a viable account of shame *and* guilt is not just a matter of where the standards come from: it is a matter of how the standards relate to the person's own views or attitudes even as he submits to them.

'Even as he submits to them.' For radical heteronomy implies no diminution of the special authority that these standards undoubtedly exercise. Nor could it, so long as it is shame and guilt of which we speak, or to which we attribute radical heteronomy, for such authority is essential to the very nature of these emotions. Without it, we would not have either emotion.

In this lecture there will be much discussion of what this authority amounts to, and how – how, but not whether, for that I take for granted – it is compatible with heteronomy. But, in anticipation of what is to come, this much may now be said: that, when the person is made aware that he has fallen short of the required standards, and is thus held in less regard, he is led to see himself as he would if he accepted these standards, which he may well not. We may say that the authority regulates the person's attitude without necessarily touching his opinions. The person's attitude, or his view of himself, is in line with certain standards, which need not be in accord with his opinions, or what he thinks of himself. An early lesson to be learnt in the inquiry into shame and guilt is that we must not let either our acceptance of the heteronomy of shame and guilt lead us into a denial of the special authority implicit in these emotions, or our acceptance of this special authority lead us into a denial of the heteronomy they can exhibit.

And we should still go wrong if, having conceded variation within heteronomy, or kinds of heteronomy, we were then to think of autonomy as a simple, undifferentiated phenomenon. It was an insight, to which the greatest of the eighteenth-century moralists tried to do justice, that the moral emotions, and morality itself, never fully achieve that form of autonomy which the life of inquiry, and often the life of pleasure, effortlessly attain to. Even when we are completely in accord with the judgments from which shame and guilt originate, there is the phenomeno-logical sense that these judgments are those of a higher author-ity. They speak to us, however ready listeners we may be.[8]

The next question is, If it is true that, at least in some cases, when we experience shame or guilt, it is in another's regard that we fall, who is this other? Is there someone who it must be? Or can it be just anyone other than ourselves, provided only that this person can muster the special authority that shame and guilt pre-suppose? The answer will turn out not to be obvious, or short, and its complexity will require us to stretch somewhat our picture of the mind, and in a direction for which the discussion of phan-tasy at the end of the last lecture has prepared us.

Though the answers to these last questions are still ahead of us, and their detail cannot be foreseen, there is a broader, and extremely important, conclusion that we are in a position to anticipate. It is that the phenomena of shame and guilt cannot be accommodated within the conception of the simple, undi-vided self: such a conception must be rejected now, though the need for doing so, which is over-determined, should always have been apparent.[9]

And, to conclude this section, let me make it clear that, in talking of falls in the person's sense of security, or of changes in the regard in which the person is held, I am using the terms 'fall' and 'change' in the same broad way that, in the previous two lectures, I used, in connexion with desire, the terms 'satisfaction' and 'frustration'. In other words, I include both real changes and merely believed-in changes, both actual changes and anticipated or likely changes. This is for the now familiar reason that invariably belief in, and sometimes anticipation of, some event can contribute as effectively as the real or actual event to genuine psychological change: for instance, the formation of an emotion.

In this section, I have, it will be noted, talked of the originating condition of shame and guilt. But the originating condition of shame and guilt is not itself shame or guilt. To arrive at the emotion requires the formation of an attitude on our part. I shall return to this all-important distinction later, and how, for all its importance, and, more remarkably, for all its obviousness, it can get overlooked. It can get misplaced.

4. There are major differences as well as major similarities between shame and guilt. I turn to the immediate differences before looking at each emotion in greater detail.

In the first place, in the case of shame, we feel criticized for the kind of person we have become: in the case of guilt, we feel criticized for what we have done or left undone.

Secondly, in the case of shame, the criticism invokes an ideal, which we have failed to live up to: in the case of guilt, the criticism invokes a set of injunctions, which we have transgressed. Neither the ideal nor the injunctions, which are what I have been referring to as the standards of shame and guilt, may be immediately apparent to us: they may require excavation, and, when they are brought up into the light of day, we may not succeed in making them fully intelligible to others, or even to ourselves.

Thirdly – and this is a matter of degree – in the case of shame, the criticism is based less, and, in the case of guilt, it is based more, on identifiable harm or damage that we are supposed to have caused, though not necessarily intentionally. There are, as we shall see, circumstances in which guilt arises though no-one has been harmed.

Fourthly, in the case of shame, the criticism can be met, met and turned, only by an attempt on our part to change how we are. In the case of guilt, the criticism can be turned only by an attempt to compensate for what we have done. For this reason, shame will tend to generate the desire to change, guilt will tend to generate the desire to repair. But, as with other emotions, the generation of an appropriate desire is not intrinsic to the emotion: it is only one possible outcome, and it may not happen.

Fifthly, if both emotions call for a response on the part of others, what shame calls for is that others should forget what we have become, and what guilt calls for is that others should forgive what we have done.[10]

And, finally, in the case of shame, the criticism is experienced as being conveyed to us by a look: we feel the eyes of disapproval upon us. In the case of guilt, the criticism is experienced as being conveyed in words: we hear the voice of disapproval.[11]

In the writings of philosophers or psychologists, these distinctions are sometimes expressed more neatly than the emotions themselves allow for. There are several reasons that can account for this, but one is the dubious methodological belief that the best way to examine the differing natures of shame and guilt is through a consideration of social institutions in which these emotions are, in Plato's famous phrase, 'writ large'. What we should do, the claim goes, is to get clear about the finer points of difference between shame and guilt by looking at the grosser contrasts between what some anthropologists call, respectively, 'shame cultures' and 'guilt cultures.' Shame is best grasped through considering a society whose members fear falling outside of it through losing honour or face, and guilt through considering a society dominated by a legal system, which, once its citizens have violated its conditions, holds them to account for what they have done.[12] Since these external counterparts to shame and guilt presumably lend themselves to reasonably succinct ethnographical description, it is a short and pleasant step away to think that the emotions will lend themselves to comparably succinct psychological description.

But the method is decisively flawed. For, when we come to examine the institutions that are supposed to parallel shame and guilt, there are two broad possibilities. One is that the institution, under closer inspection, fails to embody some crucial aspect of the emotion to which it is taken to provide the analogue: for instance, there is nothing comparable to the particular kind of authority, or the particular kind of inescapability, that is associated with the emotion. The other is that the institution embodies every crucial aspect of the relevant emotion, but does so only derivatively. It does so only because those who live within it, and regulate its practices, or comply with its ways, are motivated to do so by the emotion itself, and surreptitiously this motivation becomes, for the ethnographer, criterial of the institution. So, for instance, nothing counts as breaching society's code of honour unless shame is felt: or nothing counts as falling foul of the law unless guilt is experienced.

We can see that, once either of these steps is taken, we shall not get what we were promised. Neither way round will the institution be able to teach us the nature of the corresponding emotion. For, in the first case, if we try to read off the emotion from what the institution is like, we shall end up misinformed: something will be missing from the picture of the psychological phenomenon. In the second case, we can be convinced that the institution suitably exemplifies the emotion that we are interested in only if we draw upon the very knowledge of the emotion that the institution is supposed to give us. And there is the ever-present danger that, along the way, psychology will coarsen itself into the image of sociology, or that we shall model the finer texture of the emotions upon the coarser structure of public institutions.

4. I turn now to a closer consideration of the two emotions, and I start with shame.

I shall consider two stories, both of which derive from the philosophical literature, and which have been held to illustrate the conditions for the onset of shame. I shall tell the stories, and then say how I believe that they have to be understood – what has to be put in, what taken out – before they can do this adequately.

The first story, as it stands, is very skeletal. It comes to us from Sartre.[13]

A man makes an awkward or coarse gesture. Let us say, half-way through a meal he blows his nose on his napkin, or, as is reported of a well-known English man of letters, he uses a rasher of bacon to mark his place in the book he is reading, or he crouches down to look through the keyhole of the door. At first, he believes that the gesture has gone unnoticed. Then he realizes that he has been observed. The observer goes out of his way to make this clear to him. Our man is covered with shame.

Let us go back over the story, isolating the significant steps.

In the first place, the person begins by not looking upon his gesture with disapproval. Secondly, the observer disapproves of the gesture. Thirdly, he conveys this disapproval by the look that he gives the person who made it. Fourthly, the look conveys to the person disapproval, not only of the gesture, but of the kind of person he has become through making it. Fifthly, the look conveys all this in such a way that the person feels threatened. The person has no choice but to assimilate it to an attack, a physical attack, with the result that his sense of security is dimin-ished to the point of anxiety. He feels shame.

But let it be noted that, all the while, there is no point at which the person need share the observer's opinion of what he has become: nor need he sympathize with the reasons that the observer has for finding him an object of shame: nor need he even think that such reasons exist: certainly he does not have to believe that the gesture he made, which is the cause of the offence, was done intentionally, or that he is in any way respon-sible for it.

In this story, the look, the eyes, are, it will be noted, assigned a very strong role in the generation of shame: they are the car-riers of disapproval, and, to fulfil this role, they are responded to by the person who experiences shame as though they had a power that they do not, that they could not, and that he is unlikely to believe that they actually, have.

However the situation must not be misunderstood. For there is something that, in this case, the eyes do not do, but that, in a number of other cases, they do do. There are cases where the eyes, or observation, convert acts that would not otherwise be shameful acts into shameful acts. Certain acts when observed, and only when observed, are shameful: the very same acts when unobserved are not – though the shamefulness of these acts is not merely a matter of their being observed. (What it is is, of course, a further question.) On this point, consider urinating. No sane person is ashamed of urinating as such, though most people are ashamed of being observed urinating. People who are not ashamed of masturbating are invariably ashamed of being observed masturbating. In both cases the shamefulness of the act is to be explained by reference to something special about the conjunction of the act and its being observed.

However our present concern is not with these latter cases, for the vulgar gesture is not one of them. The vulgar gesture is something of which to be ashamed, whether or not it is observed. In the story the person who made the gesture just happened not to feel shame. Accordingly, if observation makes a difference here too – and the claim is that it does – the difference must derive from some general connexion between shame and being under observation, which is to be investigated. Another way of putting the matter is to say that, in the explanation of some shameful acts, such as urinating when observed, being under observation occurs twice over: but it has a place, or occurs once, in the explanation of every shameful act.

I turn now to the second story to see what light it throws on the general connexion.

This story, cited by various moral psychologists, comes from the writings of Max Scheler.[14]

A model has been posing for a famous artist. She finds the work congenial. It allows her to indulge to the full her taste for innocent daydreaming, and she enjoys the company of the great man. He draws her carefully, and she likes the attention she receives. Then one day she becomes aware that he is no longer looking at her exclusively as someone to draw. He has noticed her attractions as a woman, which she assumes that he hadn't done up till then. His interest in her warms, and he now considers her as someone to whom it would be agreeable to make love. He thinks, as he draws her, of the pleasure in store. His eyes convey this to her, and we do not have to fall in with the prudery that assumes that this gives her no pleasure. It would be plausible to think that it gives her some pleasure, at least in so far as she continues to retain all the control over the situation that she feels she needs. However she – that is, the particular model whom I have in mind – certainly feels shame.

If this story also provides us with an originating condition of shame, how does it fit in with the previous story? Does one story contain something that the other is without, and, if so, which way round, and how does it bear upon the nature of shame?

A crucial figure in the first story was the observer. Who, we might ask ourselves, plays this role in the second story? One answer might be, The artist. For the artist observes. It is through his eyes that the artist becomes aware of the model's sexual appeal, and it is through them that he conveys this awareness back to her.

Nevertheless the artist differs in various ways from the observer who noted the vulgar gesture. And there is one difference that seems decisive, so that the two men cannot possibly play the same role. For, whereas the observer of the coarse gesture disapproved of it, and conveyed his disapproval unambiguously, this being the central use to which he puts his eyes, there is no reason to think that the artist, as he becomes aware of the model's sexual attractions, disapproves of her, or holds her in lower regard, nor is there reason to think that the model herself thinks that he does. Once the artist starts to think of her as a sexual woman, or someone to go to bed with, and not just as a female body, or something to draw, she may stand higher in his regard, and she may feel this: she may feel that she is viewed less as an object. (And, if she did think that the artist held her in lower regard, and held her in lower regard just because he found her attractive, as Angelo does Isabella,[15] might she not, other complications apart, find the occasion one more for anger, or even for indignation, than for shame? I shall return to this, and similar, possibilities.)

If the artist is not the counterpart to the observer of the vulgar gesture, but there is a general connexion between shame and being observed, then it looks as though, compared to the first story, the second story, despite its greater narrative fullness, under-describes the situation as an originating condition for shame. To get the story to adequacy, we must introduce another, a further, observer who, modelled on the observer in the first story, will, as the artist changes from viewing the model without sexual interest to viewing her with sexual interest, hold her in lesser regard. He will convey this lesser regard, and what kind of person she has become for him, through the look that he gives her. It is in his eyes that the model suffers a decline in regard – and 'suffers' here must be given something close to a physical sense – and this has the consequence that she feels less safe, and knows why. And it is then that shame sets in.[16]

However, once again, what is not necessary for the onset of shame is that the model should concur with the opinion that the observer has of her, or with the reasons that he has for doing so, nor need she think that whatever it is that has offended the observer was something over which she had any control. The model does not have to feel that she has been provocative, or careless of her reputation, or collusive with the artist's designs. All that is necessary is that she should be aware of how she appears in the observer's eyes, that his eyes should make her aware of this, and that this should in turn make her anxious. And then it is for her as if, as if for practical purposes, she concurred with the observer's opinion of her.

But the introduction of this further observer raises two questions. The first is, What consequences does his existence have for the role that the artist continues to play? Does his presence make that of the artist otiose, or at least peripheral? The second question is, How does the new observer get into the narrative, given that he has no obvious contribution to make to the story-line?

I start with the first question, or the residual role of the artist in the narrative.

There is a trivial way in which the artist must remain essential to the story, to this particular story as it has been told, if it is to terminate on shame. For he is part of what the observer disapproves of. Of course, his part could be taken – or, better, could have been taken – by someone else, or perhaps the role of the model herself could have swollen so that there would be no need for anyone else. But then we would have had a different story. So, unless the story is to change out of all recognition, we can say that the artist, the artist and his desire, are essential.

But initially it seemed as though something more specific about the artist was essential: that is, the eyes of the artist. It seemed crucial that the artist resembled the observer in the first story in also being an observer. Was that a misapprehension? So long as the new observer disapproves of what has happened to the model, and this has to do with the artist, is it additionally required that what provokes the observer involves her appearing a certain way in the eyes of another? Is it not sufficient that she appears a certain way in *his*, the observer's, eyes? Would it be much the same if the observer had seen the two of them swimming naked at midnight, or had been told of their gambling for stakes much higher than they could possibly afford, or had read in the newspaper that she had put her daughter out to adoption so that the two of them could go and live in the sun – provided only that these were all things that he, the observer, though not, of course, necessarily she, thought shameful, and let colour his view of her?

To these questions, the answer is, strictly speaking, It would be the same. That the artist looks at her a certain way is only a contingent feature of what excites the observer's disapproval, and so, at one remove on, of what precipitates the model's shame. And this is confirmed by the fact that the first story, where there is no equivalent to the artist, hence no equivalent to the artist's gaze, is still a story of shame. The occasion of shame is fully supplied by the gesture that the man made and the look that the observer gave him for making it.

Nevertheless, though there is no necessity, there is an appropriateness, to this further detail. For it fits in with the fact that shame is specific to a phase dominated by the eyes. In the thematic patterning of looking and being looked at across the whole narrative, the Scheler story does justice to the deeper associations of shame. Ultimately the young woman falls victim to the eyes of an observer: it is of a piece with this that the woman should experience the observer as offended by the way another's eyes fall upon her.

I turn to the second question, How does the new observer, who turns out to play such a crucial role in the onset of shame, get into the narrative? If the narrative is to be adequate, does he have to occupy an actual, physical location in the setting where the emotion forms?

It seems an unlikely demand on the plausibility of the narrative that the observer should have to push his way into the artist's studio, and there adopt a vantage point from which he can keep both model and artist under close, unfriendly surveillance. Indeed, if this is what the narrative has to insist upon, it will take on a different character. The motivation of the artist, and, more profoundly perhaps, that of the observer, would mutate. Were it the case that the artist was evidently undeterred by the presence of a close observer as he pressed his attentions upon the model, we might start to wonder whether the artist was not in fact excited by the presence of the observer, and whether the observer was not expressly enflaming something of which he could then disapprove. We might start to wonder whether, once again, the model should not feel anger, or indignation, rather than shame: indignation at being so set up.

As to how we should account for the observer's presence in the narrative, I suggest an answer, which will move the discussion forward, though later we shall need to improve upon it. For the moment we may think of the observer, not as a physical presence in the studio, but as someone who figures in the narrative only because he is imagined by the model. The model finds herself imagining him. She imagines him observing her under the artist's gaze: she imagines him thinking less well of her just because of this exposure: she imagines him conveying this to her through the look that he gives her: and she imagines this hurting.

At this stage in our inquiry, we might wonder how it can be that, in one story, a purely imagined figure can have the power over our emotions that, in the other story, calls for a flesh-and-blood figure. This raises an important issue, but what I can say is that this will not remain the best way of putting the matter.

6. I turn from shame to guilt, and guilt I propose to illustrate from two famous autobiographies.

My first illustration comes from Rousseau's *Confessions*.[17]

If Rousseau is to be trusted, which he may not be, the passage that I choose recounts the very incident to which the *Confessions* owes its existence. For, in two separate places, Rousseau tells us that he wrote the book principally to dispel the burden of guilt that the memory of this event laid upon him.[18] Of what he did on that occasion, he protests that it was 'the sole offence I have committed', and that it was something that he had never been able to confide even to his most intimate friends.

As a young man, Rousseau had, in the course of his wanderings, been employed as a footman in the house of a certain Madame de Vercellis. On her death an inventory was taken of all her belongings, and the only thing that was missing – though just how this fact came to light is obscure – was an old piece of pink and silver ribbon. Rousseau had stolen it, and, when, in the course of the investigation, his belongings were searched and it was discovered amongst them, he denied stealing it. Asked how it came to be in his possession, he accused a young woman who worked in the house as a cook, Marion, a pretty, sweet-natured peasant girl, who was totally trustworthy. She, Rousseau said, had stolen the missing article, and, when further questioned, he repeated the accusations to her face. The young woman did not trouble to defend herself, and all she said was 'Oh Rousseau, I thought you were a good man. You make me very sad, but I should not like to be in your place.' Thereupon the nephew, who was winding up the estate, dismissed both Rousseau and Marion, and he expressed his bafflement by saying that he hoped that the guilty one's conscience would amply avenge the innocent one. And so, Rousseau wrote, it had. On sleepless nights, in times of crisis or distress, the girl's words of gentle, unfailing reproach returned to torment him.

If we take this story as illustrative of how guilt arises, the features that we have seen to differentiate guilt from shame are present in a comparatively florid form, and they may be brought under two broad headings. In the first place, what provokes the fall in the regard in which Rousseau is held, in this case in Marion's regard, is something that he has done rather than some way he has become. And, secondly, what conveys this diminished regard back to Rousseau, and so precipitates a fall in his sense of security – although this aspect of the story is not something he dwells upon – is the voice, Marion's voice, and what it utters, and the tone in which it does so, rather than the eyes, and the look they give.

And this story also shows us how in one, one important, respect guilt replicates shame. It is that, not only does criticism come to the person from an outside source – that is, from a source not identical with himself – but the person is not required to be in any kind of accord with the critic. Rousseau does not participate in the lower regard in which the critic holds him, nor does he sympathize with what motivated this fall in regard, nor does he even think of himself as responsible for the deed that occasioned it: all things that he would have to do on the view of guilt as essentially autonomous. And that Rousseau's guilt caused him real suffering should not blind us to any of these facts, nor they to it. Significantly, after Rousseau recounts the story of his 'sole offence', after he has elaborated on the sorrow and the pain that he has endured over the years on its account, he then lets the reader know, for he would be less than frank if he didn't, that, however bad the consequences of what he did, in his motivation he could not have been further from any wickedness. When he accused the girl, friendship was the cause. For it was friendship for her that put her in his thoughts, and, when he said that she had given him the ribbon rather than that he had taken it, this was because he had stolen the ribbon in order to give it to her. And that he stuck to his story even when the ugly results of his doing so began to emerge was due to just one thing: shame. He was shamed into doing something which, as things turned out, would make him, and would go on making him, feel guilty.

We may set beside this narrative, which is comparatively full, particularly when we put together what is explicitly said and what is implicitly but distinctly implied, the skeletal account offered by St Augustine in his *Confessions* of a youthful act that seems to have haunted him for a long time.[19]

Late one night, with some companions, Augustine raided a pear-tree next to his family vineyard, and carried off most of the fruit. At the time, even as he did it, Augustine clearly felt guilty about the act, for it made him miserable. However this feeling did not prevent his doing it. Indeed the contrary: for, when he reflected upon it, the guilt that he felt about the act, or what he called its 'sinfulness', was the only reason that he could find in himself for having done it. The pears themselves in no way attracted Augustine and his companions: they were unripe, and were immediately fed to the pigs, and such seems always to have been the intention. It was not just the sinfulness of the act, it was its delinquency, or the fact that it was committed for its sinfulness, for the guilt that he might expect to feel over it, that made it at once so hard for Augustine to condone and so impossible for him to forget.

When, elsewhere in the *Confessions*, Augustine talks of guilt, he connects its originating condition with a voice, which he himself thinks of as an imagined, or imaginary, voice. He doesn't do so here, but an explanation suggests itself. The voice that Augustine imagines hearing, or that he imagines speaking, is ultimately God's voice. Sometimes this voice speaks through another voice. When, for instance, he was a student, and had frequented the brothels, the reproving voice that had rung in his ears, begging him to abandon his sexual excesses, was invariably his mother's.[20] A woman tearfully begs him to desist from women. On such occasions he reports the voice to the reader. However, since God is also the intended reader of the *Confessions*, it is understandable that, when the voice was imagined in God's own person, any reference to, or description of, the voice was thought by Augustine to be unnecessary. Silence, silence on the part of the writer when he came to write, should not be taken as evidence for silence, silence in the head of the writer at the time of the incident.

7. With these instances of shame and guilt before us, we may now go back to the nature of the criticizing agency, which plays such a prominent part in their originating conditions.

If we review the four stories I assembled, we see that, for each emotion, there is one case where there is a real-life person with whom the agency could be identified, and one case where there is no such person. In the last section, it looked as though, where there is no such person, the most plausible candidate for the role is an imagined, or imaginary, figure. That was how I have described the cases. Both the man who made the coarse gesture and Rousseau confront a real-life critic. By contrast, the model suffers under a non-real, hence an imagined, or imaginary, pair of eyes, and Augustine suffers from a non-real, hence an imagined, or imaginary, voice.

The natural thing to think is that the kind of case where the critic is a real-life figure is fundamental, and that the second kind of case can be understood only derivatively, or as parasitic upon it. This would be natural, for, when we ordinarily pair off cases of doing something with cases of imagining doing that thing, we take the former as primary, and then try to understand the latter through the former.

My present proposal is that, in the case of the criticizing agency, we reverse this familiar order, and that we think of the case where the criticizing agency is non-real as primary, and we then use it to explain the case where there is a real-life critic. However, as we do this, we must make another adjustment. This second adjustment will presuppose a revision in the way we conceive the resources of the mind. For, in those cases which we are now to regard as primary, I further propose that, instead of thinking of the critic, the non-real critic, in terms of the imagination, we should substitute for the notion of the imagination that of phantasy as it was introduced in the last lecture. The model and Augustine are reproved by phantasized critics: the eyes that rest accusingly upon one, the voice that rebukes the other, are the products of phantasy.

I start with the first part of this proposal. But it will not prove practical to treat the two parts altogether separately.

8. If the primacy of the real-life critic is a natural starting-point, in fact it early on runs into so many difficulties that to abandon it will not turn out to be such a wrench.

Indisputably there are situations in our lives when we do something, and we might well be expected to feel shame because of what we feel we have become through doing it, or to feel guilt because of what we think of the thing itself, and yet, initially, we feel neither of these things. And then we become aware that we are under observation, and, in a flash, shame or guilt, as the case may be, sweeps over us. These are not, let me emphasize, cases of the sort briefly considered where being observed converts something we do into a shameful or guilty act, which it would not otherwise have been. In the cases I have in mind, being observed, or the presence of a real-life figure, without making any difference to the nature of the act, makes all the difference to what we feel about it. Do these cases not establish the primacy of the real-life observer?

I answer No. For, if these cases are ex-hypothesi clear or unproblematic, it is hard to see what could make them so except a bond of accord that may be assumed to hold between ourselves and the observer about the circumstances in which it is appropriate to feel shame or guilt. The only irregularity in these cases is that, though we acknowledge the circumstances to be appropriate, we happen not to feel the appropriate emotion. Hence the need for the observer, whose role is to nudge us into doing so. Vary the situation perhaps only by the smallest amount, and there would have been no such need, and we would have had the feeling unaided.

But, if this is how these cases have to be understood for them to be unproblematic, they cannot establish the primacy of the real-life critic. For they themselves are barely central cases. On two counts they omit central aspects of shame and guilt. In the first place, they exclude the phenomenon that, as we have seen, any account of shame and guilt must allow for: that is, that shame and guilt can function heteronomously. Secondly, even within these limitations, they reveal the real-life critic acting in a wholly ancillary, or dependent, fashion. For the fact of an accord between ourselves and the real-life critic entails that we were independently in a position to feel shame or guilt, or that whatever is required in the way of a criticizing agency had already been set up internally by the time the real-life critic appeared on the scene.

But, it will be objected, Who says that the only situations with a real-life critic that are unproblematic are those where there is a bond of accord between the critic and the person? Why should we accept this? Indeed to accept this, it will be argued, is to prejudge the matter at issue. It is to take for granted, it is not to argue, that the real-life critic has no independent authority. Why should we believe that the hold of such a critic over the person necessarily depends upon the prior installation within the person of a criticizing agency whose part the real-life critic only reduplicates? Why, in other words, should we not take the stories of the man who is observed making a vulgar gesture, or of Rousseau upbraided by Marion, as telling us, as we have them, all that we need to know in order to understand why one of them, the man, was made to feel ashamed of what he had become, and the other, Rousseau, was made to feel guilty over what he had done?

Certainly there is nothing problematic in general about an external agent trying to induce in us an emotion that we are, at least initially, reluctant to experience, or that we feel is inappropriate to the circumstances as we see them. Someone might want to induce in us, against the grain, fear, or anger, and might succeed. Indeed, if someone wants to make us feel frightened, or angry, and takes the obvious steps, success is likely to attend his efforts, and nothing has to be presupposed on our part over and above a basic human endowment. It is unnecessary to imagine that some special sensitivity has been set up in us, which the agent then leans on like someone might lean on a lever to induce a change in the outer world. That being so, why should the situation be any different if an agent tries to make us ashamed or guilty?

Reflexion shows us that an external agent who sets out to induce in us shame or guilt has two obstacles to overcome, which do not exist in the case of the non-moral emotions. These two obstacles are significant for our understanding of the moral emotions.

In the first place, the agent must be able, through the weapon of criticism, or the display of a lower regard for us, to bring about a mental state that we experience as an assault upon our sense of self, and that thus triggers anxiety. This stands in contrast with what is needed if someone is tries to induce in us fear, or anger. For, in such circumstances, all that the person must make us experience is the frustration of a desire.

Secondly, having made us feel that we are imperilled in our innermost sense of ourselves, an external agent would then have to bring it about that, as we start to wonder who, or what, it was that precipitated this experience, and we settle for an answer, an attitude forms that is directed, not on to some outside fact or figure, not, for instance, though this might seem the obvious target, on to the agent himself, who has been in this crude way endeavouring to tamper with our feelings, but back on to ourselves. The attitude that must be induced is a reflexive attitude. This again is in contrast with what has to be brought about by someone who tries to induce in us fear, or anger. For, in that case, what an agent has to induce in us is an attitude that takes someone or something other than ourselves as its object.

So far, in talking about the appropriate authority of the criticizing agency, I have said little about what it amounts to except that it can oblige us to adopt an attitude that is not necessarily in line with our opinion. This can now be further spelt out. The authority of the criticizing agency must be such that it can, despite its heteronomy, bring about two things. It can cause the anxiety that goes with the self in danger, and it can arouse an attitude that turns, not outwards, or on to another, but inwards, or back upon ourselves. Furthermore it must cause the latter through the former. We end up criticizing ourselves because of the anxiety we have caused ourselves. And I suggest that there is no clear route by which a real-life critic, or an external agent who would have no difficulty in bringing about fear, or anger, could come by such authority.

If this is so, and if the real-life critic is not the primary instance of the criticizing agency, we must look to what is by now the alternative. We must look to the non-real life critic, and, to explain the non-real life critic, we must, I have proposed, look to phantasy.

9. In the last lecture, in introducing phantasy, I associated it with a hierarchy of roles or functions that it can discharge, each role calling for its own level of complexity in the way in which phantasy works.

I shall go over these levels, expanding somewhat what I said then.

On the lowest level, phantasy serves as the internal representation of desire. Associated with each desire is a dispositional phantasy, which manifests itself by occurently phantasizing the satisfaction of that desire.

However, in representing desire, phantasy is open to a particular failing, or abuse, which derives from an infantile mode of mental functioning, which phantasy never completely outgrows. What happens is that the person, whose sense of reality is either inchoate or temporarily suspended, readily confuses an occurent state of phantasy in which one of his desires is represented as satisfied with the state of affairs in which that desire would be satisfied. This has various consequences, one of which is that the desire will terminate, if only momentarily. Under the impact of phantasy, the desire will react as if it were satisfied. Freud called this confused state 'hallucination'.

This very last point is ultimately of the greatest importance, for what it exhibits is how a state of phantasy can, in favourable circumstances, cast an influence over our dispositions. In this case, a desire is modified through its satisfaction being phantasized, but this causal power has wide-ranging applications, and it directly explains the second level on which dispositional phantasy operates. For, on this next level, phantasy exploits the failing to which it is exposed in operating on the present level.

On the second level then, the person, still firmly in the grip of an infantile mode of functioning, will be disposed to phantasize some object of his desire so that, confusing merely represented satisfaction with real and actual satisfaction, he can enjoy, without the intervention of reality, the pleasures of satisfaction. Of course, both the confusion, at any rate in its florid form, and the attendant pleasures, will be short-lived. Phantasy operating on this level Freud referred to as 'wish-fulfilment', and wish-fulfilment is teleological, without being intentional. That is, it rests upon a mechanism, and this mechanism would not survive in our repertoire if it did not bring about the consequences that it does. That does not mean that these consequences are, from the point of view of the person, overall beneficial. They are not. Wish-fulfilment, in anything except the short run, is a baneful phenomenon, and we have to struggle hard to exorcize it.

On the next level too, phantasy occurs because of its causal

influence upon the dispositions of the person. But these consequences exhibit a much greater complexity.

The person – and this time the person may be comparatively
freed from the influence of the infantile mode of functioning –
finds that some phenomenon, internal or external, mental or
physical, a loved figure or a troublesome desire, gives rise to
anxiety. This anxiety may stem either from fear for the thing, the
thing being found benign, or from fear of the thing, the thing
being found malign. Either way round, anxiety causes the person
to phantasize a relocation of the thing. If the thing is external,
the person phantasizes his taking the thing into himself: this is
introjection. If the thing is internal, the person phantasizes his
putting it into the outer world: this is projection. Within the
phantasy, the thing, the way it changes position, and the inner
location, are all represented in a singularly concrete or corporeal
way. The thing will be represented as a part or product of the
body, the way it changes position will be represented by some
bodily process like swallowing or excretion, and the inner location is invariably identified as inside the person's body, the outer
location as external to the body.

This use of phantasy is in the service of defence, and it brings,
not just pleasure, but relief from anxiety. It brings relief from
anxiety because the person tends to view the world and himself
as though the change of location that he has phantasized, whether
from outer to inner, or from inner to outer, had actually happened. There are various mechanisms of defence – in addition to
introjection and projection, there are splitting, denial, and projective identification – and each mechanism is realized through
its own kind of phantasy, with its own distinctive content. Once
again, though the phantasy occurs because of its consequences, it
is not right to regard it as intentional. It occurs without benefit
of instrumental beliefs.[21]

On the next level, the task of phantasy is to represent the consequences of defence, and I shall, for ease of exposition, confine
myself to the consequences of defence as employed against
figures.

Once a figure that is the cause of anxiety has been introjected,
the effect of this initial incorporative process – in part because

of the highly concrete way in which the process is experienced – will be to establish a dispositional phantasy: that is to say, a disposition to phantasize the figure as now inside one. The object of any such phantasy has been called an 'internal figure', and an internal figure is a generalization of the special instance that Freud isolated and called the 'superego'. It may be assumed that the dispositional phantasy that is responsible for the continuing life of an internal figure is endowed with a true narrative richness. The narrative will incorporate the various feelings that the figure excites in the person, either because of the characteristics with which it is endowed or because of the characteristics possessed by, or attributed to, its prototype, or the figure in the real world from whom it descends.

Introjection is not a final solution: in this respect, introspection resembles any other defensive operation of the mind. Internal figures will give rise to similar anxieties as external figures, and for this reason introjection is likely to be followed, sooner or later, by projection. Projection, as we have seen, has the same structure as introjection, involving phantasy twice over: a phantasy of expulsion, corporeally envisaged, brings into existence a disposition to phantasize the inner figure now as outside one.

The final level on which I want to consider phantasy is as the internal representation of emotion. Basically what is represented is the attitude that lies at the core of emotion, and, to do so, the narrative aspect of phantasy is exploited. The person represents a given emotion by phantasizing various incidents involving the object of the emotion. In each case, the object of the emotion will be phantasized doing, enduring, acting upon the world in ways that the attitude suggests. But these phantasies will not only concur with the emotion, but, from time to time, they will test the emotion. And, all the while, the phantasies will go back, will circle round, will reenact, the originating condition, thus further justifying the description I offered of emotion as a quasi-mnemic phenomenon.

For our present task, or for the understanding of the criticizing agency, it is with the top, or last three, levels on which phantasy operates, and with their closely linked roles, that we are concerned.

However, even in this somewhat expanded recapitulation, what I said in the previous lecture about how phantasy fulfils these different roles is too perfunctory for our present needs. It requires elaboration and refinement at four points.

(One), whenever I have spoken of introjection and projection, I have spoken of them in that order, and that may have given rise to a misunderstanding. The misunderstanding would be that projection is somehow ancillary to, if not merely corrective of, introjection. That is not so. The two mechanisms are more closely associated, are more on a par, than this indicates. In the texture of ordinary life, the two are so inextricably bound up that they can be thought of as two phases in a recurrent cycle: the mind now breathing in, now breathing out.[22]

Nowhere is this alternation of introjection and projection of greater moment than in the context of the formation of internal figures. For, in many cases of introjection, its immediate explanation, or why it is called for, lies with prior projection. It is only as a result of the projection of properties, properties felt to be either bad and therefore dangerous, or good and therefore vulnerable, on to a figure in the environment that the figure starts to arouse anxiety. Its actual properties would never have justified such an attitude. But, once overlaid with these projected properties, it is either feared or feared for, and, both ways round, the anxiety triggers introjection. But, with introjection invoked, and the figure internalized, the effects of prior projection are not at an end. There is a special likelihood that the projected properties, which the internalized figure still bears along with its original properties, will be a source of continuing anxiety, indeed of forms of anxiety specific to them. It is characteristic of internal figures that, decked out with unwanted parts and aspects of the person, they will tend to be phantasized as mounting, from the inside, endless attacks upon those who, once their donors, are now their hosts.[23]

But even this is not quite right. Further expansion is called for, and that consists in setting beside projection the somewhat different mechanism of projective identification, casually mentioned in the last lecture. The three distinctive features of projective identification are these: (First), whereas properties are projected, it is parts of the self, preeminently internal figures, which projective identification relocates: (secondly), whereas properties are projected on to something, parts of the self are projectively identified into something; and (thirdly), whereas projection is largely defensive, there is a multiplicity of purposes that projective identification can be made to serve. Projective identification is characteristically envisaged in at least as corporeal terms as introjection or projection. For something to be projectively identified, it must first be thought of as a thing, preferably a bodily part or product, and then phantasized as being expelled from the person's own body, and launched into another's. The mode of expulsion is conceived of on the model of corporeal processes of elimination. Once the expelled figure is relocated, not merely is the person temporarily quit of it, but it can in turn be used to control, to damage, to seduce, to communicate with, others.[24]

(Two), though I have talked as if a single incorporative phantasy would suffice to set up an internal figure, or a single expulsive phantasy to remove it, this is unrealistic. More realistic is to think that the disposition to phantasize the introjected figure as inside one, or the disposition to phantasize the projected figure as outside one, comes into being only when the same occurrent phantasy, directed on to the same figure, is reiterated with the same content, the same attendant anxieties, and, above all, the same expectations that phantasy will bring relief, or some measure of relief, from these anxieties.

'The same expectations.' Here the underlying point, which is of great importance, is that the causal power that mental states of phantasy have over the person's mind is heavily bound up with the way, or ways, in which the mind in general and phantasy in particular are conceived of.[25] States of phantasy would not have the power they have were it not for the fact that we conceive of them, implicitly that is, as having this power, and, for that matter, other and wider powers: though this does not mean that we have it in our power to conceive of them otherwise. And, by other and wider powers, what I mean is this: Notoriously we credit states of phantasy with the power to change the world locally. And it is in large part because of their failure to do this, and of our incapacity to admit this failure, that we reinvoke phantasy to alter the world more globally. Freud's patient, the Rat Man, who was unable to bring his father back to life through phantasy, phantasized for him a ghostly existence between death and this world, and did so even though this ran completely counter to his otherwise rational cast of mind.[26]

(It is a further question whether, when a particular mental state of phantasy establishes a disposition to phantasize in a certain way – say, an incorporative phantasy causes the disposition to phantasize the corresponding figure as inside us – we should place the relevant conception of the phantasy on the side of the cause, and thus alongside the phantasy itself, or on the side of the disposition, and thus regard it as a further and concomitant effect of the phantasy. This question, which I shall not attempt to answer, is of a piece with the question whether, when the external world causes a perception of it, we should think of the belief that the perception is of the world, which almost invariably accompanies the perception, as part of the cause of the perception, and thus alongside the world, or as a further part of the effect of the world upon us.)

(Three), when an incorporative phantasy that has a figure in the world as its object does indeed bring about the disposition to phantasize a figure as inside us, the relation between the external figure and the internal figure is never, strictly speaking, one of identity. I may in places have suggested otherwise, but this was only for simplicity of presentation. The internal figure is not the same figure as the external figure from whom it derives.

Ultimately this claim can be expressed in Leibnitzian terms. The two figures are non-identical because they differ in their properties. However it is worth going below this blanket explanation and looking at the different sources of this discrepancy.

In the first place, the internal figure will differ from the external figure as it actually is in that the internal figure will possess those properties which were projected on to it some time before its introjection, and which may partially account for the need to introject it.

Secondly, the internal figure will possess properties that, taken either as a set or individually, are unique to phantasized figures.

'As a set': in that, though none of the properties may be in itself exceptionable, they could not be co-instantiated in the real world without either supplementation or alteration. The set may be incomplete, as when the internal figure is phantasized as without a past, or an age, or a sex: or the set may be inconsistent as when the figure is phantasized as combining the contrary aspects of the mother and the father. 'Individually': in that some properties assigned to the internal figure may admit of no clear actualization in the real world, as when an internal figure is phantasized as invulnerable, or as omniscient, or as having some special direct access to the inner life of the person in whom it is lodged.

And, thirdly, the internal figure is often so susceptible to the desires, needs, and anxieties of the person that its life exhibits a flexibility, a fluidity, totally inconsistent with the ordinary constraints of personal identity over time. This alone would set it apart from any external figure.

One overall, and necessarily approximate, way of thinking of the relationship between the external figure who is introjected and the internal figure who is the product of the introjective process is to liken it to that between a real-life figure and a fictional character modelled upon it. When a fictional character metamorphizes from its real-life model, though it will inherit some of its qualities from its prototype, some will come from its creator, others from the exigencies of the narrative, and yet others, which could never be realized in this world, can be traced to the very nature of fiction. More particularly, we might find the analogue for an internal figure in a fictional character that departs from its pallid original through the grandeur, the extravagance, the horror, that it would take the imagination of Dickens, or Dostoievsky, or Proust, to impart to it.

(Four), when the process of introjection is complete, and the disposition to phantasize an internal figure is established, there is a spectrum of ways in which this figure may be phantasized as standing to the person. At one end of the spectrum, and standard when the external figure is introjected out of fear of it, the internal figure will be phantasized as in sharp opposition to, or as standing over and against, the person. The figure is in most ways alien to the person who hosts it, even though every aspect, every property, that it possesses depends upon the way it is phantasized, and so ultimately upon the person who phantasizes it. At the other end of the spectrum, and standard when the external figure is introjected out of fear for it, the internal figure will be phantasized as on the side of the person, and aligned both with his interests and with his values, and the person will in turn hasten to conform to whatever the figure counsels or enjoins. Now the person identifies with the figure.

An internal figure that starts life at one end of this spectrum may shift to the other, and how this transition is effected is a rich topic, to which I shall return in a later section.

I conclude this discussion by pointing out that, if, as I have still to show, we cannot understand shame and guilt without reference to internal figures, we must also recognize that only some internal figures are connected with these emotions. Others, because of their repertoire, or of what the person who houses them is disposed to phantasize their doing and saying, are in no way suited to the part of the criticizing agency.

10. But, knowing what we now know about internal figures, why should we think that any are qualified to play this role?

If they are, the reason must be that they, and they alone, can accommodate the two central features distinctive of the criticizing agency. Internal figures must be capable of realizing an agency that can be, from the point of view of the person whom it regulates, heteronomous, and yet possessed of the appropriate authority: that is, it can, through the impact that it makes upon the person's sense of self, oblige him to adopt towards himself the attitude implicit in shame or guilt, alien though it may seem to him. Furthermore, internal figures must have a way, not just of instantiating, but also of reconciling, these two attributes. The authority that they wield must be one that is undiminished by heteronomy, and they do not have to compromise on their heteronomy to acquire the authority they need.

How, we might ask, can internal figures do something that is evidently beyond the scope both of an external figure and of the simple, undivided self? The answer is twofold. That internal figures can stand in for an agency that can be heteronomous derives from how they come into being. That they can exercise the appropriate authority derives from how they are phantasized.

I shall take each answer in turn.

First, then, it is because internal figures originate, through an incorporative phantasy, from external figures, that, once they have been internalized, they may well continue to address the person who now harbours them as an alien force. They may set themselves to make the person feel shame or guilt on occasions when the person finds no reason to do so. How they actually succeed in what they try to do is, of course, another matter: it is the separate, though related, issue of authority, which comes next.

To this account there is an objection, which, though anticipated, has not been met. It is this: Given that everything that we phantasize internal figures' doing is something that comes from us, or that it is *we* who phantasize what they carry out, how can we phantasize their doing to us anything so evidently against the grain as causing us to feel shame or guilt when we are not inclined to do so? Undeniably internal figures start out as external figures, but does not internalization strip them of the externality that they would need to retain if they were to function as the vehicles of heteronomy?

This objection fails to take seriously the nature of introjection. For, once we have internalized a figure, and a disposition to phantasize a counterpart figure as inside us has been established, then how, or when, or to what effect, we phantasize that figure are not matters over which we are likely to have discretion. The explanation is that, in internalizing a figure, we internalize, along with it, a whole repertoire on which its identity depends. Over time we can, as we shall see, bring about certain internal changes in ourselves, which in turn can modify or attenuate the strict repertoire that governs what an internal figure is phantasized as doing, saying, thinking. But that is an arduous, oblique, not an immediate, process, and, in the meanwhile, the life of internal figures has its own momentum. Error is to think, against all the evidence that our inner life offers us, that everything that goes on in the mind, at least in the thinking part of the mind, is under our control.[27] The repertoire of internal figures is often no more under our control than the rules of a foreign language, which we have internalized, and which we speak out of this internalized knowledge.

Secondly, I have traced the special authority that internal figures have over the person to how they are phantasized.

But, since the special authority that internal figures have matches the authority of the criticizing agency, and that authority is, as we saw at the end of the last section but one, fundamentally the authority to induce in us the appropriate attitude, it is time to bring to the fore something that has not yet in this lecture received more than passing attention: that is, the attitude at the core of shame and guilt. To this I shall now turn. But it must, from the beginning be borne in mind that, when internal figures, acting as vehicles of the criticizing agency, bring about this attitude, they bring it about, not immediately, but mediately. What they bring about immediately is the attack upon the sense of self, and the subsequent anxiety. The attitude is the person's response to this experience.

11. The comparative neglect so far of the attitude in shame and guilt may seem the more surprising when we reflect that, from the point of view of these lectures, or the philosophical topic of the emotions, the most significant thing that shame and guilt have in common is that each involves an attitude. For this is what makes, or helps to make, them emotions.

So what, in the case of shame and guilt, is the nature of the attitude?

It can now be seen with hindsight that, when, in the last lecture, I considered the attitude in the case of the non-moral emotions, the account that I gave implicitly presented the attitude as made up out of two major elements. They are the object of the attitude, and, though I did not use the term, the content of the attitude. The object of the attitude is what the attitude is directed on to, and the content is how the attitude views the object. The object may be a thing or a fact, and it may be real, but it need not be. The content may have a propositional core, but it need not, and, when it does, this propositional core could not exhaust the content of the attitude, for the content is, if circuitously, bound up with feeling. This account is not an analysis, because it does not provide us with the materials out of which we can understand what an attitude is, and there is no accompanying claim that, once the object and the content have been subtracted, there is nothing left over to the attitude.

If this is a structural account, it is important to see that, though it supplements the historical account that these lectures have largely favoured, it is also underpinned by it. Object and content provide the armature for the attitude, but, in doing so, they root the attitude in its history, hence in the history of the emotion as I have been using this phrase. This is because the account traces back, first object, then content, to a specific source, and, in each case, the source is located at a crucial, a nodal, point in the formation of the emotion.

Let us look at these two sources in turn: First, the object. The object of the attitude is heir to the precipitating factor, and the precipitating factor is that to which the person's thoughts turn, turn and cling, as he is driven to reflect upon what brought about the originating condition. In this way the object can be traced back to the earliest stages in the formation of an emotion. The content of the emotion is only a little less entrenched: it belongs to what is conceptually, but barely temporally, the next stage in the formation of the emotion. For, once the originating condition has been experienced, the content comes about through the turning outwards, or the extroversion, of this experience. The content of the emotion is the result of turning outwards the experience of satisfied or frustrated desire.

If this account of the attitude, worked out with the non-moral emotions in mind, should turn out to be valid also for the moral emotions, this would be a boon. Such a result would, in the first place, enhance our confidence in the account as it applies to the non-moral emotions. An account that held only for one kind of emotion would hold only dubiously for it: one that held for both would be relatively secure. But furthermore a common account might also be expected to help us with our present inquiries into the special authority of the criticizing agency. Is a common account available?

That, with the moral emotions too, the attitude can be segmented into object and content is a plausible thing to assume. A more difficult question is whether, for both kinds of emotion, object and content can be traced back to the same sources. Not the least of the difficulties here is to know how to understand 'same' in the present context. For, if there is a common account across the emotions, it will not be an account that has been transposed bodily and intact from one kind to the other. It will be an account that has been transferred *mutatis mutandis*. What then are the *mutanda*, and how do they appear when they are *mutata*?

That alteration is required in the details of the account if its spirit is to be preserved follows from the fact that there is a big difference between the two kinds of emotion. Furthermore it is precisely of a sort that cannot fail to show up when we inquire whether a common account of the attitude is available in principle. For the fundamental point of difference between the two kinds of emotion is in their originating conditions: the non-moral emotions arising out of satisfaction or frustration of desire, the moral emotions arising out of an assault upon the person's sense of self.

The question therefore arises, Can the account that we might well think of as the best account that we can provide of the attitude in the non-moral emotions be recycled for shame and guilt, deviating only in ways that can be fully explained by differences in the originating conditions of the two kinds of emotion? For, if it can be, then we have, in the appropriate sense, a common account.

I shall ask this question in turn of (one) the object, and (two) the content, of the attitude in shame and guilt. Can each be explained by a common account, which preserves certain broad structural features and, at the same time, allows for the peculiarities of the histories of these emotions?

I start with the object.

As we have seen, what is distinctive of the object in shame and guilt is that it displays *specificity*, and *necessity*. *Specificity*, in that invariably the object is precisely the person himself. It is not some person other than himself, nor is it some fact about, or some property of, himself. *Necessity*, in that the object, not merely invariably is, but must be, the person himself. The emotion could not be a case of shame or of guilt if the object were otherwise.

These two restrictions, or the *fixity* of the object, as I shall call it, have no parallel in the case of the non-moral emotions, which may, with only very few, though undoubtedly very important, exceptions, be directed on to a range of facts and figures alike. How are these restrictions to be accounted for?

I start with an explanation of a sort to which mid-twentieth-century philosophy has familiarized us. It proposes that these restrictions follow from the meaning of the words 'shame' and 'guilt': they follow from the way these terms have been defined. Clearly such an explanation would run counter to anything that the would-be common account suggests.

If we accept this mode of explanation, then it has two consequences, by which it may be judged. First, and more generally, it makes the identity of the emotions solely an artifice of language. Shame and guilt are circumscribed by the dictionary. Secondly, and more particularly, it permits a situation of the following kind to arise: An emotion forms within the person that is in all ways either like shame, or like guilt, except that it happens not to be directed back on to the person. The emotion, not being reflexive, cannot be either shame, or guilt: that is to say, it cannot be called by either of these two names. To the question, What are such emotions to be called? two strategies can be invoked, ultimately indifferently. Further nomenclature can be introduced, which would reflect the closeness of these aberrant emotions to old-style shame and guilt, or existing nomenclature can be redefined. We can refer to the new emotions as 'quasi-shame', or 'quasi-guilt', or we can stipulate that, from now onwards, someone can perfectly correctly be said to feel shame or guilt for another, or on another's behalf. Now, if these are held to be adequate solutions to the problem, then, either way round, the fixity of the object in shame and guilt emerges as something totally superficial. The explanation of fixity is that a situation such as that currently under consideration was not foreseen, therefore its possibility was, misguidedly it turns out, foreclosed upon.

To many these two consequences are not acceptable. They will look for an alternative way of grounding the identity of the emotions, hence for an alternative mode of explanation for the fixity of the object in shame and guilt.

I suggest that anyone who finds this stipulative view of how the emotions are distinguished impoverished will look for an account of the matter according to which any criterial distinction between two emotions, or any difference in how the corresponding emotion-terms are defined, will go along with, and will reflect, some further difference betwen them. There will be some difference either in what makes each of the emotions what it is, or – according to these lectures, more or less the same thing – in their characteristic histories. Once we have such an account, our natural resistance to the idea that the nomenclature of the emotions can be gerrymandered at will, and without serious consequence, will be vindicated.

And now my claim is that an account of the foregoing sort is precisely what the would-be common account of the attitude in emotion has to offer. For let us consider, first in outline, then in greater detail, how the common account would explain the fixity of the object in shame and guilt, and why there is, in this respect, a difference between the moral and the non-moral emotions.

In outline, the common account would say this: If the object in shame and guilt does exhibit fixity, then it must be that, once the originating condition of shame or guilt has occurred, and our nature prompts us to look for what precipitated it, we are, invariably and of necessity, led back to ourselves. By contrast, at the corresponding moment in the history of the non-moral emotions, we are, except in exceptional circumstances, led further afield.

But this is skeletal. Let us next try to imagine, on the basis of these lectures to date, and out of our own experience of the moral emotions, what the infilling would be.

When shame and guilt form, there has been a fall in our sense of self: distinctively, a fall in our sense of self that has been caused by a drop in the regard in which we are held by another, a drop then passed on to us in a judgment conveyed by the eyes or the voice. This drop is due to something that we have become, or to something that we have done.

However it is crucial that this condition, this complex condition, is understood appropriately. And appropriately means experientially: each step in the process is experienced as such.

There is an instructive parallel here between the two kinds of emotion. For, just as the non-moral emotions are caused, not by the mere fact that one of our desires has been satisfied or frustrated, but by the satisfaction or the frustration itself, which is partly constituted by an experience of ours, so similarly, in the case of the moral emotions, the cause is an experienced fall in the sense of self. And this experience is as complex as the condition that it registers. For the fall in the sense of self is experienced, in the first place, as a situation of hurt, or grave damage. It is further experienced as caused by the lesser regard in which we are now held by some agency. And there is a further aspect to the experience, for this drop in regard is felt to be communicated to us in a certain sensory way.

If, from one point of view, it is quite surprising how much gets packed into this experience, from another point of view, which is that of our present concern, there are two omissions that are highly significant. It is only later, or with the attainment of maturity, that these omissions are, one way or another, benignly or malignly, made good. First, there is no register of the criticizing agency acting as a free force, with its own motivation. The agency is recorded impersonally, or as pure insistence. Although the fact that the judgment is phantasized as being enunciated by a criticizing agency is why it is felt by us to be damaging, it is the judgment – as opposed to, say, the agency via the judgment, which is an alternative we shall consider later – that is experienced as damaging, the agency appearing in the phantasy as a mere conduit, or vehicle, of the damage. As far as our experience is concerned, the agency is transparent on to the judgment. Secondly, there is no register of the standards that determine the judgment. As we have seen, we are not expected to agree or disagree with them. But, more than that, we are not expected to be apprised of them, except in this one respect: The standards are such that any judgment derived from them is a judgment passed on the person as such, on the person himself, not on some aspect of the person, or on the person in so far as he has become this, or done that.

These two omissions work together when it comes to the present topic, or to our tracing our lowered sense of self to its precipitating factor. For, if the gravity of the damage we suffer, or the way it appears to have been directed to where it hurts most, makes us see it as the handiwork of a person, and thus leads us to trace it to a figure, to a figure rather than to an insensate fact, at this point the two omissions take over, and their joint effect is to ensure that the figure to whom we ascribe the doing of the damage is none other than ourselves. We are the agents of the hurt from which we suffer. It is we who ultimately have damaged our own sense of self.

This self-incriminatory process, which is central to the establishment of the attitude in shame and guilt, may be reconstructed somewhat as follows: The first omission, or the depersonalization of the criticizing agency, means that there is no-one, no person, for us to pick upon other than ourselves. The second omission means that one consideration we might very well have for not picking upon ourselves – that is, our innocence in our own eyes – is made to count for nothing. We have brought down damage upon ourselves through incurring an adverse judgment, and the fact that the judgment may be, in our own eyes, indefensible accompanies the standards that determined the judgment into limbo. Both are effaced. If we have to blame someone, which we feel we do, there is no-one but ourselves to blame.

Now, before I turn from the object to the content of the attitude involved in shame and guilt, and ask how far this can be explained by the would-be common account of the attitude, let me clarify one matter. I must emphasize that, in keeping with what I have said about the heteronomy of shame and guilt, what I have been doing is to trace the natural history of two emotions. These histories weave experiences, attitudes, reactions, ascriptions, accusations, into their narratives. But all these occur, or form, independently of the person's beliefs. The histories fall outside what a more scientistic terminology calls the person's belief-system.

So now I ask, Can the content of the attitude in shame and guilt be understood as the turning outward, the extroversion, of what we have just seen to be the complex experience in which the originating condition was realized? I believe that it can be, but this turning outward must, despite the element of artificiality that this introduces, be observed layer by layer.

The core of the originating experience is an experience of damage: deep damage, or damage to the sense of self. Turned outwards, this leads us to view the object of the attitude as having it in it to bring about, indeed to have brought about, such damage. We come to see ourselves – for we are the object – as, not just potentially, but actually, dangerous: this is the first layer of the attitude. However, since the damage that we have brought about is damage to us, and is experienced as such, the next layer to the attitude is our coming to see ourselves as, specifically, a danger to ourselves. Experientially we are, in Baudelaire's phrase, '*la victime et le bourreau*'.[28] We are the victim as well as the executioner, and this is how we must seem to ourselves. But to seem so, or to keep alive in ourselves this awareness of how self-directed the danger is that we represent, we must also keep alive some persisting awareness of the damage itself. Hence the next layer to the attitude: we hurt. If shame and guilt are negative emotions, they are so twice over: in this respect, they resemble jealousy amongst the non-moral emotions. They are negative in that they view their object in an unpleasurable light: and they are also negative in that viewing their object as they require is a painful experience for the person. Next, it must be remembered that the damage that we have done to ourselves, which the hurt of shame and guilt commemorate, was, and will necessarily be experienced by ourselves as being, something that we did to ourselves indirectly: we damaged ourselves by bringing down upon ourselves a hostile judgment. But, since the judgment is not necessarily one with which we concur, the judgment is experienced primarily as the brute impact of the world upon us. This part of the experience, when extroverted, gives shame and guilt their layer of self-protectiveness. And the final layer of the experience that is extroverted records a distinctive aspect of the disapproval that fuels shame and guilt: that is, that it is directed against us as an integral person. Once this is turned outwards, and the attitude common to shame and guilt thus completed, we become ashamed, or we feel guilty, of ourselves, not in so far as we have become this, or done that — though this is why we are ashamed, or feel guilty, of ourselves — but totally. My shame, my guilt, adhere to me as a person.

So much for those aspects of the originating experience which are common to shame and guilt, and their extroversion. But also turned outwards so as to supply the attitude with further content are aspects of the experience that are peculiar to one emotion or the other. As we have seen, one aspect of the experience out of which shame is formed is that the hostile judgment is conveyed to us by the eyes, and one aspect of the experience out of which guilt is formed is that the hostile judgment is conveyed to us by the voice. When these particular aspects of the experience are turned outwards, they register in a very concrete way an aspect of shame and guilt not so far discussed: their inescapability. More specifically, the eyes and the voice are used to bridge the gap between the circumstances in which these emotions arise and the way they persist. We are ashamed of ourselves, and must continue to be so, so long as there are eyes to see us: we feel guilty, and must continue to feel so, so long as there are voices to reach us.

These are phantasies, and it is barely surprising that it should be in the area of the moral emotions that the nexus between attitude and phantasy should be strongest. The continuing phantasy of the eyes that perpetuate shame or of the voice that enforces guilt are then reflected in the defences that we mobilize against these painful emotions. Turning a blind eye, or a deaf ear, can be more than metaphors. They describe operations that we carry out in phantasy against the internal figures that service the criticizing agency.[29] A full step beyond these purely internal operations are the acting-out of them in the real world. Literature and myth are full of such examples, horrendous in their literalness. Cornwall blinds Gloucester so as to free himself from shame,[30] Terreus cuts out the tongue of Philomela to silence guilt.[31]

Finally, there is, exclusive to guilt, a further element to the attitude. Guilt arises because of something that we have done: often, but not invariably, to someone. When there is such a further person, this secondary figure functions within the originating experience as part of the reason why the agency passes down judgment on us. However, when at the next stage, the originating experience is turned outwards, this further person takes on a new role. The person becomes the secondary object, first, of the attitude, then of the emotion. If the primary object of Rousseau's guilt is necessarily Rousseau himself, the secondary object is Marion, whom he also damaged. In the case of Augustine, by contrast, there seems to be no secondary object, unless perhaps the shadowy figure of the neighbour whose orchard he ransacked. It seems essential to guilt that there *can be* a secondary object, though there *need not be*. Guilt can arise through the mere transgression of rules, without any suggestion of harm or damage to others.[32]

The foregoing discussion clears the ground for the adoption of a common account of the attitude across both kinds of emotion. For the explanation it provides of object and content in the case of shame and guilt is *mutatis mutandis* the same as that which holds for the the non-moral emotions.

I now want to support this argument by considering an experience subtly but significantly different from the complex experience in which shame and guilt originate, and show how, when this experience is turned outwards, it leads to an attitude, hence to an emotion, that, both in its object and in its content, differs from shame and guilt. Furthermore it differs from shame and guilt in just those ways that, given the differences between their originating conditions, the common account would lead us to expect.

This new kind of experience occurs in a situation of the following kind: We have dropped in someone's regard. Let us call him a critic, and it makes no difference whether he is an external or an internal critic: if he is an internal critic, he is unqualified, as we shall see, to represent the criticizing agency. The next thing to happen is that, because of this lower regard in which he holds us, our critic feels entitled to act against us. And he does so. Or, at least, he is experienced as doing so. This time – and this is what makes the situation different – it is what the critic does, and not the mere drop in his regard, that damages us. And the difference is perfectly compatible with the critic's choosing as the instrument of damage that he employs against us the mere enunciation of the drop in the regard in which he holds us. From an external point of view, what this hostile critic does may be indistinguishable from what the criticizing agency, or some internal figure representing it, did in the originating condition of shame or guilt. But, from the critic's point of view, or how what he did was intended, or from our point of view, or how what he did is experienced by us, there is a massive difference. When the critic's adverse judgment reaches us, it is taken, not as what I have called the brute impact of the world upon us, but as a motivated attack. The critic has made use of how he thinks of us in order to cause us hurt, and it is impossible for us to regard the judgment as impersonal.

Now, when this second kind of experience is turned outwards, or becomes the originating condition of an emotion, there are two features of oncoming attitude that can be anticipated. First, as we start to identify the precipitating factor, the natural direction in which we shall turn is, not towards ourselves, but towards our critic. Our critic, with his motivation bared, has lost the transparency enjoyed by the internal figure who originates shame or guilt. In exposing himself to our hostility, he interposes himself between us and ourselves. Secondly, the damage that the critic has done to us is now experienced, not as the total attack that the criticizing agency in guilt and shame launches against us in our innermost sense of self, but as something more local, or as an attempt to frustrate a desire of ours.

Put these two differences together, and we see that this new experience, when extroverted, converts itself into an attitude that, both in object and in content, is characteristic of a non-moral, rather than a moral, emotion. Indeed it is not hard to predict, within broad limits, the emotion that is likely to form in the situation that I have outlined. Dependent on exactly how the person interprets the critic's hostile motivation, anger or fear or hatred or indignation will form.

In *Crime and Punishment*, Dostoevsky recounts how Raskolnikov, a young student filled with ideas and resolutely impervious to self-knowledge, gradually comes to feel guilt over his murder of the old money-lender, and the fortuitous killing of her younger sister. Raskolnikov modulates through a succession of emotions, and the process of change, as Dostoevsky describes it, which he does in great psychological detail, corresponds closely to a struggle within Raskolnikov's mind between the two kinds of originating condition that we have just been considering.

Initially Raskolnikov assumes a Napoleonic conception of himself as superior to the ordinary moral law. In finding the courage to kill, for the greater benefit of mankind, someone whom he looks upon as a louse, he hopes to fulfil a higher destiny. So long as this remains his attitude, he finds a way of attributing to his various critics, who, at their own pace, come to suspect the great crime that he has committed, a specific motivation. They misunderstand him, they want to humiliate him, they are intent on suffocating him with mindless affection, and to each he responds with the appropriate emotion: contempt, or anger, or murderous irritability. Only gradually is he able to turn his attention from the motivation of the critic to the content of the criticism, and, as he does, two things happen, which initiate a change of attitude. First, he experiences directly the hurt that the criticism does to him as a person. Secondly, he sees himself as the cause, the indirect cause, of his own hurt. He says to Sonia, 'Did I murder the old woman? I murdered myself, not her!'[33] The last two words apart, he now concedes guilt, which we may assume him to feel.

However it must be observed – and this accords with a persistent theme of this lecture – that, even when Raskolnikov accepts the criticism to the point of being opened up to the experience of guilt, he still contrives to think of the criticism itself, or that to which the guilt is a response, as completely unjustified. Desperately trying to maintain his failing illusion of grandiosity, he is pained by something that he does not, that he cannot, acknowledge. Dostoevsky too thinks that there is a further stage through which Raskolnikov's change of heart must pass. His transformation will be complete only when he acknowledges the justice of the criticism, and Dostoevsky shows us, thereby raising a psychological aspect of the matter that falls outside the scope of this lecture, that this is in turn something that he will be able to do only when he simultaneously accepts his love for Sonia. If the first stage of Raskolnikov's transformation takes him from some miscellany of non-moral emotions to the experience of guilt, what still lies ahead of him is the second

stage, which will move him from guilt experienced heteronomously to guilt experienced autonomously. Dostoevsky, who
was probably daunted by the literary task involved, abbreviates
this part of the narrative, and it is confined to the final pages,
which make up the Epilogue of the novel.

Readers of *Crime and Punishment* will note that, before
Raskolnikov concedes guilt, there are some brief moments when
it looks as though, in response to criticism, guilt is about to break
through. On each occasion, it does not. Instead Raskolnikov continues to experience criticism as a motivated attack, and correspondingly responds, as we have seen, with anger, or spleen, or
self-righteousness. I want to suggest that we should not think of
these regressions solely as evidence of immaturity, or inability to
experience his true situation, or lack of self-awareness. They are
that, but they are also something more. They are the symptoms
of defence. Defence is triggered in Raskolnikov by the inability
to tolerate, not the experience of frustration, but the graver hurt
that he glimpses will come, once he truly confronts the criticism
levelled against him, in his deepest sense of self. We can now think
of the various hostile emotions that Raskolnikov, in his efforts to
ward off guilt, directs against his family, against Sonia, against the
police, as so many malformed emotions.

At the end of this extended discussion of the attitude in shame
and guilt, it is worth making explicit a difficulty that has plagued
its exposition, and that may well make it that much harder to
follow. The difficulty is unexpected: though what I said in an
earlier section may have alerted us to it. It is the difficulty, greater
in the case of the moral emotions than elsewhere, of keeping
clear a distinction that is fundamental to my account of the emotions. It is the fundamental nature of the distinction that makes
the difficulty unexpected. The distinction is between (one) the
originating condition of the emotion, and (two) the attitude
which is at the core of the emotion, and which forms in response
to the originating condition.

It is because the two are, specifically in the case of shame and
guilt, cut largely out of the same cloth that confusion threatens.
For, with the moral emotions, we, we ourselves, are at the centre
both of the originating experience and of the attitude. A moral

emotion arises, it can be said, when we transform criticism of ourselves, as it comes at us from another – this being the originating condition – into hostility which we adopt towards ourselves – this being the attitude. However, if we fail to distinguish the two, if indeed we confuse them, just because they are both antagonistic and they are both directed against us, we shall, amongst other errors, backslide into that of the necessary autonomy of shame and guilt.[34]

13. This reminder of a distinction that might be thought to need no reminder will prove salutary as we return to the question, left hanging, of the special authority of internal figures, and how they come by it, and how their coming by it allows them to implement the criticizing agency. If we want to find an answer to the question, then we must keep in the forefront of our minds the difference between the two antagonisms that dominate the formation of shame and guilt: the criticizing agency versus us, then us versus ourselves – the second of these being the heir to, or the transform of, the first.

In assessing the power of internal figures to exercize the authority appropriate to the criticizing agency, we must guard against a cardinal error: that of measuring up the way in which internal figures bring about shame or guilt against the way in which an external figure might bring about a non-moral emotion by satisfying or frustrating a desire of ours. The larger mistake that this would involve – a mistake that the flow of this lecture might seem to have encouraged – is to think that, when we ask whether internal figures or external figures are better equipped to induce some psychological condition, we are comparing like with like. Another way of making the same error is to treat the authority of an internal figure, and how far it reaches, as though this rested upon the empirical properties of the figure. I have tried to counteract this last mistake by claiming that the authority that internal figures wield derives from how they are phantasized. It is to this claim that I now turn.

Before I substantiate this claim, let me note a happy ambiguity in the word 'how'. Suppose that I phantasize a certain figure criticizing me, and I am asked, How do I phantasize it? and the

answer is, Remorselessly, then this can be understood in two
ways. It can be understood as saying either (one) that I phantasize this figure as remorseless in its criticism of me, or (two) that
I am remorseless in phantasizing it as criticizing me. 'How', in
other words, can cover the content of the phantasy that I engage
in and the manner in which I engage in the phantasy. This
ambiguity is happy in that, not only are the content and the
manner likely to be conjoined, but they are certain to conspire
in the effect that they cause. When I phantasize an internal critic
as something from which I cannot escape, I am also likely to be
unable to escape from doing so, and, in the circumstances, this
conjunction is crucial to understanding the full authority that the
criticizing agency has over me.

Of course, of content and manner, content is primary, and,
when we turn to the content of the phantasies in which
internal figures appear, let us start from the fact, already observed,
that internal figures can be phantasized as having properties that
are not open to external figures to possess. Amongst these exclusive, or proprietary, properties lie a special set that might be called
'achievement-properties'. For internal figures can be phantasized
as doing certain things, and as doing them successfully, where
success in no way depends, as it does in the real world, upon
planning, or the favourable conjunction of circumstances, or,
when all else fails, good luck. The success that, in these cases,
attends what internal figures do is internal to their doing it: it is
part of what we phantasize their doing. 'Successfully' as a qualifier
of the way in which these figures are phantasized as criticizing
us is as much a part of the content of the phantasy as 'harshly',
or 'superciliously', might be. The relevance of such achievement-
properties at this juncture is this: Suppose that we ask ourselves
the question, Why is it that the judgments that our internal critics
pass upon us, or that we phantasize their passing upon us, so hurt
us that, when we start to look for what precipitated our distress,
it is not available to us to pick upon the critics, who, after all,
asserted these judgments, but we must turn upon ourselves, who
merely provoked them? The short answer to this question is, That
was what we phantasized. We phantasized these judgments as
having this kind of effect built into them. And, if we next ask,

What is the difference between phantasizing these judgments one way and phantasizing them another way? What is the difference between phantasizing them so that we have the licence to rebel against them and phantasizing them so that we are obliged, however reluctantly, to lie down under them? there is no further answer. There is no answer over and above the way we respond – the way we respond, note, not the way we phantasize we respond – to the phantasized judgment. The content of the phantasy and the impact of the phantasy upon us are obverse and reverse of the same coin. The two sides can be separately observed, but they are not separable, so long as they circulate as the currency of our psychology. Deny this, and we are deep into thinking that the authority of an internal figure, like that of an external figure, rests upon its empirical properties.

However it would be wrong to conclude that the internal figures who are vehicles of the criticizing agency gain the requisite authority solely from the fact that they are internal figures. That they originate in an incorporative phantasy, and then continue to be phantasized doing this or that inside us, is not the whole of the relevant story. What is also relevant is their earlier history, or which external figures they descend from, and how, and why. It is, in large part, what we might think of as their pre-history that distinguishes them from those other internal figures who are unsuited to the part of the criticizing agency.

Freud provided a well-known account of the origins of the super-ego, which, as we have seen, is how he referred to the internal figure, or figures, who represent the criticizing agency. I say 'figure or figures', because Freud was imprecise whether there is one, or many, and thought this of little consequence.[35] According to him, the superego of the male child – and he had difficulties, which do not concern us, about the case of the female child – originates in what he calls the 'dissolution of the Oedipus complex'.[36] The boy's earliest sexual desires have been directed on to the mother, whereupon the father, as defender of his exclusive rights to the mother's body, is phantasized as threatening the boy with castration. In terror, the boy introjects the father, thereby exchanging a frightening external danger for enduring internal torment. The superego now harangues, upbraids, chastizes, the boy according to standards that make no allowances for, indeed often expressly run counter to, the boy's own wishes.

From Melanie Klein we get a different and somewhat more protracted narrative of the infant's troubled relations with its parents, and one that now covers both the little boy and the little girl. This begins with the infant's phantasized explorations of the mother's body, and its preoccupation with its own insides. These phantasies have a strong sadistic colouring. In contradistinction, Klein reserved the term 'Oedipus complex' for a phase that is emotionally more mature, though, in point of fact, still chronologically earlier, than anything Freud envisaged. Sexual, or, more specifically, genital, phantasy, so far from pitting the infant against the parents, compensates for the predominantly aggressive phantasy that had gone before. The Oedipus complex is, for Klein, a phase of reparation, and the bitter triadic conflict that Freud placed at its centre she has brought forward in time, and makes it coincide with the infant's phantasized discovery of the father's penis lodged inside the mother's body. For Klein it is this that is at the core of the infant's jealousy.

However the more benign view Klein took of the Oedipus complex did not lead her to a necessarily more benign view of the criticizing agency, or the superego.

For, in the first place, she chronologically uncoupled the establishment of the superego and the Oedipus complex. According to her, the superego did not come into being at the dissolution, nor even, as she first thought,[37] at the advent, of the Oedipus complex, but already presided over the earliest phantasies about the mother's body.[38] Secondly, it was important for Klein, unlike Freud, to insist on the multiplicity of internal figures who make up the superego: at one point, she proposed the phrase 'superego organization'.[39] This collective of internal figures, or the person's 'inner world', were the residues of the various external figures, or aspects of figures, maternal as well as paternal, who had brought about the infant's earliest satisfactions and earliest frustrations, and were subsequently introjected. Accordingly, if this had the consequence that some of these internal figures were supportive rather than critical, it is only the latter who could be thought of as realizing the critical agency, and thus responsible for shame and guilt.[40] And these figures are not envisaged by Klein as in any way blander than the internalized castrating father of Freudian theory.

But now it must be pointed out that there is no philosophical need to choose between these two accounts, or to appropriate from either anything except those structural features of the origins of the internal critics which can explain their particular authority.

First and foremost is the fact that the criticizing agency is invariably heir to a figure that the person feels fear of: fear of, rather than, or more than, fear for.

Secondly, this frightening figure in no small measure owes the badness that it is experienced as possessing to the infant's prior projection on to it, or, more to the point, projective identification into it, of the infant's own badness.

And, thirdly, this figure exhibited its badness, and made itself feared, primarily through its blind opposition to the infant's desires.

At first, it might seem counter-intuitive to try to explain the authority of those internal figures who implement the criticizing agency by reference to the fact that they derive from external figures who once induced fear in us. For, as we know, precisely what these internal figures do not do is to induce fear in us. They do not induce in us, either directly or indirectly, an emotion that, like fear, takes another as its object. On the contrary, what they do is that they induce directly in us an experience, which causes an emotion, which therefore they indirectly induce, that takes us, or ourselves, as its object.

What, then, is the relevance of the first of these structural conditions?

The answer lies in the trade-off that defence, or, more specifically, introjection, effects between outer and inner dangers. For, in introjection, we get rid of an external source of fear, and, in exchange, set up something internal, over which we hope to have more control, but to which we assign powers that no external figure could possibly enjoy. The internal figure damages us, but we are not moved to retaliate against it, at least in any straightforward way. Rather, as we respond to the damage, we turn against ourselves. These are the terms of the trade-off, and they are cemented by the other structural conditions in which the criticizing agency is formed. The trade-off, it will be appreciated, is not a pact that we enter into as free signatories: rather it is part of the natural history of our emotions, and of ourselves.

An essential aspect of the criticizing agency is its irresistibility. We go along with its demands upon us. And we do so for two reasons, which are connected with the second and the third of the structural conditions upon its genesis. That the figure owes much of its ferocity to prior projection on our part will have the consequence that, once introjected, it will direct this ferocity against its original source.[41] That the figure was experienced as in blind opposition to our desires places it, once internalized, beyond our immediate comprehesion so that we shall tend not to question its judgments, or their targets.

Indisputably the power of the internal critic will with maturity be reinforced by the power of love and sympathy. But that these emotional bonds cannot unaided account for shame and guilt is conclusively shown by the following considerations: In the first place, shame and guilt can, as we have seen, arise in cases where there is no injured party, or the injured party is ourselves. Secondly, we can feel shame or guilt when there is an injured party, but it is one who falls decisively outside the scope of our love or sympathy. Thirdly, it requires explanation why love and sympathy should be adequate to arouse shame or guilt in us, it is also to be observed that they have such little pre-emptive power: that is, they prove inadequate to prevent our becoming or our doing that over which we shall later feel shame and guilt. And, fourthly, why, if love and sympathy are the driving forces behind shame and guilt, should shame and guilt attach themselves so tenaciously, not just to our public actions, but to thoughts and feelings entertained in the deepest privacy of our being, from which no-one suffers?

What needs to be remembered is that, if an adequate explanation of shame and guilt in terms of love and sympathy were to be found, it is unlikely to be one that would postulate a simpler, or less structured, conception of the self. At the minimum, it would require postulation of some mechanism of identification.[42]

14. In his last book, *The Drowned and the Saved*,[43] Primo Levi, the melancholic genius who survived Auschwitz only to die at his own hands in 1987, wonders why it was that, for so many inmates of the concentration camps, the great Fidelio-like moment of jubilation that should have happened when the camps were overrun, and the prisoners were set free, never occurred. The chapter of the book in which an explanation is sought has the disturbing title 'Shame'. Are we to infer that Levi believed that what prevented the prisoners from celebrating their liberation was shame at their wretched condition? Surely, even if this was, as he claims, how the emotion was perceived at the time, this cannot be what the emotion was.

In the first place, if we exclude those prisoners who, in one capacity or another, and to varying degrees of culpability, served as functionaries of the Lager – that is, as scribes in the Work Office, or as workers in the *Sonderkommandos,* servicing the crematoriums until they descended into them, or as *Kapos*, administering harsh and mindless punishment to their fellow prisoners – how could the others, the vast majority, think of themselves as having done anything to bring themselves to the condition they were in? Even the ethic of me-first, or, at best, us-first, which dominated their daily lives, was not one they had adopted, rather than one that had been thrust upon them.

But, if 'do', or 'adopt', here have the meaning of something that we do intentionally, or something for which we accept responsibility, then this is a weak objection. For we know that lack of responsibility, or, for that matter, lack of intention, are fully compatible with deep, burning shame about what we have become.

But a second, and seemingly stronger, objection would be to query how it could be – and now we may assume all questions of responsibility or intention set aside – that the prisoners could have traced their condition back to themselves? Surely, when they thought about what they had become, they could think only of

what others had done to them? If that is so, then the central condition of shame seems violated: there is no reflexivity.

Perhaps we should listen to what Levi said, for he obviously
was not oblivious of these considerations. The shame of which
he speaks was shame that the prisoners felt on their own behalf
– *and also more*. It was shame felt on behalf of themselves, and on
behalf of humanity, of the whole human species.

But how is that comprehensible? For so far we have understood reflexivity as requiring that the shame that a person felt
should be felt by him on his behalf – *and neither less nor more*.

To accommodate Levi's suggestion within my proposals, we
must note that it moves to a seemingly deeper level.

Let us first recognize that, whenever we experience shame or
guilt, there is a presupposition to it. For any criticism that is levelled against us by an internal critic is invariably levelled against
us as a person, as a member of a certain species, and it is as a
person that we receive it, and this we acknowledge when we
experience the criticism as an attack upon our sense of self. For
the relevant sense of self is that awareness which a person has of
himself as an ongoing creature, related to his past, to his present,
and to his future, in the ways in which we persons necessarily
are. It is the awareness of ourselves as a member of the human
race.

Now what Levi argues for is that there can be events that
human beings live through, or are forced to live through, that are
so inherently terrible that they make this awareness of ourselves
as a person, as a member of a species, something totally unbearable. In consequence, any occasion on which this awareness is
brought to the surface – and this includes any form of criticism,
no matter what we are criticized for, whether it seems to us just
or not, and, for that matter, any form of praise, and indeed any
other form of reflexion – will suffice to submerge us in shame.
In these special circumstances, shame is brought home to us, not
through the content of what is said, but through its bare presupposition. And Levi is further telling us, and out of his own
experience, that life in the Lager, life as it was made, not, of
course, by the prisoners, but for the prisoners by their captors,
was of such an abject nature that merely to survive it and to go

on existing, thinking of oneself as a person as life requires, was a permanent occasion for shame. Anyone who even raised the question whether he, as a human being, had cause to be ashamed of this thing that he did, or of that thing that he omitted to do, must straightway feel shame. For he now knew that 'man, the human species – we, in short – had the potential to construct an infinite enormity of pain, and that pain is the only force created from nothing, without cost and without effort.'[44]

A word of caution: The foregoing discussion shows us how, in situations of enormity, shame can become pervasive. Everything that brings home to us who, or what, we are covers us with shame. And I have tried to show what kind of structural, or philosophical, account can be given of this phenomenon. But, having in the last lecture criticized Sartre for turning what is a psychological issue – that is, the malformation of emotion – into a metaphysical issue, I must emphasize that this is not what Levi does. Nor, I hope, do I, in commenting on Levi's thoughts, give any encouragement to such a way of thinking. Levi's account asks to be supplemented by a psychological account of how what he describes actually came about, or how it was that, for many innocent men and women, the very broadest way they had of looking at themselves, that is, as persons, became so shot through with mistrust that they mistrusted everything that involved it. Hence what might have been expected to be experienced as the coming true of one of their deepest desires – the desire to escape from ignominy, and constant fear, and certain death – could not be. There was only one way to experience it: as an occasion for shame.

This is not the end of the matter, and it seems as though there is a mode of shame that is even more pervasive than that invoked by Primo Levi's account of what happened when the concentration camps were overrun. For cannot shame form, not only when we have changed but through nothing that we have in any sense done, but also when there has been no change at all? I call such shame pervasive because it leads us to be ashamed, not of what we have become, but of what we are. More specifically, we are ashamed of the body that is ours, and outside of which it is hard to make much sense of our existence.

Shame in this mode belongs to what Nietzsche called the 'ascetic ideal', or, more provocatively, the morality of 'sickliness'.[45] However much credit may be due here to Nietzsche's powers of observation and descriptive ingenuity, it is relevant to the course of the present argument that his explanation of asceticism as the turning inwards, the turning back upon oneself, of the reactive emotions, specifically of the *ressentiment* of the weak, an explanation that significantly fails to introduce a further, or criticizing, agency, to that degree fails to account for certain features of shame. For instance, Nietzsche makes a simple contrast between those who follow an ascetic ideal, and are self-accusatory, morbid, envious, and passive, and those who have a healthier ideal, and are self-confident, strong, prepared to be cruel, and active. What he thereby overlooks is the way in which the ascetic can, from time to time, rebel against what he suffers at the hands of the criticizing agency, and display cruelty. Nietzsche left no space for Shakespeare's Richard III.

15. I now turn from the core of shame and guilt to their manifestations, first internal, then external.

What is distinctive of *the internal manifestations of shame and guilt* is that they are distributed across the person's dealings with the object of the emotion and his dealings with the criticizing agency. There is no parallel to this with the non-moral emotions, where the person's thoughts, desires, and wishes are preoccupied with the object. In the case of shame and guilt, they certainly turn back upon the object − that is to say, the person himself − but they also turn towards those internal figures but for whom he would have no need to be so self-preoccupied.

Since it is the person's dealings with the criticizing agency that are distinctive of the moral emotions, I shall concentrate upon them. These, it may be conjectured, are predominantly embedded in phantasy, and, given the limited degree to which phantasy can be retrieved for consciousness, our awareness of this part of the ongoing life of shame and guilt is curtailed. However we can safely assume that some of these phantasies, hence some of our dealings with the criticizing agency, leave it comparatively unchanged, whereas others have the effect, and, in some cases, the purpose, of modifying the agency.

Dealings with the internal critic that reinforce its hold over us form the standing interior condition of any instance of shame or guilt, and, in a more or less overt fashion, they supply the core narrative that is threaded through these emotions. The critic reiterates his charges, the person continues to suffer under them: the person incites the critic, the critic responds with severity: the critic relents, the person wonders, To what end? However the repetitive character that the phantasies may be assumed to have can be obscured from us, and indeed from the person himself, by the way they are regularly acted out, or realized in an external arena where the fluid cast of characters and the constant change of scenery are deceptive. The variety, the relief, are entirely superficial. Below the surface the repetition is rigid.

I shall illustrate this whole process from one of the most single-minded studies of the inflexibility of shame and guilt.

Set in seventeenth-century New England, *The Scarlet Letter* traces the aftermath of an illicit liaison. One of the lovers is Hester Prynne, a woman of commanding beauty, who, some few years earlier, and in another country, had contracted a loveless marriage with an elderly, dessicated scholar. The other is a man whose identity she refuses to reveal, even under the direst abuse. The birth of a child, and the publicity attached to this event, bring the liaison to a close, and the lives of the two lovers follow very different courses. In each case, there is the persisting influence of an emotion that is deep and intransigent.[46]

Hester is brought to trial for adultery. Her life is spared, and she is expelled in ignominy from the community. Though she is free to go anywhere, she establishes herself in a lonely cottage by the ocean shore, not far from the town, where, on her regular visits in pursuit of work, she is treated by all with scorn and repugnance. Two desires prevent her from moving away. One, which she recognizes as vain and sinful, is to be reunited, at some distant moment, with her lover. The other is to suffer at the scene of her offence. The outward signs of her disgrace, which are her illegitimate child, a wild creature, who accompanies her everywhere, and the great scarlet 'A', embroidered by her own hands, and which, by sentence of the court, she is required to wear on her breast at all times, ensure that her desire for suffering is satisfied to the full. The constant stare of inquisitive, mocking, censorious eyes, young and old, familiar and unfamiliar, gives her no peace. Often tempted to cover the scarlet letter with her hand, she never does.

Her lover, the novel eventually reveals, is the Reverend Mr Dimmesdale, a young clergyman, trained in Oxford, eloquent, fervent, learned beyond his years, physically delicate, and with a seraphic sweetness of character. Of all his great gifts, it is supremely his capacity to talk directly to the heart of his audience, his possession of the pentecostal gift, the 'Tongue of Flame', that has won him the unique position he enjoys in the estimation of his flock. He is a saint in their eyes. And it is this position, and his concern not to betray the trust that his congregation had placed in him – misguidedly, as he sees it – as well as a tendency to regard the world as shadow-like, that has prevented him from publicly acknowledging his own offence. Continually tempted to do so, he never can. More than once, in the course of a sermon, he has cleared his throat, ready to confess his sin, but when, in tremulous tones, he would start to denounce his own vileness or the baseness of his character, lower than the low, his congregation heard his words very differently from how they were intended, and revered him all the more for his humility. He resorts to penances of a kind favoured by Rome: to fasts, to all-night vigils, and to scourging himself. Tortured by what he cannot say, he develops the habit of placing one hand over his heart on the spot, where, or so it was claimed after his death, his body had developed its own red stigma of sin.

A revealing moment is when Hester comes before the Governor, and the custody of her daughter is to be settled, and Dimmesdale is asked his opinion. Speaking, presumably with theological nicety, he speaks of the girl as 'the child of its father's guilt and its mother's shame'.[47]

If this is how Hawthorne would have us think of the situation, and of the emotions under the dominance of which his two characters live, then it must be that the constant publicity in which the woman leads her life, and the constant secrecy from which the man cannot break free, correspond on the outside to the ongoing internal life of, respectively, shame and guilt. Each emotion at once motivates, and is reinforced by, the way of life that houses it. But what, in each case, shapes the correspondence between the way of life and the emotion? And the answer must be that the way of life provides the external setting under cover of which the original, internal criticism, from which the emotion springs, can be most readily, most remorselessly, most repetitively, reenacted. Hester, in seeking exposure, seeks out eyes that, like the eyes of her internal accusers, will never cease to torment her, and to transfix her with pain. Dimmesdale, by accepting the admiration, the reverence, the reputation for sanctity, that he cannot find it in himself to repudiate, constructs around himself a wall of silence behind which the original condemnatory voices harangue him with, we must assume, bell-like clarity.

From this ongoing drama of shame and guilt, which accommodates itself to the circumstances of daily life as Hawthorne describes them, it is only Hester Prynne's remarkable sense of herself as a woman that allows even the possibility of relief or escape, and it is to this broad issue of how the criticizing agency can be made to abate or attenuate its attacks upon the person that I now turn.

Any philosophical account of shame and guilt must, I have contended, find a place for the inordinate, or imperious, character that these emotions can, and do, assume, particularly when they derive from judgments with which the person is not in agreement. But that is not the whole story. Shame and guilt can be in accord with what we touchingly call our finer instincts, and it would be a serious defect if philosophy could not also show how, in time, these emotions may approximate to what conventionally is held to be the truth about them. An account that roots these emotions in criticism coming from internal figures is, I believe, best able to do this through the narrative it can provide of what happens to these figures in the aftermath of introjection. We may note three different, though clearly interrelated, strands of development.

In the first place, the internal figures modify. Their more fearful characteristics are joined, joined and tempered, by sunnier characteristics. They are reassembled in the image of a more complex or nuancé person.

Secondly, the phantasies in which these figures have thus far been repetitiously implicated with their monotonous turns of fortune are slowly worked through and understood, at any rate to some degree. Their remorseless, fateful character starts to give.

And, finally, the internal figures slowly approximate, not just to how an actual person might be, but to how their real-life proto-types are.

These are just three themes in what is called by Melanie Klein the 'depressive position', but to these changes, which, being changes in the criticizing agency, are therefore changes in the person's inner world, it is possible to associate some major dif-ferences in the evolution of shame and guilt: though a strict one–one pairing is not possible.

First of all, the person ceases to treat the criticisms coming from the agency as solely persecuting onslaughts. He starts to treat them as mere criticisms, or as what I have called the brute impact of the world. Now he attends to their content, and tries to assess it.

Secondly, the person gradually acquires a new motivation for complying with this criticism, in so far as he judges that it merits his doing so. For, now that, in the person's mind, the agency has benign as well as malign characteristics, he has the motivation that love or concern additionally provide. Indeed the presence of the malign characteristics serves to bring home to him the painful fact that the figure whom he now loves is one and the same as the figure whom he once hated, and that hate never required the totally destructive attacks that were in phantasy launched against the figure. The complex identity of the figure, good and bad entwined, being brought home to him, shame or guilt now take on a very special modulation: they refine into regret and grati-tude, and generates the desire to make reparation.

And, finally, the approximation of the internal critic to its external prototype will increasingly make it seem appropriate to the person to respond to the criticizing agency, not merely, as the medieval thinkers used to say, *in foro interno*, or in the mind, but, *in foro externo*, or in the outer world. Reparation, to seem adequate, must take on characteristics that make it realistically appropriate.

It is natural to suppose that these differences in grade will go along with, or be indicated by, corresponding differences in the phenomenology of the phantasy. They will go along with differences in the way in which the internal figure is represented. This is correct. A hostile figure, who stands apart from the person, will be envisaged from the outside, or what I call peripherally, whereas the benign figure, who is in some accord with the person, will be envisaged from the inside, or what I call centrally.[48]

In a later section, we shall see how the criticizing agency can sometimes merely seem to to be modified, when in fact modification has been evaded, and instead defence has been invoked.

16. Next, to *the outward manifestations of shame and guilt*, and I begin with the claim, already made in connexion with the non-moral emotions, that emotion has no direct motivational force. By contrast, indirect motivational force is within its reach, for emotion may generate desire, and then desire may, in conjunction with instrumental belief of the right sort, motivate action.

However it might be argued that the case for the lack of direct motivational force does not obviously carry over from the non-moral to the moral emotions. That is because, of the four considerations that I drew upon in mounting the case, two start from the premiss that the attitude, hence the emotion, arises from the satisfaction or frustration of desire, which, we know, is not the case with shame and guilt.

In point of fact, I shall, in arguing for the non-motivational character of shame and guilt, base myself solely upon the third consideration, or that, with emotion, whether moral or non-moral, there is no consummatory notion comparable to that of satisfaction as this applies to desire. In consequence there is nothing, no end, towards which emotion motivates us.

I shall concede this much to my opponent: If there were an end in the case of shame and guilt, it is not difficult in each case to see what it would be. In the case of shame, it would be that what I am ashamed of is forgotten. In the case of guilt, it would be that what I am guilty about is forgiven. But, though shame is all but certain to generate the desire that something should be forgotten, and guilt the desire that something should be forgiven, the states towards which these desires are directed, and which may be expected to be consummatory of them, are not in the same way consummatory of the emotions from which they derive. So the person who is ashamed of what he has become might well want that, and why, forgotten. But suppose it were, he might still feel that he should go on being ashamed. And similarly for the man who feels guilty.

Not surprisingly, why the notion of consummation is inappropriate to shame and guilt is an issue that has most urgency in a theological context, or in a discussion of sin and divine mercy. In what follows, I shall adopt an argument, secularizing it as I go, from Cardinal Newman.[49]

Newman asks us to contrast two persons, each of whom reflects upon something in his past. In one case, it is something that he did: in the other case, it is something that he might have done. Both are occasions for shame. (Newman talks only of shame, and I shall follow him in this respect: but what he says can be extended to guilt.) Each person asks himself the same question. The question is not whether it was, or would have been, appropriate for him to have felt shame over the action. The answer, Yes, is assumed. It is whether it is, or would have been, appropriate for him to have gone on feeling shame once something becomes clear, and, in each case, the something has to do with the chances of his offence being forgotten. Can that, in other words, be a relevant consideration? The two people think differently. One, we are led to see, thinks clearly. The other is deeply confused in his thinking. If Newman puts the matter by saying that one thinks as a Christian should think in the face of God's judgment, and that the other does not know what sin is, we may rephrase this by saying that one understands shame, and the other does not.

Let us look at the two cases.

The first person reflects on something he has become of which he is ashamed. He wonders whether it has been, whether it ever

will be, forgotten, and he realizes that he has no reason whatsoever to have beliefs either way. However he does not chafe under
the uncertainty, and he realizes that, if anything, the emotion from
which he is offered no escape should reconcile him to the uncertainty. If he truly accepts the shame, then he should be able to
accept the pain of the uncertainty. That pain might well serve a
role.

The second person reflects upon a situation that is hypothetical. Early on in his life, he encountered many temptations,
as young people do, from which he was deterred, in some
measure at least, by the shame that he would undoubtedly have
felt, had he given in. Now, as he thinks over his past, one of these
temptations starts to exert its pull over him afresh. Suppose, he
begins to think, he had submitted. He reflects that, if he had, by
now he would have got what he wanted, and, since most probably what he became through getting it would have been forgotten, the shame would have passed. Such reflexion engenders
regret. The best way he can now find of describing his situation
is, Newman tells us, this: that, by standing out against temptation,
he 'lost an opportunity'.[50]

However different our perspective, we can surely agree with
Newman in his assessment of his two imaginary characters. One
understands shame, but clearly the other does not: his casuistry
betrays him. What separates the two? I suggest that we can explain
the difference between them by thinking of the second as implicitly assimilating the way in which forgetting stands to shame to
the way in which satisfaction stands to desire. The first person
totally rejects such an assimilation.

To test this explanation, let us imagine someone who did make
this assimilation, and put him in the situation of the second
person, and consider what his thought-processes would be.

Such a person, in thinking about his past, thinks sequentially.
So, first, he recalls a certain desire he once had, but which,
because he found it reprehensible, he did not act upon. But now
he thinks, Suppose I had. If he had, he would, he reflects, most
probably have got what he wanted. In that case, his desire would
have terminated, and the desire, as well as the pleasure that he
got from the desire, would all be past history. Next he reflects

that, since he found the desire reprehensible, acting upon it, and what he would have become as a result of acting upon it, would have produced shame in him. His thoughts now turn to this shame, and they do so as if to a separate factor. Shame, unlike acting upon the desire, would have produced unpleasure. But what he would have become through acting upon the desire, or what would have made himself an object of shame to himself, would, by a certain moment, have been forgotten. That moment would, he is certain, have been over by now. In that case, the shame, as well as the unpleasure that he would have got from it, would all be past history. Now, he further reflects, suppose that the pleasure that he got at the time from satisfying the desire had outweighed the unpleasure that he would subsequently have got from the shame that ensued, and further suppose that there was no additional shame to factor in, then it would have been better overall for him to have done what he didn't do. It would have been better for him if all the following things had happened: he had satisfied his desire, he had experienced shame, and the shameful person that he had become had been forgotten. That being so, he can only feel regret. – And these, it will now be observed, are, spelt out, the exact thought-processes of the second person that Newman considers. So what is wrong with the second person can fairly be traced to the assimilation of forgotten shame to satisfied desire. He treats forgetting as the consummation of shame.

But what is it, we might now ask, about how the first person thinks that shows that he does not make the same assimilation, and that gives his thinking a certain appropriateness?

In the first place, he recognizes that, though he wishes that what he has become might be forgotten, the forgetting that he wishes for is not an event that is purely external to him, and to the shame that he feels. For instance, so long as he continues to feel shame, he can never be fully convinced that it has happened. Secondly, he recognizes that the forgetting by itself will not dissolve the shame. What he has to do is to accept that what he has become has been forgotten, and this in turn requires that he should have changed: that he should no longer be as he became. Thirdly, though, while in the grip of shame, he is likely to desire what would dissolve his shame, this does not necessarily mean that he desires his shame to dissolve. He may find his shame in some way appropriate. Fourthly – and this is probably the most important point – even when the shame has dissolved, he will not think of it as past history. Past instances of shame, shame and guilt, must always colour the way we view ourselves. If it is true that the incident of Marion and the stolen ribbon and the lie is integral to Rousseau's decision to write the *Confessions*, this was not likely to have been so as to exorcize the incident. Rather it was an attempt to bring it once again before his consciousness in order to understand it, hence to understand himself the better.

It might be thought that the point that I have been making about the non-motivational character of emotion, including the moral emotions, is incompatible with a distinction that some psychoanalysts make between *persecutory guilt* (or *anxiety*) and *reparative guilt*.[51] For this distinction appears to divide guilt into two depending upon the kind of action, or inaction, that it motivates.

This would be so if this distinction is taken, as the nomenclature suggests, as one holding between two different kinds of guilt, where the difference between them lies in the different motivational force that is essential to each. However I believe that the distinction is to be understood as one within the one emotion of guilt, and it makes the point that, though there is no motivational force that is essential to it, guilt can, at different times, for reasons to do with the developmental stage that the person has reached, associate itself with different forms of response. So sometimes the response will be a matter of enduring the suffering, and trying to avoid the worst of the consequences. At other times the response will be to make recompense to what I have called the secondary object of the guilt.[52]

17. Some might feel that I have been peremptory in my dismissal of the connexion between the emotions and rationality.

The truth is that there are two different contexts in which the connexion may be asserted.

The two contexts may be called, not altogether happily, an *internal*, and an *external, context*. As I use these terms, an emotion is assessed for its rationality externally when the principal factor taken into account is the precipitating factor, later the object, of the emotion. By contrast, an emotion is assessed for its rationality internally when the principal factor taken into account is the other emotions that the person has, and thus the general distribution of his interests, and what else he had on his mind. The evident crudity of this classification is that any assessment of the rationality of an emotion that is properly thought of as external would also have to take into account many factors that are surely internal.

My scepticism to date about the rational assessment of the emotions relates exclusively to external assessment. (And, even then, I do not want to commit myself either way on a comparatively trivial issue, which is the status of emotions assessed as irrational because they are based on false beliefs about their objects. What seems to me at stake here is, in the first instance, the rationality, or irrationality, of the beliefs.)[53]

However, raised internally, the issue of rationality has more bite. If a homeless man, without family, without friends, without future, and with a past that no longer has any meaning for him, has a dog, and the dog dies, what limits can be set upon what it would be rational for him to feel? However grief of this order would be out of place if a world statesman, or a general on the eve of battle, or a much feted pianist about to set out on a concert tour of the major American cities, was to suffer the same kind of loss. The claims of other preoccupations would make such an outpouring of emotion seem irrational. When the duchesse de Guermantes, about to go out to dinner, is called upon by Swann, and hears from him that he is dying, and nevertheless finds time to go upstairs, at her husband's insistence, but complicitous with it, and change out of her black shoes into red shoes,[54] her action offends us, not because we externally calculate that, whereas it would be reasonable for someone to care such-and-such an amount about an old dying friend, it is unreasonable for someone to care more than such-and-such another amount about the shoes that she wears out to dinner. It offends us because it confirms what we had come to suspect: that, for her, the world, which had once been, as she had once been, so full of spontaneity, has shrunk to a cold and empty place in which nothing really exists except the miseries and splendours of social life. The wrong colour of shoes, and the embarrassment that this might cause her, have become for her like the death of his dog, and the emptiness this produces in his life, are for the old tramp. And that she declares that she despises such trivialities, and does, does not weaken their hold over her, or reduce how much of life they occlude.

18. A note on the title of this lecture: Why 'the so-called moral emotions'? Why are not the emotions I have been discussing to be thought of as 'the moral emotions' without qualifier?

My idea here is simple. Its consequences are considerable. I briefly referred to the idea in the Introduction, where I call these lectures lectures in applied philosophy. It is an idea that I have considered on other occasions.[55]

As I see things, there are two broad ways of conceiving of morality.

The first way conceives of morality as primarily a set of propositions, or a code, like the Code of Hammurabi, or the Ten Commandments. These propositions, once we know of them, we may come to believe, and, if we do, we may then employ them to guide, or at least to influence, directly or indirectly, our conduct. Precisely what it is that sets these propositions off from other propositions, or the mark of morality, is a matter on which there is room for disagreement. Except for those who take an anti-moralistic stance, there is agreement that it is something important.

It is certain that, in the ordinary course of life, only a random selection of such propositions will come our way. The selection will depend on the circumstances in which we happen to find ourselves, the edifying books that we read, and what our teachers tell us. We are certain to find ourselves dissatisfied with our particular sample. It will strike us as an imperfect set: either it will be less than complete, or it will contain interlopers, or false claimants to the status of morality. Accordingly we shall inevitably be committed to scrutinizing, sifting out, refining upon, these propositions so as to arrive at something that we find assertible. This critique of morality, as we may call the project, is in part a practical, in part a philosophical, inquiry, though any hope of drawing a sharp line between these two parts of the project is regularly dashed. As to the criteria that the project employs, they are close in nature to whatever we, in the first place, hold to be the marks of morality, or that by which we distinguish between propositions of morality and other propositions. What we attain to, or what we are left with, after this project has run its course we shall think of as *our* morality.

The second way conceives of morality differently, or as primarily the output of a certain part of our psychology. Under this conception morality will have a more heterogeneous character, comprising, as well as propositions, a miscellany of attitudes, beliefs, dispositions to act, and dispositions to refrain from action, the whole, in virtue of its origins in the psyche, shot through with feelings, and anxieties. As to which part of our psychology it is from which morality issues, we can say in advance two things: it is a part that is implicated in our relations with others – but, we may well ask, Is there any part that isn't? – and it has some connexion with the resolution of inner conflict.

Under this conception of morality too, a critique of morality is soon forced upon us: and for two reasons. In the first place, we shall want to know whether what presents itself to us as morality has in fact the right genealogy, whether it derives from the relevant part of our psychology. But then, secondly, we shall have a further question to ask, which is how to separate off, within that which has the right origins, what is – to use a broad term – acceptable from what we find unacceptable: acceptability itself being a psychological, if a higher-order psychological, notion. But, it is to be noted, though this conception of morality sanctions such a critique, it is not at all helpful about what are the criteria, or standards, to be invoked at the second stage. A matter on which it is declarative is that it is against thinking of this project as though it were primarily an intellectual procedure. For, true to its initial psychological inspiration, it insists that there is little merit, or even sense, in declaring something acceptable unless we are ourselves inclined to accept it.

Of these two conceptions of morality, the first tends to aggrandize morality, and it does this through taking as the mark of morality something honorific, such as truth, rationality, divine origin, or our own best interests. However to elevate the status of morality is one thing: to provide morality with a motivational basis, or to present it as something that we have an urge to follow, which is generally taken to be essential to morality, is a harder task. In so far as this first conception of morality lends itself to this part of its task, it generally does so through what many would regard as an overkill. It claims for morality, not just some, but overarching, motivational force. Morality is said to 'trump' all other motives.

In both these respects, the second conception of morality stands in marked contrast to the first conception. It is not concerned to show morality in any independently favourable light, and it has no obvious resources for doing so: though it certainly stresses that the entry into morality is a considerable psychological achievement. However, by rooting morality in our psychology, it has little difficulty in showing that morality has whatever is required of it in the way of motivational force. Any difficulties that this conception has in this area arise only when it is expected to justify this motivational force. Some philosophers have argued, with considerable force, that such a demand is illicit.

So much for the two conceptions of morality, and now the question arises, If shame and guilt are to be thought of as moral emotions without qualifier, within which conception of morality would this claim have least difficulty in getting itself accepted?

This question breaks itself down. We can ask, (one) Which conception assigns, from the start, a place to shame and guilt within morality? and (two) Which conception assigns a constructive role to shame and guilt within the critique of morality?

The obvious answer to both questions would seem to be, Not the first conception.

For, when morality is viewed primarily as a code, with no psychological content, then shame and guilt seem extraneous to it. The only question that can arise is whether they have a substantive role to play in the critique of morality, and again the answer seems to be in the negative. And that is because, for most upholders of this conception, any substantive appeal to shame and guilt as indices of what morality should condemn would seem to implicate morality, to an uncongenial degree, with the facts of empirical human nature.

If we turn to the second conception of morality, we appear to get very different answers.

For, in the first place, in so far as this conception is readily able, as I have suggested that it is, to ascribe motivational force to morality, this in large part comes from what I have called elsewhere[56] the psychic force of shame and guilt: that is, the force that manifestations of these emotions, or the mental states in which they issue, have over our thoughts and conduct in virtue of their phenomenology.

However whether this conception of morality is able to assign shame and guilt a sufficiently crucial role in the critique of morality is a more difficult question. Can shame and guilt contribute positively to the refinement and reinforcement of morality?

The first thing to be noted is that, in this context, the notions of refinement and reinforcement do not sit too comfortably together. For, contrary to conventional views about the development of the moral sense, the problem is that, at the early stages of development, morality, and the forces that sustain it, specifically the criticizing agency, appear to stand in need, not so much of reinforcement, as of attenuation, if they are then to be refined. The urgings of the criticizing agency are too crude and savage to allow for the softening effect of reflexion.[57]

If it is now proposed that shame and guilt should be applied serially, so that they first refine morality, and only then reinforce it, this is simplistic. For it assumes that these emotions are more under our control, and, in turn, freer of the standards of the criticizing agency, than is the case.

There are three distinct ways in which the primitive functioning of shame and guilt serve as obstacles to the softening of morality.

In the first place, there is the phenomenon that Freud called the 'conservatism of the instincts',[58] or the resistance to change that all the emotions display, but none so much as shame and guilt. If initially this means only that the same emotion forms in the same broad conditions, no matter what either their finer detail or the person's attitude might be, gradually this takes on greater complexity. For, over time, as the person starts to question this rigid patterning of emotion over his life, the pattern starts to reinforce itself. In the case of shame and guilt, this requires that the standards of the criticizing agency, upon which shame and guilt supervene, harden. Shame and guilt reinforce the standards from which they gain whatever legitimacy they have. The process of moral scrutiny is set back.

Secondly, there is the phenomenon that Freud, borrowing a phrase from Nietzsche, called 'pale criminality'.[59] The pale criminal is a person who suffers deeply from shame or guilt, the sources of which remain concealed from him. In order to make these emotions more comprehensible to himself, and ultimately to purge himself of them, he is led to commit actions that are, in his own eyes, by his own standards, heinous. These actions do two things for him: they at once justify him in what he feels, and help to draw down punishment from others, which may eventually purge the feelings themselves. If 'the pale criminal' might seem to the outside world to care insufficiently about punishment or disapprobation, the truth is that he lives for them. Once again, shame and guilt subvert moral refinement.

In one crucial respect, the conservatism of the emotions and pale criminality are the converse of one another. In both cases, the excess, or the inappropriateness, of the shame or guilt that the person experiences leads him to seek justification. In both cases, he finds it only through forcing upon himself something that goes against the grain. In one case, it is the standards of the criticizing agency, which he has otherwise outgrown. In the other case, it is behaviour that he looks upon with deep disapproval. The standards that he reinforces are those which would make the emotions seem appropriate, given the behaviour upon which they follow. The behaviour on which he embarks is that which would make the emotions seem appropriate, given the standards that he accepts.

The third phenomenon not merely slows down the process of moral scrutiny, it reverses it. When the emotions that the criticizing agency controls prove unbearable, the person invokes defence, and tries, with some measure of success, to rid himself, as it were for ever, of the criticizing agency.[60]

What occurs next is an instance of a more general phenomenon, which we have noted: the projection of an unwanted internal figure on to, or, more likely, its projective identification into, the outside world, or some particular part of it, such as another figure. I have already suggested that this takes place through the invocation of a phantasy that is the mirror-image of the phantasy that inaugurated the incorporative process. However this process does not simply restore the status quo, or return the figure, and the line between the inner and the outer world, to where both were before introjection disturbed them. The figure who is now in the external world is still in essence an internal figure. To say this is, of course, to say something about how the process of expulsion and the expelled figure are phantasized. It is to say something about the concern that the person has for the figure, and the fear that he has of it, and the different steps that he will take to feel neither kind of anxiety.[61]

When the figure who is projected into the external world is a vehicle of the criticizing agency, there is a special range of consequences to be anticipated.

In the extreme case, which is unstable, and therefore the relief that it brings from punishment is short-lived, the person loses all direct contact with the projected figure, and proceeds to phantasize a total freedom from all restraint. However, in order to reassure himself that he possesses this freedom, the person will experience the need to avail himself of it: that is, to do everything that the criticizing agency forbad. In the Saturnalia that ensues, the standards of the criticizing agency still dominate the person's life, but now in their negative version. Flagrant transgression displaces terrorized compliance. Under the guise of self-assertion and experimentation, what we observe is the depleted life of the psychopath, excitement coating repetition, as this is glorified in the novels of Sade, and satirized in those of Dostoevsky.

If this radical way of dealing with the exigencies of the criticizing agency brings with it massive anxiety, one possibility is that the sequence of projection and introjection recommences. Expelled into the environment, the internal critic is then reingested back into the inner world, and some amends is attempted. Then, as this fails, the figure is again projected. And, as this cycle of defence turns and returns, so a corresponding pattern of emotion passes across the inner life of the person, and a matching pattern of behaviour is enacted in the outer world. A notorious serial murderer picks up young men, takes them home, offers them food and drink, strangles them from behind, buries them under the floorboards, then, at regular intervals over the next few weeks, brings them out, props them up against the bed, and talks and drinks with them.[62] The solicitousness evinced in these strange incidents fulfils more than one role. Now it attempts to placate the reinstated critic, now it attempts to assuage the loneliness brought about by its absence, now it displays an indifference, which belongs to the surface of life.

A less extreme case is where the person retains contact with the critical figure, once it is expelled into the outside world, and he tries to take advantage of the relocation of the figure to soften the emotional relations in which the two are locked. He does so, for instance, by replacing punitive relations with relations of a more erotic kind. A patient, Mr B., projects his internal critic into various women of his acquaintance. Then he endeavours to lure them into sado-masochistic affairs. Being beaten, and the prospect of being beaten, and the excitement of this prospect, overlay, and sweeten, the guilt that his merciless inner critic would otherwise induce in him.[63]

Finally, the projection of the criticizing agency can be carried out to constructive ends. The person projects it on to, or into, the environment in order, for instance, to come to terms with those in authority, or to find a measure of shared agreement with friends and acquaintances.[64] We may believe that something of this kind occurred, though in an adulterated form, when Rousseau fell victim to guilt on hearing Marion's gentle but determined rebuke. The unexpected witness, the young woman with no vindictiveness in her, provided a bridge between the inner tribunal and the demands of social justice. She did, on the inside, what the young nephew, the executor of the estate, evidently failed to achieve on the outside.

This very last phenomenon, unlike those previously considered in this section, finds a place for shame and guilt in the process of moral scrutiny.

19. What is an emotion?

I started these lectures with the question, What are the emotions? by which I meant, What kind of phenomenon is an emotion? Emotions, I claimed, are mental dispositions, and this gave rise to the question, How do we distinguish emotions from other kinds of mental disposition, such as beliefs and desires? And now I conclude these lectures by asking, What is an emotion? meaning by this, How do we distinguish one emotion from another? Is there a general way of individuating anger and fear and jealousy and gratitude?

If I have so far provided no more than hints about how this question is to be answered, I shall, in choosing between various proposals, stick to the abiding theme of these lectures, and be influenced by the degree to which they contribute to the psychologization, or the repsychologization, of the concept of emotion.

The first proposal is one that, having postulated a general state of emotionality, then equates the particular emotion that a person has with the emotion that he attributes to himself. I call this view self-attributionism.

Apart from the gap that this proposal opens up between the emotions of language users and the emotions of animals without language, which are left totally unaccounted for, it remains problematic how much weight the proposal places on the person's actual ability to identify in words the emotion that he feels. For the person might have, through immaturity, or lack of self-reflexion, either an impoverished emotional vocabulary, or an inhibition about applying it autobiographically. Indeed the very weight of emotion itself might make the task of attribution too difficult to carry out. At the end of *Andromaque*, is Hermione to say that she loves, or hates, Pyrrhus?[65] Accordingly, the test that this proposal provides must be taken as giving at best a hypothetical criterion. The emotion that a person has is that which he would attribute to himself in conditions from which these deficiencies have been idealized away.

However there is still the difficulty of knowing how this proposal wants us to understand the nature of the emotion. One way, which may seem facile, but which it is difficult to see how the proposal can avoid, is to think that there is nothing to the emotion over and above the self-attribution. In other words, the proposal, which starts off by equating the emotion that a person has with the emotion that he is disposed to attribute to himself, concludes by equating that emotion with the disposition to attribute it to himself. By this time, the problem is not so much that the emotion has been reduced to something that it seems not to be – namely, an attribution – as that the attribution has been deprived of the one thing by which we would identify it: that is, its meaning. What permits us to assign substantive meaning, let alone substantive psychological meaning, to these attributions?

A quite different way of understanding the proposal, and one which is close in spirit to the philosophy of Wittgenstein, is to take it as claiming that, though there is evidently more to an emotion than the mere attribution of it, there is still no better way of understanding any emotion, or of understanding the differences between the emotions, than through the language that we use to pick them out individually, or to distinguish between them. And this is not simply to go round in a circle – from understanding a phenomenon to understanding the word that has it as its reference, and then back again – is because the relation between the language of the emotions and the emotions is, it is claimed, not exhausted by the relation of word and reference. There are innumerable ways in which the words for the emotions are woven into the fabric of daily life. A more extreme version of this view holds that even to think of the reference-relation, at any rate outside the context of name and place or person, is to entertain a myth.

This last point could be true – although the marginal role that it too assigns to the emotions of those outside language strongly suggests that it isn't – and yet there could be something general left to be said about how the domain of emotion is divided up into the emotions.[66]

The second proposal identifies the emotions through its originating condition, though the proposal does not necessarily – indeed it is almost certain not to – take the same view as I do of how emotions originate. So: Fear is the emotion that forms in dangerous circumstances: indignation the emotion that greets unjust behaviour: jealousy the emotion that arises when we have been balked of something that we desire by a rival.

The initial deficiency of this proposal is that it generally associates itself with a view that, presumably in the interests of simplicity, identifies the various originating conditions objectively, or in terms of the external world. But, at the very least, the person must be aware of the originating condition for the appropriate emotion to form. And the introduction of awareness into the originating condition introduces other aspects of the person's psychology, other dispositions, through which the objective conditions are necessarily filtered.

However it is still not enough to try to use the originating condition as it is experienced to individuate the emotion. For, the ultimate significance of the originating condition is that it triggers the quest for the precipitating factor, and where this quest terminates is not determined by the originating condition itself. As I have tried to bring out, the amount of leeway that the person has in the pursuit of the precipitating factor is considerable, though it will vary from case to case. Broadly speaking, it is likely to be greater when the emotion derives from an external condition than when the emotion derives from a wholly internal condition, as happens with the moral emotions.

But the point needs closer attention. In the last lecture, in considering the case of the man left by a woman with whom he had been living for some years, and who now vacillates between despair, jealousy, and regret, I noted that – though I was not in a position to put it in these terms – the object and the content of his attitude will fluctuate in tandem. I do not now wish to give the appearance of underwriting the view that, in these fluctuations, it is always the object that is the prime mover. Initially it is compelling to think that the object must come first, but the motivation here is provided by a propositional view of the attitude, which identifies the object with a subject-term, the content with a predicative expression. Once we can free ourselves from this view, the natural priority of the object loses its appeal.

A third proposal is that the identity of an emotion is given by its manifestation in action, actual or hypothetical.

This answer has much to be said against it. It depsychologizes emotion. At the same time it overlooks what I have stressed at various points in these lectures: that is, the contingency of the connexion between emotion and action, which depends upon the fortuitous formation of desire.

A final and acceptable proposal is, as I hope these lectures have suggested, that the essence of emotion lies in the attitude.

At the beginning of these lectures, I said that emotion tints, or colours, the world. This was, it will be appreciated, a metaphor, and it is a useful metaphor if it indicates what kind of thing an emotion is. But it has another use if it also allows us to see the inherent difficulty that there is in trying to make explicit, or to define, the nature of the individual emotions, or what is distinctive about the attitudes that lie at their core. The task is as promising as trying to make explicit, or to define, a colour, or the shade of a colour.

But here is another opportunity for error. For colours, and shades of colour, are simple. True, we talk of shot colours, but a shot colour is not a colour, it is a combination of colours.

Emotions are inherently complex, and they have a complexity that cannot be reduced to ambivalence. Ambivalent emotions are shot emotions, the warp coming from one emotion, the weft coming from another. But take each one of these strands, and we shall find that, as we follow it along, it is continuously complex, so that its identity lies, not in a simple quality, but in a narrative, in the story of its life.

Philosophers who talk of the appropriateness of emotions to their objects are additionally wrong if they fail to see that emotions are essentially interactive. Some of this we have already seen: A desire forms. We are thereby sensitized to the world. The world satisfies or frustrates our desire: we experience the impact of the world. We respond to this impact by forming an attitude. But this attitude, we must recognize, anticipates a reaction from the world. And to this reaction, we have in turn some idea of how we would expect ourselves to respond. And so on.

This interaction is embedded in the narratives that we associate to our emotions, and in these narratives, conscious or unconscious, lie the identities of the emotions. But we must not think that these narratives are stories that we can make up at whim or at will. They are probably as deep as anything that we know about ourselves.

I end with a final supposition: Suppose that the world blocked the interaction that I am suggesting is essential to the emotions. Suppose that the world either was impervious to our emotions, or instantly and utterly capitulated before them. Suppose, for instance, that, whenever we loved someone, our love was never returned, not out of indifference or because love had been pledged elsewhere, but because the thought of such reciprocity never occurred to the person. Or suppose that, whenever we were angry, the object of our anger dropped down dead. Our emotions either totally determined the lives of others, or made no impact on them whatsoever. Furthermore suppose that this was, not only how the world was, but how, in our phantasies, we represented it. Our emotions would, I suspect, die of the lack of interaction, of the lack of narrative.[67]

NOTES TO THE TEXT

ENDNOTES TO LECTURE ONE

1 The map of the mind that follows is something set out at greater length in Richard Wollheim, *The Thread of Life* (Cambridge, Mass.: Harvard University Press, 1984), Lecture II.

  Forceful advocacy of the distinction between mental states and mental dispositions is to be found in Gilbert Ryle, *The Concept of Mind* (London: Hutchinson's University Library, 1949), especially Chapter V. However Ryle has a very different conception of the distinction from that which I advance. For him, as will emerge later in the main text, a mental disposition is not a psychological phenomenon at all. As to mental states, Ryle, *Concept of Mind*, p. 92, appears to take a view of some of them, which he refers to slightingly as itches, pangs, and throbs, which is closer to mine. However he clearly regards such mental states as peripheral, and his treatment of them is perfunctory. For the rest, though he emphasizes what they are not, he does not make it clear what he thinks that they are.

2 For this phrase, see William James, *The Principles of Psychology* (New York: Holt, 1890), Chapter IX, p. 239, where James talks of '*the stream of thought, of consciousness, or of subjective life*'. Chapter IX is itself entitled 'The Stream of Thought'. I use the term 'consciousness' in a broad sense, or as a determinable, of which 'unconscious', 'preconscious', and 'conscious' would be the determinates. However this is neither how James used the phrase, nor how he wanted it understood.

3 David Hume, *A Treatise of Human Nature* (1739), Book II, 'Of the Passions', Part III, sec. III.

4 When Ryle, *Concept of Mind*, pp. 94–95, writes, 'To say [of a person] that his motives [i.e., his dispositions, and, more particularly, his desires] have such and such strengths

is simply to say that he tends to distribute his activities in such and such ways', not merely does he reject the idea that the strength, or weakness, of a person's dispositions might *explain* his activities, but the purely descriptive account that he provides of how these notions link up with behaviour is arbitrary. For it denies what seems to be a fact of experience: that, in certain circumstances, a person might have strong desires, and yet not act on them. He might, through inertia, or through guilt, or through perversity, come to act on a weaker desire. Possibly such a person would pay a sizeable price for doing so in the way of anxiety, or tension, or resentment: but these are not aspects of the situation on which Ryle has anything to say. Mark Platts, *Moral Realities: An Essay in Philosophical Psychology* (London and New York: Routledge, 1991), criticizes the association of strength of desire with tendency to act upon the desire, but he does so from a point of view with which I am out of sympathy. Platts, as I shall later put it, maximally 'depsychologizes' desire.

5   In point of fact, Ryle, *Concept of Mind*, pp. 93–98, does assign what he calls 'agitations' to the person at the point of intersection either between two conflicting dispositions or between one disposition and the world, which frustrates it. However he leaves it unclear whether he thinks of these agitations as mental states, and, given his treatment of mental dispositions, hence of conflict of dispositions, he has no real reason to think that this is what they are. Why should one person be agitated just because another cannot decide how to describe him?

6   Ryle, *Concept of Mind*, p. 93. The lack of explanatory value that attaches to Ryle's view of dispositions is a theme both of D. M. Armstrong, *A Materialist Theory of the Mind* (London: Routledge & Kegan Paul, 1968), and of Jerry A. Fodor, *Psychological Explanation* (New York: Random House, 1968).

7   This usage, it should be appreciated, is stipulative. A number of philosophers, of whom Brentano is pre-eminent, use the term 'intentionality' to refer to the directedness of mental phenomena, and they are then likely to refer to what I call 'intentionality', or the thought-content of mental phenomena, as 'cognitive content'. For me intentionality is not the directedness of mental phenomena, but what accounts for it.

8   John Deigh, 'Cognitivism in

the Theory of Emotion: A Survey Article', *Ethics*, 104 (July 1994), pp. 824–54, distinguishes within the philosophy of mind between 'traditional cognitivism', which insists only on as much thought-content as is needed for mental phenomena to pick out things in the world, and 'contemporary cognitivism', which insists that the thought-content of a mental phenomenon is invariably propositional.

9 This phrase comes from Thomas Nagel, 'What is it Like to be a Bat?', reprinted in his *Mortal Questions* (Cambridge, England, and Cambridge, Mass.: Cambridge University Press, 1979). Nagel stresses that the phrase is misunderstood if 'what it is like' is taken to mean 'what it is similar to'. If I ask of a guest, 'What is the soup like?', and he replies, not with some remark like 'Too salty', or 'Tasteless', but by saying, 'Exactly like the soup you gave me last time', then, if I intended my question in a Nagel-like sense, he has misunderstood it. Semantically Nagel moves 'what it is like' away from 'what it resembles', and approximates it to 'how it strikes one'.

10 For arguments of this sort, the contemporary source is Wittgenstein: see especially Ludwig Wittgenstein, *The Blue and Brown Books* (Oxford: Basil Blackwell, 1958). But no-one has argued more forcefully, or more brilliantly, against the Empiricist thesis that the meaning of an 'idea' derives directly from its psychological content, or, in the terminology that I am using, that its intentionality *is* its subjectivity, than the English Idealist philosopher F. H. Bradley: see F. H. Bradley, *The Principles of Logic* (Oxford: Clarendon Press, 1883), Vol. I, Book I, Chapter I.

I have noted that those contemporary philosophers who are strongly committed to the *prima facie* connexion between the intentionality of mental phenomena and language, when, unlike, e.g., Donald Davidson, 'Thought and Talk', reprinted in his *Inquiries into Truth and Interpretation* (Oxford: Oxford University Press, 1982), they are not expressly sceptical about allowing intentionality to non-verbal or pre-verbal creatures, tend to think that, in these special cases, a very primitive intentionality is carried by a primitive subjectivity of images and sensation. This reveals, to my mind, an over-strong preoccupation with the 'medium' of thought. For this position I have only conversational evidence.

11 I am grateful to an exchange

with Jennifer Hornsby on these issues on the occasion of a talk that I gave to the Oxford University Philosophical Society in 1985.

12   Gregory Vlastos remonstrated with me, on more than one occasion, for my using the word 'phenomenology' substantively, or as the name for a feature of our psychology, rather than as the name for the study of such features. I never heard him similarly protest against the substantive use of the word 'psychology'. I should like to put on record my gratitude to this remarkable scholar for the interest he took in my work and for the unobtrusive encouragement he gave me over many years.

13   See Ludwig Wittgenstein, *Philosophical Investigations*, trans. G. E. M. Anscombe (Oxford: Basil Blackwell, 1953), Part II, xi.

14   See Wollheim, *Thread of Life*, Lecture II, where this particular kind of causal efficacy is called 'psychic force'. It will be evident that I am committed to a strong form of mental causation, whereby not only do mental states have causal power but they have it in virtue of their mental properties. Such a view is, I believe, best accommodated by thinking of causation as fundamentally grounded in

processes rather than in laws. See Tim Crane, 'Mental Causation', *Proceedings of the Aristotelian Society*, Suppl. Vol. LXIX (1995), pp. 211–36.

15   I have discussed the question in Wollheim, *Thread of Life*, Lecture II.

16   The importance of distinguishing between emotions, which are dispositions, and the mental states in which these dispositions manifest themselves is stressed in G. F. Stout, *A Manual of Psychology* (London: University Tutorial Press, 4th ed. 1929), pp. 371 and 375, where the former are called 'emotional dispositions', and the latter 'emotions'. See also George Pitcher, 'Emotion', *Mind*, 74 (July 1965), pp. 326–46, and William P. Alston, 'Emotion and Feeling', in *The Encyclopaedia of Philosophy*, ed. Paul Edwards (New York: Macmillan, 1967), Vol. 2.

17   Certainly the weaker, and maybe the stronger, thesis is expressed by Robert Solomon when he writes that '[I]t does not even make sense to say that one feels angry if one is not angry', and 'One can identify his feeling as feeling angry only if he is angry', in Robert C. Solomon, 'Emotions and Choice', in *What is an Emotion?*, ed. Cheshire Calhoun and Robert C.

Solomon (New York and Oxford: Oxford University Press, 1984).

18 As an example of a philosopher who is aware of idiomatic usage, but insufficiently wary of that which lacks philosophical significance, see Errol Bedford, 'Emotions', *Proceedings of the Aristotelian Society*, LVII (1956–57), pp. 281–304. For a greater sensitivity to these issues, see Robert M. Gordon, *The Structure of Emotions: Investigations in Cognitive Philosophy* (Cambridge: Cambridge University Press, 1987), e.g., p. 35.

19 For the views of James and Freud on the nature of the emotions, see James, *Principles of Psychology*, Chapter XXV; and The Standard Edition of *The Complete Psychological Works of Sigmund Freud*, under the general editorship of James Strachey, in collaboration with Anna Freud (London: Hogarth Press, 1953–74), e.g., Vol. XIV, 'The Unconscious' (1915), and Vol. XVI, *Introductory Lectures on Psychoanalysis* (1915–16), Lecture XXV. For James, further see Lecture Two.

20 For this approach, see J. S. R. Wilson, *Emotion and Object* (Cambridge: Cambridge University Press, 1972), specifically pp. 70–71. Wilson compares emotions to pains, though allowing that emotions are more complex, and he contrasts emotions with beliefs. Emotions are treated as (a) complex responses to an external situation, which (b) follow upon the person's attending to the situation, when (c) this attention has in turn been caused by the situation itself. Helen Nissenbaum, *Emotion and Focus* (Stanford: CSLI, 1985), Chapters 4 and 5, criticizes Wilson for his one-sided treatment. However there are many matters on which I find myself in general agreement with both Nissenbaum and Wilson.

Malcolm Budd, *Music and the Emotions: The Philosophical Theories* (London: Routledge & Kegan Paul, 1985), p. 1, agrees that emotions can be considered both episodically and dispositionally, but nevertheless holds that 'the idea of an emotion as an episode' is basic. However he does not hold that dispositional emotion can be reduced to, or understood exhaustively in terms of, episodic emotion. He says that 'an emotion in the dispositional sense involves more than [a] tendency to undergo the emotion'.

21 That emotions are not reducible to beliefs, or desires, or some combination of these

two has been emphasized in two comparatively recent books on the topic, which have thrown considerable light on a number of issues: Gordon, *Structure of Emotions*, and Ronald de Sousa, *The Rationality of Emotion* (Cambridge, Mass.: MIT Press, 1987). But Gordon and de Sousa ground the irreducibility of emotion in different considerations. Gordon, *Structure of Emotions*, pp. 4–9, is influenced by the distinctive explanatory value of emotion, whereas de Sousa, *Rationality of Emotion*, Chapter 1, is influenced by the way that emotion resists certain classifications to which belief and desire submit readily. These include the dichotomies of rational vs irrational, objective vs subjective, active vs passive.

22 For the role of a disposition, see Wollheim, *Thread of Life*, Lecture II. The concept of role as I use it is close to that of 'proper function' as this is employed in Ruth G. Millikan, *Language, Thought, and other Biological Categories: New Foundations for Realism* (Cambridge, Mass.: MIT Press, 1984), pp. 17–18.

23 For this point, see *Collected Papers of C. S. Peirce*, ed. C. Hartshorne and P. Weiss (Cambridge, Mass.: Harvard University Press, 1931–35), Vol. V, 'The Fixation of Belief'. The relevance of Peirce's views to the present discussion was pointed out to me by Isaac Levi at a meeting of the Cambridge Moral Sciences Club, where I learnt much else. I should like to thank, in particular, Myles Burnyeat and Jane Heal.

24 On the significance of belief-formation and its mechanism for the role of belief, see Bernard Williams, 'Deciding to Believe', and 'Ethical Consistency', both reprinted in his *Problems of the Self* (Cambridge: Cambridge University Press, 1973).

25 It seems to some philosophers of a very Humean persuasion that a desire does not necessarily give us a reason to act since we can have a desire without having a reason for it. I agree with the premiss of this argument, but the conclusion does not follow. For there are various mental phenomena that can give us a reason without our having a reason for them: for instance, perceptions, prejudices, and free associations. At the other end of the spectrum is the view, no less Humean in inspiration, which is often expressed as that of the internality of reasons, according to which only a desire can give us a reason to act: see Philippa Foot, 'Reasons for Actions and Desires', reprinted in her

Virtues and Vices (Oxford: Oxford University Press, 1978); and Bernard Williams, 'Internal and External Reasons', reprinted in his *Moral Luck* (Cambridge: Cambridge University Press, 1981).

26 The term 'desirability-characterization' appears in G. E. M. Anscombe, *Intention* (Oxford: Basil Blackwell, 1957), p. 71, and Anscombe connects it with the first premiss of a practical syllogism. It is unlikely that Anscombe herself holds that every desire is grounded in a desirability-characterization. Two elisions in her presentation obscure her position. The first elision occurs when, having set out to give the requirements upon our desiring something, she shifts to specifying what is required if we (now observers) are to find the desires of another comprehensible (*ibid.*, pp. 69–71). This marks a real elision, for another's desires may be perfectly adequate as desires but be incomprehensible to us: if, for instance, we do not share them. The second elision occurs when, in the course of saying what is required if we are to find the desires of another comprehensible, Anscombe again shifts, this time to setting out what makes someone's acting on a desire that he has com-

prehensible (*ibid.*, pp. 71–74). This too marks a real elision, for, though every desire that a person has, hence every comprehensible desire that a person has, provides him with a reason for acting on it, the reason is not necessarily one on which it would be comprehensible for him to act. As far as I can see, Anscombe's conclusion is that the only desires that are surely and clearly grounded in desirability-characterizations are those which are based on a calculation of means to ends and those which are desires about how, or in what way, to do something that we already desire to do.

For another view of the relations between desires and desirability-characterizations, see Platts, *Moral Realities.*

27 See Brian O'Shaughnessy, *The Will: A Dual Aspect Theory* (Cambridge: Cambridge University Press, 1980), Vol. II, pp. 345–46.

28 For the vacuous use of 'desire', see, e.g., Alfred R. Mele, *Springs of Action: Understanding Intentional Behavior* (New York and Oxford: Oxford University Press, 1992). Philosophers who have criticized this use include Thomas Nagel, *The Possibility of Altruism* (Princeton: Princeton University Press, 1970); Mark Platts, *Ways of Meaning: An Introduction to a*

Philosophy   of   Language
(London: Routledge &
Kegan Paul, 1979); and G. F.
Schueler, *Desire: Its Role in
Practical Reason and the Expla-
nation of Action* (Cambridge,
Mass.: MIT Press, 1995).

Schueler tries to rectify the
situation by proposing a distinction between two kinds
of desire, or what he calls
two 'senses' of desire. There
are 'desires proper', and mere
'pro-attitudes' (a term bor-
rowed from Donald David-
son, but not necessarily used
as he uses it). Schueler has
two reasons for down-grading
pro-attitudes. One comes
from a reading of Nagel, *Possibility of Altruism*, pp. 29–32,
which I consider in the next
endnote. The other is that,
when I try to decide whether
to act in accordance with
a pro-attitude, I take into
account only the object of my
pro-attitude and not the fact
that I have the pro-attitude
towards it. But Schueler
ignores the fact that this is
how I standardly argue when
I decide whether to act on a
desire. If we are to make a
distinction of the kind that
Schueler advocates, the likeliest place to find the difference is in the internal state
of the agent in the aftermath
of acting upon a desire, alternatively a pro-attitude.

29 Nagel, *Possibility of Altruism*,
makes a distinction between

unmotivated and motivated
desires, which has a tenuous
similarity to the distinction
drawn here between explicit
and implicit desires. Un-
motivated desires 'assail' us,
whereas motivated desires,
which Nagel introduces in
the context of assessing the
Humean thesis that all intentional action requires the
presence of desire, clearly do
not. Nagel argues that the
Humean thesis is tenable only
if desires are taken to include
motivated desires, but, in
doing this, we thereby debili-
tate the thesis. For it could
very well be that the existence of the motivated desire
is to be explained by reference to the very considerations that motivate the
action, and these considerations need not, according to
Nagel, include any further
desire, motivated or unmotivated. Furthermore the motivated desire could be merely
a logically necessary, and not
a causally necessary, condition
of the action. It looks as
though, by this time, the
Humean thesis has been
totally trivialized. Indeed,
when Nagel says that for an
agent to have a motivated
desire 'simply follows' from
the fact there are conditions
that motivate him, by which
he presumably means that
saying the first is nothing over
and above saying the second,

this has the consequence that, when a motivated desire is posited, no genuine desire is posited. John McDowell, 'Are Moral Requirements Hypothetical Imperatives?', *Proceedings of the Aristotelian Society*, Suppl. Vol. LI (1978), pp. 13–29, is more or less in agreement with Nagel's point. Stephen Schiffer, 'The Paradox of Desire', *American Philosophical Quarterly*, 13, no. 3 (July 1976), pp. 195–203, suggests that Nagel's distinction between unmotivated and motivated desires partially matches that between reason-producing, or self-justifying, and reason-following, or self-referring, desires.

30 Kit Fine pointed out to me (in discussion) that the oratio obliqua thesis can be regarded as assimilating desire to belief only on an impoverished view of belief. For, on a better view, belief admits of the same tripartite classification as I go on to claim for desire.

31 Deigh, 'Cognitivism', p. 824, argues that, though it is plausible to think that the objects of belief are propositions, it is a substantive error to think this of the objects of emotion, and, by parity of reasoning, of the objects of desire. However Deigh may be at fault in the over-literal way in which he takes the thesis that the objects of belief are propositions. On this, see G. E. M.

Anscombe, "On the Grammar of 'Enjoy' ", reprinted in her *Metaphysics and the Philosophy of Mind: The Collected Philosophical Papers of G. E. M. Anscombe*, Vol. II (Minneapolis: University of Minnesota Press, 1981).

32 The rejection of the linguistic thesis in connexion with the philosophy of mind generally is argued for in Wilson, *Emotion and Object*, especially Introduction, and Chapter VII, and Nissenbaum, *Emotion and Focus*.

33 The argument in this paragraph is adapted from O'Shaughnessy, *The Will*, Vol. II, pp. 117–23.

34 For basic actions, see Arthur Danto, 'What We Can Do', *Journal of Philosophy*, LX (1963), pp. 434–45; Donald Davidson, 'Agency', reprinted in his *Essays on Actions and Events* (Oxford: Oxford University Press, 1980); and Jennifer Hornsby, *Action* (London: Routledge & Kegan Paul, 1980).

35 O'Shaughnessy, *The Will*, Vol. II, pp. 295–97, also Vol. I, pp. li–lv, and Vol. II, pp. 117–20.

36 The view that desires for things are fundamental seems assumed in the famous passage from St Augustine's *Confessions* about the earliest use of language with which Wittgenstein opens the *Philosophical Investigations*. For there Augustine writes, 'When they

(my elders) named *some object*, and accordingly moved towards *something*, I saw this and I grasped that *the thing* was called by the sound they uttered when they meant to point it out. Their intention was shewn by their bodily movements, as it were the natural language of all peoples: the expresssion of the face, the play of the eyes, the movement of other parts of the body, and the tone of voice which expresses our state of mind in seeking, having, rejecting, or avoiding *something*. Thus, as I heard words repeatedly used in their proper places in various sentences, I gradually learnt to understand what *objects* they signified; and after I had trained my mouth to form these signs, *I used them to express my desires*.' However it is not completely clear from the context whether the desires referred to are Augustine's desires for things or his desire to express his thoughts, which he holds to preexist language.

37 A version of this argument is found in Anthony Kenny, *Action, Emotion and Will* (London: Routledge & Kegan Paul, 1963), pp. 112–15. Kenny restricts the application of his remarks to tangible objects of desire. The argument that Kenny uses is that, unless the ascription of a desire is expanded in this way, we have no means of saying what counts as the person's getting what he wants. But a person's getting what he wants is surely to be explained in terms of what he wants, not *vice versa* as Kenny appears to assume.

38 See *The Writings of Melanie Klein*, under the general editorship of Roger Money-Kyrle (London: Hogarth Press, and the Institute of Psycho-Analysis, 1957), Vol. III, *Envy and Gratitude* (1957).

39 For these considerations, though not for the argument, see Kenny, *Action, Emotion and Will*, pp. 112–15.

40 *Ibid.*, p. 125, gives some support to this view. Kenny's argument is employed by John Searle, *Intentionality: An Essay in the Philosophy of Mind* (Cambridge: Cambridge University Press, 1983), p. 30, though Searle draws a different conclusion.

41 On the method of thought-experiment, see Wollheim, *Thread of Life*, Lecture I, and 'Danto's Gallery of Indiscernibles', in *Danto and his Critics*, ed. Mark Rollins (Oxford: Blackwells, 1993).

42 Adam Morton, *Frames of Mind* (Oxford: Clarendon Press, 1980), p. 139, advances the view that a desire can be satisfied without its coming true when he writes, 'It isn't as if the desire says, 'I want

that', and then to satisfy it one has to produce just that. Rather, it says, 'I want something, and here's what it must do for me', and then one can search round offering it various things until something satisfies it.' However, as this quotation makes clear, Morton thinks that this view requires him to uncouple a desire from its object in a way that I am unprepared to consider.

43 On King Lear's assimilation of the demands of love to the demands of loyalty, and the havoc that this wreaks on his attempts to satisfy the natural desires of a father, see Stanley Cavell's haunting essay 'The Avoidance of Love' in his *Must We Mean What We Say?* (New York: Charles Scribner's Sons, 1969).

44 Dependence upon criteria, or upon the meaning of terms, to give us unaided the conditions for their application has been criticized in different areas by very different thinkers. See Fodor, *Psychological Explanation*, and Ronald Dworkin, *Law's Empire* (London: Collins, 1986), Chapters I and II, where this method of argument is called the 'semantic sting'.

45 The objection that no way has been provided of distinguishing between the mere termination of a desire and its satisfaction has frequently been levelled at the theory of desire to be found in Bertrand Russell, *The Analysis of Mind* (London: George Allen and Unwin, 1921), Chapter III. See, e.g., Kenny, *Action, Emotion and Will*, Chapter V, especially pp. 100–11, and, for a more sympathetic treatment, see David Pears, *Questions in the Philosophy of Mind* (London: Duckworth, 1975), Chapter X.

As both Kenny and Pears are careful to point out, there are several layers to Russell's theory in that it says something about (one) animal desire, (two) conscious human desire, and (three) unconscious human desire. It is on the bottom level that the criticism most obviously holds, and the source of Russell's difficulty lies in his identification of an animal desire with a 'behaviour-cycle', given the meagre, i.e., purely behavioural, materials that he allows himself for the construction of a behaviour-cycle. For Russell needs to have ways of determining (one) when a behaviour-cycle begins, (two) whether some new event belongs to it or not, and (three) what brings it to its natural end, which is for him the satisfaction of the desire. A full or fully comprehensible answer to any one of these problems would have to convey what the unity of a behaviour-cycle resides in, and so would be an answer to the other two, but, for our present purposes, it is the third problem that gives concern. The difficulty that faces Russell is well illustrated by the example that he himself uses of animal desire. He asks us to consider a bird that mates, builds a nest, lays eggs in it, sits on the eggs, feeds its young, and cares for them until they are fully grown. All this, he tells us, 'constitutes one behaviour-cycle'. We appear to follow what we are told, and we find the story intelligible. But suppose the bird had mated, built a nest, laid eggs in it – and then flown away. We would be inclined to say that the behaviour-cycle had not come to its natural end. We would say that it had been interrupted, or postponed, or been superseded by another behaviour-cycle. But with what reason would we say any one of these things, and why would we say one rather than another? Or vary the example, and imagine another kind of bird, which, after mating, building a nest, and laying eggs, flies away, and is generally held to do so, not for any of the reasons given in the case of the first bird, but because its desire is now satisfied. Why should we say this? How can one behav-iour-cycle be complete at the very point at which another would have been broken off?

When Russell's account ascends to human desire, he adds what is, at any rate, on the most natural interpreta-tion of his original materials, a new item. He adds a sensa-tion, and this sensation causes the behaviour-cycle to start, and ceases only when the purpose of the cycle is achieved. Undoubtedly the account gains from this addi-tion, but it does little to ease the problem considered in this endnote: that is, the unity of the behaviour-cycle in which the core of the desire is thought to reside. For, if the identity of the sensation is expected to account for the identity of the behaviour-cycle, then as Pears remarks, the trouble is that the only cases that lend themselves readily to this kind of treat-ment are cases that are closer to need than to desire.

It must be observed that the clear-cut distinction between human and non-human desire is not some-thing that Russell goes along with all the time. There is the suggestion that animal desire has more to it than behaviour, and there is the complementary suggestion that the sensation that seems to be the distinc-tive mark of human desire is a mere causal power, which does not have the phenomenological aspect that Russell's words initially ascribe to it.

46 I owe this example to Hermione Gee. The failure to recognize the way in which desire sensitizes us to the world underlies certain abstract principles in Welfare economics, such as the Compensation Principle, in so far as these purport to introduce commensurability between the frustration of desire and some transfer-payment. This is not to deny that there are many situations where such principles operate in an unobjectionable fashion.

47 Pears, *Questions*, pp. 253–54, makes a similar point in evaluating Russell's account of desire. However his point is broader than that which I seek to establish in that he stresses that, in this context, internal does not necessarily mean mental.

48 I owe this suggestion to Bernard Williams.

49 This is a point that I have emphasized in, e.g., Wollheim, *Thread of Life*, Lecture II. Pears, *Questions*, treats the issue with great subtlety, and raises the deep question why, if the satisfaction of a person's desire and the satisfaction of the person can diverge, we adhere to the practice of classifying desires, and, specifically, unconscious desires, by reference to their objects. Why do we not classify them in the same way as we classify needs: that is, by reference to what will bring the person satisfaction?

50 I am grateful to Ariela Lazar for pointing out to me the need to make this point.

51 An amalgam of the two versions of the semantic view is to be found in Searle, *Intentionality*, Chapter 1.

52 The notion of direction of fit has been employed by a number of writers in somewhat different ways from that I have in mind. These include J. L. Austin and G. E. M. Anscombe. But the view that I consider is to be found in its most explicit form in Platts, *Ways of Meaning*, p. 257. I am grateful to David Pears for several long discussions on this issue, though we continue not to see the matter eye-to-eye.

53 The transition from an analytic to a prescriptive use of the thesis of direction of fit is clearly observable in Searle, *Intentionality*, p. 8, n. 2. Searle writes, 'Since fitting is a symmetrical relationship it might seem puzzling that there can be different *directions* of fit. If *a* fits *b*, *b* fits *a*. Perhaps it will alleviate this worry to consider an uncontroversial non-linguistic case: If Cinderella goes into a shoe store to buy

a new pair of shoes, she takes her foot size as given and seeks shoes to fit (shoe-to-foot direction of fit). But when the prince seeks the owner of the shoe, he takes the shoe as given and seeks a foot to fit the shoe (foot-to-shoe direction of fit).' It is not clear what Searle wishes this argument to establish, or which worry it is that it is supposed to alleviate. But two things are clear. One is that Searle shifts the issue from whether, if the shoe fits the foot, the foot fits the shoe, to the issue of the difference between finding a shoe to fit a foot and finding a foot to fit a shoe. The other is that he has, by implication, removed the whole question of direction of fit from anything to do with the nature of belief or desire to something purely prescriptive. Contrast L. L. Humberstone, 'Direction of Fit', *Mind*, 101 (January 1992), pp. 59–83, who insists on combining the interpretation of fit as the non-symmetrical getting-to-fit with the idea that direction of fit is essentially, and not just prescriptively, connected with the difference between belief and desire. It is connected with the nature of belief and desire. He tries to do this by inserting a third term, and this is what he calls the two 'controlling   background

intentions', with which we form, respectively, beliefs and desires. So, very roughly, when we form a belief, we do so with the background intention that our attitude is successful only if its propositional content is true, whereas, when we form a desire, we do so with the background intention that our attitude is successful only when the world fulfils it. Such controlling background intentions I have now come to think of as inconsistent with any psychologically plausible account of how we come to form either beliefs or desires.

Humberstone's idea has something in common with what I once thought of as the 'conception', or 'Master Thought', by reference to which we could distinguish the activities of imagination or phantasy. See Richard Wollheim, 'The Mind and the Mind's Image of Itself', and 'Imagination and Identification', both reprinted in my *On Art and the Mind* (Cambridge, Mass.: Harvard University Press, 1974), and 'Identification and Imagination', in *Freud: A Collection of Critical Essays*, ed. Richard Wollheim (New York: Doubleday, 1974).

54 The maxim 'Enough is enough' is advocated as one of the central principles of

epistemology in J. L. Austin, *Philosophical Papers*, ed. J. O. Urmson and G. J. Warnock (Oxford: Clarendon Press, 1961), 'Other Minds'.

55 Jens Peter Jacobsen, *Niels Lyhne* (1880), Chapter XIV.

56 See Bernard Williams, 'Deciding to Believe', in his *Problems of the Self*.

57 The most interesting version of the claim that desires of ours with which we do not identify are not really desires of ours is to be found in Harry G. Frankfurt, *The Importance of What We Care About* (Cambridge: Cambridge University Press, 1988). However any such argument is doomed to failure because it has to begin by asserting what it concludes by denying. The relevant relation of identifying with, or not identifying with, which holds between, or has as its terms, a person, on the one hand, and a desire, on the other, is intelligible only as a relation between a person and one of *his* desires. Unless a desire has already been identified as a particular person's desire, the question whether he does, or does not, identify with it cannot arise. For criticism of Frankfurt, see Gary Watson, 'Free Agency', *Journal of Philosophy*, LXXII (1975), pp. 205–20, and Irving Thalberg, *Misconceptions of Mind and Freedom*

(Lanham, Md.: University Press of America, 1983), Chapter 5.

58 The concern to shrink desire to the circumstances of the world was, for slightly different reasons, adopted by all the major Hellenistic and Roman schools of philosophy. It is to be found in, e.g., Chrysippus, Epicurus, Lucretius, Seneca, Sextus Empiricus. For a contemporary reading of the discussion, see Martha Nussbaum, *The Therapy of Desire* (Princeton: Princeton University Press, 1994).

59 On the relationship of perception to perceptual belief, I find myself in broad agreement with the views expressed in Fred Dretske, *Knowledge and the Flow of Information* (Cambridge, Mass.: MIT Press, 1981). Personally I find the use of the word 'information' in Dretske, and in, e.g., Gareth Evans, *The Varieties of Reference* (Oxford: Oxford University Press, 1982), to pick out the non-discursive aspect of experience unperspicuous. But the idea itself satisfies a real philosophical need.

60 It is to be observed that Kenny, *Action, Emotion and Will*, p. 124, endorses, in a rather special context, the notion of prospective satisfaction. The context is that of act-desires that have a temporal indicator that refers to the

more remote future. He quotes as examples the desire to go to Greece next summer, and the desire to marry a girl once one has found a job. Of such desires, he writes that they 'are in one sense satisfied as soon as one has certainty that they will be realized'. Kenny does not give the rationale for this view, and I doubt if it is one with which I would concur.

61 For the special phenomenology of imagination, see Wollheim, *Thread of Life*, Lecture III.

62 On the distinction between the positive and the negative emotions, see the remarks by Gordon, *Structure of Emotions*, pp. 27–32. Careful examination of these pages will also reveal the extent to which Gordon is sympathetic, and the extent to which he is not, to my view of the relations betwen emotion and the satisfaction and frustration of desire. I owe Gordon's book a great debt of gratitude for getting me to think hard about this issue, even if ultimately I adopt a position that Gordon might well find exaggerated.

63 Seneca, *De Ira*, Book II, XXXIII, 3–5. I have left out of the story the fact that Pastor had another son, for whose life he undoubtedly feared.

64 Michel de Montaigne, *Essais* (1588), Book I, 18, 'De la peur'.

65 Henry James, 'The Beast in the Jungle' (1903).

66 This is the central theme of a work, which has been unduly overlooked, probably as a direct result of its formidable awkwardness of expression: Patricia S. Greenspan, *Emotions and Reasons: An Inquiry into Emotional Justification* (London and New York: Routledge, 1988).

ENDNOTES TO LECTURE TWO

1 This point is emphasized in Donald Davidson, 'Actions, Causes and Reasons' and other essays, reprinted in his *Essays on Actions and Events* (Oxford: Oxford University Press, 1980).

2 William Shakespeare, *Twelfth Night* (1599–1600), Act II, scene V.

3 William Shakespeare, *Richard the Second* (1595–96), Act III, scene II.

4 See the argument in J. S. R. Wilson, *Emotion and Object* (Cambridge: Cambridge University Press, 1972), Chapters II and III. Similarly concerned to preserve the claim that the object of an emotion is causally related to it, though differently motivated, he too weakens what is required of the causal relation. He substi-

tutes for the notion of cause that of causal relatedness.

5 Thomas Hardy, *Far from the Madding Crowd* (1874).

6 Jean Racine, *Berenice* (1670), Act III, scene III.

7 E.g., Jonathan Lear, *Love and its Place in Nature* (New York: Farrar, Strauss, and Giroux, 1990): and Malcolm Budd, *Music and the Emotions: The Philosophical Theories* (London: Routledge & Kegan Paul, 1985). The same view, though it does not use the word 'attitude', is expressed in Allan Gibbard, *Wise Choices, Apt Feelings: A Theory of Normative Judgment* (Cambridge, Mass.: Harvard University Press, 1990), p. 131, when he writes, 'An emotion, we can say, involves a special way of experiencing one's world, a way that will be difficult to express and perhaps can only be whistled.'

8 For objectless emotions, see, e.g., Anthony Kenny, *Action, Emotion and Will* (London: Routledge & Kegan Paul, 1963), pp. 60–62; and Wilson, *Emotion and Object*, Chapter VI. It goes without saying that we should not include amongst objectless emotions those whose objects are merely inaccessible to consciousness.

9 At this point, which is the first substantial mention of the *object*, I should mention two things: (one) that I am in agreement with David Hume, *A Treatise of Human Nature* (1739), Book II, in that I think that the concepts of cause of an emotion and of object of an emotion are different concepts, though I do not believe that there is a clear point at which the notion of object proves appropriate, and (two) that I disagree with Hume in that it seems to me clear that one and the same fact or figure can be the cause and the object of the same emotion. To Hume's argument against this – that, in the case of two conflicting emotions that had the same objects, it would follow that they had the same cause, and then we should have to concede that, appearances to the contrary, they were the same emotion – I should respond, in keeping with what is said in the text, that the nature of an emotion is not given wholly by its cause. Hume's argument overlooks the role of the experience of satisfaction or frustration and its successor, the attitude.

10 For such a claim, see A. Michotte, *La Perception de la causalité* (Louvain: Institut Supérieur de la Philosophie, 1946).

11 See Richard Wollheim, *Art and its Objects* (Cambridge: Cambridge University Press, 2nd ed. 1980), and

'Correspondence, Projective Properties, and Expression', in his *The Mind and its Depths* (Cambridge, Mass.: Harvard University Press, 1993).

12   Stendhal, *De l'amour* (1822), Chapter II, and Complément, 'Le Rameau de Salzbourg'.

13   *ibid.*, Chapter XV, fn.

14   *ibid.*, Chapter II.

15   For the significance of this transformation, see The Standard Edition of *The Complete Psychological Works of Sigmund Freud*, under the general editorship of James Strachey, in collaboration with Anna Freud (London: Hogarth Press, 1953–74) (hereinafter *Freud*), e.g., Vol. VII, *Three Essays on the Theory of Sexuality* (1905), and Vol. XVIII, *Beyond the Pleasure Principle* (1920). The idea is fundamental to Spinoza's thinking about human freedom.

16   For the connexion between emotion, on the one hand, and activity and passivity, on the other, see R. S. Peters, 'Emotion and the Category of Passivity', *Proceedings of the Aristotelian Society*, LXII (1961–62); Robert C. Solomon, *The Passions: The Myth and Nature of Human Emotion* (Garden City, N.Y.: Doubleday, 1976); Jerome Neu, *Emotion, Theory and Therapy* (London: Routledge & Kegan Paul, 1977); and Robert M. Gordon, *The Structure of Emotions: Investiga-* *tions in Cognitive Philosophy* (Cambridge: Cambridge University Press, 1987).

17   That the formation of an emotion is the product of an action of ours is asserted by Solomon, *The Passions*, p. 185 (his italics), where he writes, 'An emotion is . . . something we *do*.'

18   *ibid.*, Chapters 9 and 10, where Solomon talks of our emotions as strategies that we pursue.

19   Jean-Paul Sartre, *Esquisse d'une theorie des émotions* (Paris: Éditions Scientifiques Hermann, 1939), trans. as *Sketch for a Theory of the Emotions*, trans. Philip Mairet (London: Methuen, 1962), particularly III.

20   Sartre, *Sketch*, pp. 66–68.

21   *ibid.*, pp. 68–71.

22   *ibid.*, pp. 71–74.

23   *ibid.*, pp. 62–63.

24   *ibid.*, pp. 72–73.

25   *ibid.*, p. 72.

26   *ibid.*, p. 63.

27   The term 'magic' is scattered through Sartre's discussion of the formation, or malformation as I would call it, of emotion.

28   The patient was called by Freud 'the Ran Man'. See *Freud*, Vol. X, 'Notes upon a Case of Obsessional Neurosis' (1909).

29   Sartre, *Sketch*, pp. 64–75.

30   *ibid.*, p. 67.

31   *ibid.*, p. 73.

32   *ibid.*, p. 67.

33   *ibid.*

34   For the notion of a compromise-formation, see *Freud,*
e.g., Vol. V, *The Interpretation of
Dreams* (1900), Chapter VII,
and Vol. XVII, 'From the
History of an Infantile Neurosis' (1914); and Vol. XIX,
'A Short Account of Psycho-
Analysis' (1923), sec. 2. The
first occurrence of the idea,
though not described as such,
appears to be *Freud,* Vol. I,
Extracts from the Fliess Papers,
letter Freud–Fliess 105, pp.
278–79.

35   Sartre, *Sketch,* pp. 65–66.

36   See *The Writings of Melanie
Klein,* under the general edi-
torship of Roger Money-
Kyrle (London: Hogarth
Press, and the Institute of
Psycho-Analysis, 1957) (here-
inafter *Klein*), Vol. III, *Envy
and Gratitude.* The history of
the idea is traced in *A
Dictionary of Kleinian Thought*
(London: Free Association
Books, 2nd ed. 1991), entry
'Envy'. See also, e.g., Herbert
Rosenfeld, 'Notes on the Psy-
choanalysis of the Superego
Conflict in an Acute Schizo-
phrenic', reprinted in his *Psy-
chotic States: A PsychoAnalytical
Approach* (London: Hogarth,
1968), and Betty Joseph, 'Envy
in Everyday Life', reprinted
in her *Psychic Equilibrium and
Psychic Change* (London: Tavi-
stock/Routledge, 1989).

37   For a closely similar notion
of helplessness as a traumatic

condition, see *Freud,* Vol. XX,
*Inhibitions, Symptoms and
Anxiety* (1926), secs. VIII–X
and Addendum B.

38   *Klein,* Vol. III, p. 183.

39   The standard way of dealing
with such situations, while
preserving the philosophically
appropriate generality, is to
say that emotions take
'intensional objects'. This is
the position of, e.g., Amelie
Rorty, 'Explaining Emotions',
and Robert Solomon,
'Emotion and Choice', both
in *Explaining Emotions,* ed.
Amelie Rorty (Berkeley and
Los Angeles: University of
California Press, 1980).
However the appeal to
intensional objects does not
really meet the problem of
how emotions can be directed
on to non-existent objects.
At best it explains how, given
such objects, we can coher-
ently talk about them. For
the term 'intensional object' is
equally appropriate when
the mental state is directed
on to something that exists
and when it is directed on
to something that doesn't
exist. For a careful and
interesting, if sometimes over-
subtle, treatment of the issue,
see G. E. M. Anscombe,
'The Intensionality of Sensation', reprinted in her
*Metaphysics and the Philosophy
of Mind: The Collected
Philosophical Papers of G.
E. M. Anscombe,* Vol. II

(Minneapolis: University of Minnesota Press, 1981).

40 Wilson, whom we have already considered as a critic of the linguistic thesis as applied generally to the philosophy of mind, specifically criticizes the use of 'logico-grammatical criteria' to pick out the object of an emotion. He argues, *Emotion and Object*, Chapter VIII, that these criteria will work only if we apply it in the light of 'some prior notion of object-possession'. He goes on to say that Chisholm's proposal of improving upon Brentano's thesis of Intentionality by casting it in terms of the language that we use to talk about the mental was 'a step in the wrong direction'. Helen Nissenbaum, *Emotion and Focus* (Stanford: CSLI, 1985), is equally critical of the linguistic approach to the study of the emotions. What is distinctive of Nissenbaum's approach, and diminishes the value of her essay, is her insistence that different accounts of the object of an emotion are invariably accounts of different things. What she fails to allow for is the fact that sometimes these different accounts are to be explained by reference to different philosophical assumptions. However sometimes she is right to point out that philosophers, while appearing to engage one another, are in fact at cross-purposes. Ronald de Sousa, *The Rationality of Emotion* (Cambridge, Mass.: MIT Press, 1987), who reaches the same broad conclusion as Nissenbaum, differs from her in that he gives specific reasons for multiplying kinds of object of emotion, though I do not find all his arguments compelling.

41 Wilson, *Emotion and Object*, Chapter VIII, contrasts two possible approaches to the nature of object-directedness, hence to the nature of the emotion. The first 'starts from the inside', and tries to capture the first-person point of view: the other starts 'from the outside', and considers various ways in which a person might react to an event or action, some of which are to be thought of as emotional. The distinction as it stands is not all that clear, and I believe that what is really significant about the second approach, which Wilson favours, is that it starts from *the person* as a psychological unit. If that is his meaning, I agree with him.

42 See Kenny, *Action, Emotion and Will*, pp. 189–94.

43 The view that emotions are propositional attitudes is held by those philosophers who hold that emotions are, or

essentially include, evaluations: see endnote 57.

The view is also to be
found in Sebastian Gardner,
*Irrationality and the Philosophy
of Psychoanalysis* (Cambridge:
Cambridge University Press,
1993), specifically Chapter 4,
sec. 5, where it is advanced for
reasons that have nothing
to do, explicitly or implicitly,
with the linguistic thesis.
Gardner is concerned to
defend what he calls 'the
radical heterogeneity' between those mental phenomena which are essentially
unconscious, and thus fall
within the province of psychoanalysis narrowly understood, notably phantasy and
the wish, and those mental
phenomena which can be
conscious, and therefore,
when unconscious, are so
accidently. The latter include
desire, belief, and emotion,
and Gardner makes this distinction coincide with that
between propositional states
of the person and preproposi-
tional states. On this very last
point I am unconvinced.

44 See John Searle, *Intentionality:
An Essay in the Philosophy of
Mind* (Cambridge: Cambridge
University Press, 1983), p. 6,
where a contrast is made
between desires and emo-
tions. For, having insisted, as
we have seen, that all desires
must conform to the oratio
obliqua thesis, he allows that

there are emotions 'such as
love and hate whose content
need not be a whole
proposition'.

45 See a concession along these
lines in the Preface to
Gordon, *Structure of Emotions*,
p. x.

46 An abbreviated version of this
argument is to be found in
Wilson, *Emotion and Object*, p.
59.

47 See *Freud*, Vol. III, *Studies on
Hysteria* (1895), p. 156.

48 Cf. Nissenbaum, *Emotion and
Focus*, p. 35.

49 Seneca, *De Ira*, III, xii, 6–7.
See also Michel de Mon-
taigne, *Essais* (1588), Book II,
31, 'De la colère'.

50 See Montaigne, 'De la colère'.

51 George Eliot, *Middlemarch*
(1871).

52 Aristotle, *De Rhetorica*, Book
II, uses the temporal criterion
as one criterion amongst
others for distinguishing
between the emotions.

53 These objections, and the
new classification, are the
work of Gordon, *Structure
of Emotions*, Chapters 2–4.
However there is some
anticipation of Gordon in
Irving Thalberg, 'Emotion and
Thought', *American Philosophical Quarterly*, I, no. 1 (January
1964), pp. 45–55. For
Gordon's assessment of the
relations between Thalberg's
views and his own, see
Gordon, *Structure of Emotions*,
p. 27, n. 3. Spinoza, *Ethics*,

Book III, prop. XVIII, appears to favour a cognitive classification of the emotions (in terms of the presence or absence of doubt) over a temporal classification.

54   If Gordon undoubtedly understands factive emotions as requiring knowledge, he is ambiguous on the interpretation of epistemic emotions. Contrast *Structure of Emotions*, pp. 26–27 and 65, where he claims that epistemic emotions require no more than absence of knowledge, with p. 33, where the claim appears to be that they require absence of belief.

55   Those philosophers who insist on the 'relational', as opposed to the 'notional', understanding of emotions have their views dictated to them by a variety of considerations, but none produce a coherent account of what is actually the case when all the conditions of emotion except the existence of the object are satisfied. Wilson, *Emotion and Object*, p. 56, makes the helpful suggestion that we should distinguish the issue whether what he calls 'malfounded emotions', or emotions 'based ... on a mistaken existential belief', should be said to have objects from the different issue how they are to be described, or whether the normal emotion-terms should be applied to them. However,

when he comes to consider the second issue in Chapters XVI to XVIII, his position is elusive.

Donald Davidson, 'Hume's Cognitive Theory of Pride', reprinted in his *Essays on Actions and Events*, p. 279 (my italics), at once subscribes to the factivity of pride and concedes the point that I make above, when he writes, 'Hume ignores *the fact that* an attribution of propositional pride is false unless the corresponding belief is true ... ; and this seems reasonable, since it is unclear what interesting difference there is between pride founded on a true belief and an otherwise similar passion founded on a false belief.' We may infer that Davidson thinks that the taxonomy of the emotions is fundamentally an affair of convenience.

56   For these two arguments, see Gordon, *Structure of Emotions*, pp. 33–36.

57   Christopher Marlowe, *Doctor Faustus* (1593), scene XVIII.

58   I owe this point to de Sousa, *Rationality of Emotion*, p. 138n.

59   Vergil, *Aeneid*, Book I, lines 305ff. I owe this example to Philip Fisher.

60   Homer, *Iliad*, Book III, lines 33ff. Elizabeth Cropper and Charles Dempsey, *Nicolas Poussin: Friendship and the Love of Painting* (Princeton: Princeton University Press, 1996), pp. 293–94, talks of the

enduring influence of this description of death in an ancient landscape, handed down as it was through many texts, and suggests that Nicolas Poussin, *Landscape with a Snake*, which serves as the dust-jacket of this book, was conceived with it partly in mind.

61 For the view that emotions are essentially evaluative, see, e.g., Errol Bedford, 'Emotions', *Proceedings of the Aristotelian Society*, LVII (1956–57)), pp. 281–304; Magda Arnold, *Emotion and Personality* (New York: Columbia University Press, 1960), Vol. 1, p. 171: George Pitcher, 'Emotion', *Mind*, 74 (July 1965), pp. 326–46; William P. Alston, 'Emotion and Feeling', in *The Encyclopaedia of Philosophy*, ed. Paul Edwards (New York: Macmillan, 1967), Vol. 2; Solomon, *The Passions*; and William Lyons, *Emotion* (Cambridge: Cambridge University Press, 1980).

62 Both views are to be found in Bedford, 'Emotions', where the move between the two goes unrecorded.

63 Honore de Balzac, *La Cousine Bette* (1847).

64 Gibbard, *Wise Choices, Apt Feelings*, pp. 128–32, rejects the dependence of emotion upon evaluation, or what he calls 'judgmentalism', and proposes a reversal of the order of explanation. 'Perhaps we understand evaluations only because we have the relevant emotions, and emotions must be explained in terms of emotions – as I am proposing.' I hold a related view, which derives values from the projection of states of mind, but I am not invoking this view for the benefit of the present argument: see Richard Wollheim, *The Thread of Life* (Cambridge, Mass.: Harvard University Press, 1984), Lecture VII.

Gordon, *Structure of Emotions*, p. 30, also rejects the necessary connexion between emotion and evaluation, but on grounds that I find at once inadequate for the case and superficial. He thinks (one) that an evaluation can be conventional, hence not imply the corresponding attitude, which an emotion does, and (two) that an evaluation implies a disposition to say something, which an emotion does not.

65 For this intellectualist view of the emotions, which is an exaggeration of the views of Spinoza, see, e.g., Solomon, *The Passions*; Neu, *Emotion, Thought and Therapy*; and 'Jealous Thoughts', in ed. Rorty, *Explaining Emotion*; Jonathan Bennett, *A Study of Spinoza's Ethics* (Cambridge: Cambridge University Press, 1984); and Martha Nussbaum,

Love's Knowledge (Oxford: Oxford University Press, 1990), and *The Therapy of Desire* (Princeton: Princeton University Press, 1994).

66   William Shakespeare, *Othello* (1604–05), Act III, scene III, and Act IV, scene I.

67   This is the central argument of Pitcher, 'Emotion', which is deployed against what he calls the Traditional View.

68   Bedford, 'Emotions', pp. 283–84, where he writes, 'I am inclined to think that if an emotion were a feeling no sense could be made of them [e.g., judgments of 'unjustified', 'unreasonable'] at all. It may be said that an emotion is unjustified when a feeling is inappropriate or unfitting to a situation. But I find this unintelligible. Feelings do not have a character that makes this relationship possible.' The same argument occurs in Solomon, *The Passions*, pp. 161–62.

69   For a defence of the limited intentionality of sensation, see Gibbard, *Wise Choices, Apt Feelings*, pp. 134–35n.

70   It is only to be expected that those philosophers who hold that emotion is, or in large part is, evaluation should tend to think that emotion can be assessed, or partially assessed, for its rationality: the only escape-route would be to embrace some strong form of subjectivism about value. However there are also those who reject the connexion between emotion and value, and still think of emotion as something to be assessed for its rationality.

Indeed those who reject the rationality thesis are, at this juncture, comparatively lone voices, e.g., Brian O'Shaughnessy, *The Will: A Dual Aspect Theory* (Cambridge: Cambridge University Press, 1980), Vol. I, p. 21: 'Thus, there are four phenomena that can without strain be described *either* as rational *or* as irrational, viz. belief, desire, intention and action; and so far as I can tell, they exhaust the field. To be sure, emotion looks like a fifth, but here appearances are deceptive. While it could be rational to entertain the rage-inducing belief, or rational to perform the kinds of deeds that rage might prompt, . . . could it ever be rational to be smouldering with rage? It could in certain circumstances be understandable, obligatory if one is to rate as manly, justifiable even, but hardly rational. When would an absence of the emotion of rage rate as irrational? It seems that one's mood and metabolism, and the idiosyncrasies of age, temperament and sex, play too powerful a determining role to allow us to lay such phenomena at reason's door.'

71 See William James, 'The Physical Basis of Emotion', *Psychological Review*, 1 (1911), pp. 516–609, where James conceded that he had simply assumed that emotions were mental states. He wrote, 'I myself took it for granted without discussion . . . that the special emotions were names of special feelings of excitement.'

72 William James, *The Principles of Psychology* (New York: Holt, 1890), Chapter XXIV.

73 *ibid.*, pp. 442 and 449.

74 Gordon, *Structure of Emotions*, p. 89.

75 James, *Principles of Psychology*, pp. 449–50.

76 For 'secondary occurrences' of feeling, see Wollheim, *Art and its Objects*, secs. 17–18.

77 This point about how an experience that intentionally encapsulates another can have some of the same psychological effect as the encapsulated experience is something that I have urged in several places: see Wollheim, 'Imagination and Identification', in his *On Art and the Mind*, and *Thread of Life*.

78 For the argument itself – and the commentaries on it are by now too numerous to cite – see Ludwig Wittgenstein, *Philosophical Investigations*,

trans. G. E. M. Anscombe (Oxford: Basil Blackwell, 1953), Part I, secs. 256ff.

79 An argument of this nature is suggested in Wittgenstein, e.g., *ibid.*, Part II, ix.

80 See Stanley Schachter and J. E. Singer, 'Cognitive, Social, and Physiological Determinants of Emotional State', *Psychological Review*, 69 (1962), pp. 379–99.

81 Friedrich Nietzsche, *Zur Genealogie der Moral* (1887), trans. as *On the Genealogy of Morals*, ed. Walter Kaufmann, trans. Walter Kaufmann and R. J. Hollingdale (New York: Vintage Books, Random House, 1969), Third Essay, sec. 7.

82 Montaigne, 'De la peur'.

83 Gordon, *Structure of Emotions*, pp. 73–79, claims that fear normally motivates action – or, as I prefer to state it, normally generates desires that motivate action – that might be called 'vulnerability-avoidance', or is of this second sort. Gordon does not make it clear whether he wants to generalize this claim to other emotions, and, if so, which.

84 Montaigne, 'De la colère', gives the most chilling example of how anger can conserve itself. The passage is worth quoting in full for the picture that it gives of an emotion unrestrained by the pressures of polite society.

'Piso, a person of notable virtue in everything else, having become incensed at one of his soldiers because, returning alone from foraging, he could give him no account of where he had left a companion, took it for certain that he had killed him, and promptly condemned him to death. As he was at the gibbet, along comes this lost companion. The whole army made a great celebration about it, and after many hugs and embraces by the two comrades the executioner took them both into the presence of Piso, everyone present expecting confidently that it would be a great pleasure to him also. But it was quite the reverse. For through shame and vexation his fury, which was still in power, doubled; and by a subtle trick that his passion promptly suggested to him, he made the three of them guilty because he had found one of them to be innocent, and had all three dispatched: the first soldier because there was a sentence against him; the second, who had gotten lost, because he was the cause of his companion's death; and the executioner for not having obeyed the command that had been given him.'

85 Vittorio Alfieri, *Memorie*, trans. as *Memoirs of the Life and Writings of Victor Alfieri* (1816), Third Epoch, Chapter XIV.

86 The fusion of these three things is paramount in the one-time highly influential R. M. Hare, *The Language of Morals* (Oxford: Clarendon Press, 1952).

87 See Fyodor Dostoevsky, *Notes from the Underground* (1864), Part II, 'Concerning the Wet Snow', Chapter 2.

88 This traditional view of expression is denied in Nelson Goodman, *The Languages of Art* (Indianapolis and New York: Bobbs–Merrill, 1968). Goodman is able to do this because of the more abstract account that he gives of what expression is, which he frames in terms of a conjunction of metaphorical denotation and reverse denotation is preferred. Without going into the nature or the motivation of Goodman's account, it is difficult to see this as anything other than a change of subject, nor is it clear that Goodman would challenge such a response. On Goodman, see Wollheim, 'Nelson Goodman's *Languages of Art*', reprinted in his *On Art and the Mind*.

89 In conversation John Searle has told me that he regards these cases as the central cases of expression.

90 See Charles Darwin, *The Expression of the Emotions in Man and Animals* (London: John Murray, 1872).

91 The view that expression of

emotion is to be understood in terms of constant conjunction is threaded through the philosophy of mind of Bishop Berkeley. For a subtle treatment of the difficulties involved in dissociating the particular expression of an emotion from that emotion, see Wittgenstein, *Philosophical Investigations*, sec. 537. Stuart Hampshire, 'Feeling and Expression', reprinted in his *Freedom of Mind* (Oxford: Clarendon Press, 1972), argues for the primacy of physiognomic expression, so long as expression itself is understood as a type of action.

92 The French psychiatrist Jacques Lacan, following Henri Wallon, ascribed momentous importance to the child's first perception of itself in the mirror: it is partly inaugurative of what Lacan calls the '*fonction du Je*'. What Lacan appears to have overlooked is how far the infant's sense of itself as an agent has to have developed for its visual image in the mirror to make the appropriate effect on it. See Jacques Lacan, 'Le Stade du miroir', trans. as 'The Mirror Stage', in *Ecrits: A Selection*, trans. Alan Sher dan (London: Tavistock, 1977).

93 In this discussion of the expression of the emotions, I have partly drawn on earlier work of mine to be found in Wollheim, 'Expression', reprinted in my *On Art and the Mind*.

94 Still the best general account of phantasy, and its workings, is provided in Susan Isaacs, 'The Nature and Function of Phantasy', in *Developments in Psychoanalysis*, ed. Joan Riviere (London: Hogarth, 1962). See also Hanna Segal, *Introduction to the Work of Melanie Klein* (London: Heinemann, 1964), 'Phantasy and other Mental Processes', reprinted in *The Work of Hanna Segal: A Kleinian Approach to Clinical Practice* (New York: Jason Aronson, 1981), and *Dream, Phantasy and Art* (London: Tavistock/Routledge, 1991); and R. Hinshelwood, *A Dictionary of Kleinian Thought* (London: Free Association Books, 1989), entry 'Phantasy'. For clinical material illustrating the connexion between defence and phantasy, see Betty Joseph, 'Defence Mechanisms and Phantasy', reprinted in her *Psychic Equilibrium and Psychic Change.*

On the philosophical aspect of phantasy, see James Hopkins, 'Introduction', in *Philosophical Essays on Freud*, ed. Richard Wollheim and James Hopkins (Cambridge: Cambridge University Press, 1982), and the sustained discussion of the topic in Gardner, *Irrationality*, particularly Chapter 6. I refer to my disagreements with Gardner's extremely interesting views in endnote 40. See also Wollheim, *Thread of Life*, particularly Lectures IV, V, and VI.

95   For hallucination, see *Freud*, Vol. I, *Project for a Scientific Psychology* (1950, written 1895) secs. 11–18 and 21; Vol. VI, *The Interpretation of Dreams* (1900), Chapter VII, sec. E, 'The Primary and Secondary Processes'; and Vol. XXII, *An Outline of PsychoAnalysis* (1940), Chapter IV, 'Psychical Qualities'. Freud does not always distinguish carefully between hallucination and wish-fulfilment.

96   For wish-fulfilment, see *Freud*, Vol. IV, *The Interpretation of Dreams* (1900), Chapter VII, sec. C, 'Wish-Fulfilment', Vol. XII, 'Formulations on the Two Principles of Mental Functioning' (1911), and Vol. XIII, *Totem and Taboo* (1913), Part III, 'Animism, Magic and the Omnipotence of Thoughts'.

97   For the wish, see *Freud*, Vol. X, 'Notes upon a Case of Obsessional Neurosis' (1909). For a philosophical discussion, see Gardner, *Irrationality*, particularly Chapter 5.

98   The two phantasies that I consider here are both discussed in Marcia Cavell, 'Metaphor, Dreamwork and Irrationality', in *Truth and Interpretation: Perspectives in the Philosophy of Donald Davidson*,

ed. Ernest LePore (Oxford: Blackwell, 1986).

99   For this phantasy, see *Freud*, Vol. X, 'Notes upon a Case of Obsessional Neurosis' (1909), pp. 190–92, 204, 237, and 306–07. I discuss the phantasy at some length in Richard Wollheim, *Freud* (New York: Cambridge University Press, 2nd ed. 1990). See also Donald Davidson, 'Paradoxes of Irrationality', in *Philosophical Essays on Freud*.

100   *Freud*, Vol. XVII, 'A Child is being Beaten: A Contribution to the Study of the Origin of Sexual Perversions' (1919). I discuss this phantasy in Wollheim, *Thread of Life*, Lecture V.

101   *Freud*, Vol. XVII, p. 181.

ENDNOTES TO LECTURE THREE

1   Fyodor Dostoevsky, *The Brothers Karamazov* (1880), Part III, Book IX, Chapter VI.

2   I am here thinking in particular of the so-called 'social construction' theory of emotion, of which I take the following to be representative: Michelle Z. Rosaldo, *Knowledge and Passion: Ilongot Notions of Self and Social Life* (Cambridge: Cambridge University Press, 1980); Claire Armon-Jones, 'The Thesis of Social Constructionism', in *The Social Construction of Emotions*, ed. Rom Harre (Oxford:

Basil Blackwell, 1986); A. Wierzbicka, 'Human Emotions: Universal or Culture-specific?', *American Anthropology*, 88, no. 3 (September 1986), pp. 584–94; Catherine A. Lutz, *Unnatural Emotions* (Chicago and London: University of Chicago Press, 1988); and Fred R. Myers, 'The Logic and Meaning of Anger among Pantupi Aborigines', *Man*, N.S.,Vol. 23, no. 4 (December, 1988), pp. 589–610.

The strongest thesis to emerge from this somewhat confused literature is the following: Every instance of emotion has at its core an evaluation of its object, or of the fact or figure to which it is a response; the value in question is heavily constrained criterially; the capacity to identify the relevant criteria, and to recognize their presence, require a form of training, which only life in society can supply; and, the value being in this way a product of society, the emotion that is dependent on it is socially constituted.

The first thing to be noted about this thesis is that the evaluation that it places at the centre of emotion must involve what, in the last lecture, was called an *independent value*, or a value that can be identified prior to the emotion. For, if the value

were a *dependent value*, then all the thesis would establish is that all instances of emotion aim at, and profess to be, rational. No-one, would be the claim, forms an emotion towards an object unless he judges that the object merits it. Reason – and, stretching out behind reason, in virtue of the further conditions that the thesis lays down upon any value, society – constantly attempts to control emotion. But note two things. First, since the evaluation that lies at the core of any instance of an emotion might be a false evaluation, such control is not always effectively exercized. And, secondly, there is all the difference between the social control of emotion and the social constitution of emotion.

Accordingly, if we now understand the evaluation central to emotion as involving an *independent value*, and we further think, contrary to what I suggested in Lecture Two, that, for every emotion, there is such a value suitably related to it, the residual difficulty with the thesis concerns what an emotion is over and above the evaluation. Though some social constructionists – or perhaps all social constuctionists some of the time – deny that there is anything to an emotion except the evaluation, there is mostly recognition that this cannot be correct, and the presence of some feeling, or affective, element is conceded, even though it is appreciated that this will cause a problem. However there is no real agreement amongst social constructionists about what this problem is, or what is further called for when feeling is inserted into a 'social' account of the emotions.

One obvious problem – though, as we have seen, not one peculiar to social constructionism – is how, once feeling has been introduced, to avoid a conjunctive account of emotion, or one that offers a mere inventory.

According to some social constructionists, the mere introduction of any internal, or psychological, element into an account of emotion necessarily takes away its social aspect. If this is accepted, then it would have to be concluded that social constructionism necessitates an overall behaviourist, or quasi-behaviourist, account of emotion. This seems unjustified.

A more moderate contention is that the introduction of a feeling element into the account of emotion limits the degree to which emotion can be controlled by society. For, in circumstances in which the socially controlled evaluation is appropriate, but the feeling is resistant to social pressure, the emotion will not form. and so the emotion eludes society's control. The premises of any such argument, which concern the degree to which feeling is 'natural', are often left murky.

A range of views cluster round what may be thought of as the core of social constructionism, and some shelter under the label. Some of these views are extreme, some so moderate as not to warrant the appellation.

The more extreme views concern not so much emotions as the language of emotions. Characteristic would be the view that different societies classify the emotions so differently that at least some emotion-terms are not translatable from their language into ours, e.g., Wierzbicka, 'Human Emotions'. This view seems to leave us with the uneasy conclusion that, on occasions, we can know that speakers of another language are talking about emotions, but we have no way in principle of knowing what emotions they are talking about.

Amongst the more moderate views, we find it claimed, for instance, that different societies encourage different emotions, which consequently flourish, or that different societies have different expectations of, or assign different functions to, or set different values upon, the same emotion. The latter view is sometimes put, misleadingly, by saying that, in different societies, the same emotion will have a different 'meaning', e.g., Myers, 'Logic and Meaning of Anger'. What these more moderate views share is the assumption that there is somehow a preexistent pool of emotions out of which different societies pick or choose. This seems unexceptionable.

3 For this notion of the sense of self, see Richard Wollheim, *The Thread of Life* (Cambridge, Mass.: Harvard University Press, 1984), where it is central to the argument in Lecture VIII.

4 John Rawls, *A Theory of Justice* (Cambridge, Mass.: Harvard University Press, 1971), specifically connects shame with a fall in self-esteem. However Gabriele Taylor, *Pride, Shame and Guilt: Emotions of Self-Assessment* (Oxford: Clarendon Press, 1985), p. 77, though she agrees with this claim, argues that Rawls, in talking of self-esteem, confuses self-esteem and self-respect, and she suggests that he may think that they are the same thing. She distinguishes between them, and thinks that shame is connected solely with self-esteem, properly so-called.

Taylor, *Pride, Shame and Guilt*, p. 81, seems implicitly

to agree with me in another respect when she contends that shame is an emotion of self-protection. For that is another way of saying that shame is a response to an attack upon the self. From this point onwards, as the next endnote makes clear, Taylor's views and mine part company.

5 The subtitle of Taylor, *Pride, Shame and Guilt*, shows that she is committed to the autonomy of shame and guilt. She says explicitly, 'A person feeling shame judges herself adversely', *ibid.*, p. 68. That, in the next sentence, she goes on to write, 'This judgment is brought about by the realization of how her position is or may be seen from an observer's point of view' does not affect the issue as I see it. From this commitment of Taylor's follow most of the difficulties that beset this interesting and subtle study. Rawls, *Theory of Justice*, also supports the autonomy of shame and guilt.

6 Allan Gibbard, *Wise Choices, Apt Feelings: A Theory of Normative Judgment* (Cambridge, Mass.: Harvard University Press, 1990), appears to question the uncoupling of guilt and responsibility. However much depends on the level of generality on which the point is taken. When Gibbard writes, 'Guilt does not always reform a person, but it does

confine itself fairly well to the things he *can be* motivated to do or not to do', *ibid.*, p. 297 (my italics), he may well be right. What I insist on is that it does not confine itself to things that the person *has been* motivated to do. Nevertheless it must be insisted on that we can experience guilt over thoughts that enter our heads unbidden. The teaching of Christ on the topic of adultery raises the question, Are lascivious thoughts things that we can be motivated to have or not to have?

7   The view that shame derives from criticism from an external source is central to the views of Ruth Benedict, *Patterns of Culture* (Boston: Houghton Mifflin, 1934), and *The Sword and the Chrysanthemum* (Boston: Houghton Mifflin, 1946). This view has been criticized by Gerhart Singer and Miler B. Singer, *Shame and Guilt* (New York: Charles C. Thomas, 1953), who prefer to contrast shame and guilt by connecting one with the failure to attain a personal ideal and the other with the transgression of rules.

The view of shame as originating in a real-life external critic is referred to by Bernard Williams, *Shame and Necessity* (Berkeley, Los Angeles, and Oxford: University of California Press, 1993),

pp. 81–82, as 'a silly mistake'. Taylor, *Pride, Shame and Guilt*, pp. 54–57, is one of those who are careful not to make this mistake. Though she believes that standards of shame always derive from an honour-group, she insists that the person who is shamed must think of himself as an integral part of this group. In a shame-culture, there is no room for the distinction between public and private. If a person fails in the eyes of the group, he thereby fails in his own eyes. However Taylor who, as we have seen, falls into the opposite error of believing in the autonomy of shame and guilt, for this reason, or perhaps independently, thinks that we must be in agreement with any figure whom we have internalized. This is clearly wrong. She confuses, I would say, mere internalization and identification.

8   The eighteenth-century moralists I have in mind are Joseph Butler and Adam Smith. The point that I am making here in the text is a theme that runs through, and gives depth to, a work, which I greatly admire: John Deigh, *The Sources of Moral Agency: Essays in Moral Psychology and Freudian Theory* (Cambridge: Cambridge University Press, 1996), e.g., 'Conscience, I believe, is best

understood as a psychological mechanism . . . rather than as an intellective power . . . No conception, however, would be adequate to the phenomena if it did not include among the principal properties of a conscience that its dictates and reproaches appear to its possessor as the precepts and judgments of a supreme authority', *ibid.*, p. ix.

9 For the inability of the simple, undivided self to account for a number of psychological functions that possess any substantial complexity, see, e.g., Donald Davidson, 'Paradoxes of Irrationality', in *Philosophical Essays on Freud*, ed. Richard Wollheim and James Hopkins (Cambridge: Cambridge University Press, 1982). It is important to see that the rejection of the simple, undivided self does not entail the acceptance of the ultimately incoherent conception of the self as a multiplicity of selves. This ultimately incoherent conception is to be found in Richard Rorty, *Contingency, Irony and Solidarity* (Cambridge: Cambridge University Press, 1989), Chapter II, where it is explicitly adduced as a consequence of Freudian theory.

10 I owe this suggestion to Emilia Wollheim.

11 This characterization of shame and guilt broadly concurs with the way the differences are seen in Williams, *Shame and Necessity*. For the associations of shame and guilt with respectively the eyes and the voice, see Herbert Morris, *On Guilt and Innocence* (Berkeley and Los Angeles: University of California Press, 1979), a work to which I owe much of my original interest in some of the topics discussed here.

12 For a discussion of this methodology, see Taylor, *Pride, Shame and Guilt*, pp. 17–19, 54–57, and 85–89. Fundamental to this methodology is a division of societies into 'shame-cultures' and 'guilt-cultures'. This division, which gained impetus through the work of Ruth Benedict referred to in endnote 7 above, entered into the anthropology of antiquity through E. R. Dodds, *The Greeks and the Irrational* (Berkeley and Los Angeles: University of California Press, 1951). It was effectively challenged in Hugh Lloyd Jones, *The Justice of Zeus* (Berkeley and Los Angeles: University of California Press, 1971). However it remains unclear whether those who champion this division believe that psychology is ultimately to be explained in terms of social structure, or vice versa.

13 Jean Paul Sartre, *L'Être et le néant* (Paris: Gallimard, 1943), trans. as *Being and Nothingness*, trans. Hazel Barnes (London: Methuen, 1958), Part III, Chapter I.

14 Max Scheler, 'Über Scham und Schamgefühle', in his *Schriften aus dem Nachlass* (Bern: Francke Verlag, 1957), Vol. 1. The story is discussed in Taylor, *Pride, Shame and Guilt*, pp. 60ff.

15 William Shakespeare, *Measure for Measure* (1604–05), Act II, scene IV.

16 Williams, *Shame and Necessity*, p. 220, denies the need for a second observer, but his analysis of the general connexion between shame and being observed differs from how I see it.

17 Jean-Jacques Rousseau, *Les Confessions* (1781), Book II.

18 *ibid.*: see also Rousseau, *Les Rêveries d'un promeneur solitaire* (1782), 4th Promenade.

19 St Augustine, *Confessions*, Book II, secs. 9–18.

20 *ibid.*, Book II, sec. 7.

21 For this view of the defence-mechanisms, which separates them sharply from a motivated phenomenon like self-deception, I am indebted to Sebastian Gardner, *Irrationality and the Philosophy of Psychoanalysis* (Cambridge: Cambridge University Press, 1993), specifically Chapter I.

22 I owe this metaphor to Jim Hopkins.

23 For the effects of introjecting (or reintrojecting) a figure on whom one's own properties, or parts of oneself, have been projected, see *The Writings of Melanie Klein*, under the general editorship of Roger Money-Kyrle (London: Hogarth Press, and the Institute of Psycho-Analysis, 1957) (hereinafter *Klein*), Vol. III, 'Some Theoretical Conclusions Regarding the Emotional Life of the Infant' (1952), particularly p. 69.

24 For projective identification, the principal sources are *Klein*, Vol. III, 'Notes on Some Schizoid Mechanisms' (1946), 'On Identification' (1955), and *Envy and Gratitude* (1957). For the history of the idea, R. D. Hinshelwood, *A Dictionary of Kleinian Thought* (London: Free Association Books, 1989), entry 'Projective Identification', is invaluable. See also Herbert Rosenfeld, *Psychotic States: A PsychoAnalytical Approach* (London: Hogarth, 1968), and *Impasse and Interpretation* (London: Tavistock, 1987), particularly Part IV; W. R. Bion, 'Differentiation of the Psychotic from the Non-psychotic Personalities', reprinted in his *Second Thoughts* (London: Heinemann, 1967); R. D. Hinshelwood, *Clinical Klein* (London: Free Association Books, 1994), Part II, sec. 8; and Betty Joseph, 'Projective Identification: Some Clinical Aspects', in her

Psychic Equilibrium and Psychic Change (London: Tavistock/Routledge, 1989).

25 For this point, see Richard Wollheim, 'The Mind and the Mind's Image of Itself' reprinted in his *On Art and the Mind*.

26 For the Rat Man's phantasies about his father, see The Standard Edition of *The Complete Psychological Works of Sigmund Freud*, under the general editorship of James Strachey, in collaboration with Anna Freud (London: Hogarth Press, 1953–74) (hereinafter *Freud*), Vol. X, 'Notes upon a Case of Obsessional Neurosis', pp. 174–75, 204, 275, and 309.

27 This, I take it, is close to the point made by Bernard Williams, *Shame and Necessity*, p. 84 (my italics), when he writes in what he would be the first to concede is a depsychologized, or, perhaps fairer, a prepsychologized, language, 'It is a mistake ... to suppose that there are only two options: that the other in ethical thought must be an identifiable individual or a representative of the neighbours, on the one hand, or else be nothing at all except *an echo chamber for my solitary moral voice.*' For Williams' recognition of the need for psychologization, see *ibid.*,pp. 90 and 219–23.

28 Charles Baudelaire, *Les Fleurs du mal* (1861), 'L'Heautontimoroumenos'.

29 See John Steiner, 'Two Types of Pathological Organization', reprinted in his *Psychic Retreats: Pathological Organizations in Psychotic, Neurotic and Borderline Patients* (London and New York: Routledge, 1993), where he offers an arresting account of the inner manoeuvres of Oedipus as he defends himself against what he at once knows and doesn't know.

30 William Shakespeare, *King Lear* (1605–06), Act III, scene VII.

31 Ovid, *Metamorphoses*, Book VI, lines 519–62.

32 Rawls, *Theory of Justice*, Part 3, Chapter VII, p. 67, and Chapter VIII, p. 72, contends that guilt arises only when we think of ourselves as having transgressed a 'principle of right'. Rawls limits himself in a disabling fashion by considering only what he thinks of as 'rational' guilt. Rawls's view is criticized in Taylor, *Pride, Shame and Guilt*, pp. 85–89, and in Deigh, *Sources of Moral Agency*, Essay 3, 'Love, Guilt, and the Sense of Justice'.

33 Fyodor Dostoevsky, *Crime and Punishment* (1866), Part V, Chapter IV.

34 This, I believe, is the confusion that Williams, *Shame and Necessity*, p. 219, is warning us against when he denies that 'there is some internalized figure that elicits in the subject guilt or shame'. However Williams takes the

point further, and thinks that confusion arises, not simply from mislocating shame and guilt within the internal drama, but from thinking that shame and guilt belong anywhere in the internal drama. He treats shame and guilt as 'more complex', basically more social, derivatives, which are arrived at, at least partly, by 'bootstrapping' from a cruder, 'more primitive', basis. My view, by contrast, is that shame and guilt are certainly not what internal figures elicit in us: that – and here I more or less agree with Williams – is fear (or, more precisely, anxiety). Shame and guilt are the subsequent responses of the person to this anxiety. Williams thinks that our immediate internal response to fear is anger. My retort is that, along that route, we would never arrive at shame or guilt.

My disagreement with Williams is partly methodological. He holds that, since we posit the inner world to explain what happens in the outer world, we cannot allow what we are trying to explain to make an appearance on the inside. I hold that we explain what happens in the outer world by pointing to the same thing happening in the inner world.

35   Freud, Vol. XIX, The Ego and the Id (1923), sec. III, p. 29,

where he suggests the plural in talking of the superego as the precipitate of various 'abandoned object-cathexes'.

36   For the establishment of the superego, see Freud, e.g., Vol. XVIII, Group Psychology and the Ego (1921), Vol. XIX, The Ego and the Id (1923), sec. III, and 'The Dissolution of the Oedipus Complex' (1924). For the later stages of the Superego, see also Freud, Vol. XXI, Civilization and its Discontents (1930), and Vol. XXII, New Introductory Lectures on PsychoAnalysis. For the detail of Freud's thinking on the origins of morality, and the changes that it goes through, see the careful discussion in Deigh, Sources of Moral Agency, Chapters 3–6. The contribution that psychoanalytical thinking, specifically Freudian thinking, makes to the philosophical problems of morality is assessed with great insight and attention to detail in Samuel Scheffler, Human Morality (Oxford: Oxford University Press, 1992), and Deigh, Sources of Moral Agency.

37   Klein, Vol. I, 'Principles of Early Analysis' (1926), 'Symposium on Child-Analysis' (1927), and 'Early Stages of the Oedipus Conflict' (1928).

38   Klein, Vol. I, 'A Contribution to the Psychogenesis of Manic-Depressive States' (1935), and 'The Development of Mental Functioning'

(1958), particularly pp. 239 and 245.

39   *Klein*, Vol. I, 'Mourning and its Relation to Manic-Depressive States' (1940), pp. 362–63.

40   *Klein*, Vol. I, 'A Contribution to the Psychogenesis of Manic-Depressive States', pp. 267–69: '[T]he earliest utterances of conscience are associated with persecution by bad objects.' See also *Klein*, Vol. I, 'Love, Guilt and Reparation' (1937).

41   For the peculiar significance of projection prior to introjection, see *Klein*, Vol. I, 'The Early Development of Conscience in the Child' (1933).

42   Without a doubt Deigh, *Sources of Moral Agency*, pp. 41n, 56–57n, and 74n, attributes a view at once too bland and too simple to Melanie Klein, whom he describes as an 'optimist', along with John Rawls. A truly optimistic view is to be found in Marcia Cavell, 'Knowing and Valuing: Some Questions of Genealogy', in *Psychoanalysis, Mind and Art: Perspectives on Richard Wollheim*, ed. Jim Hopkins and Anthony Savile (Oxford: Blackwell, 1992).

When such labels as 'optimist' and 'pessimist' are distributed, care must be taken to distinguish between optimism about (one) the origins of shame and guilt, (two) the origins of morality narrowly considered, or the morality of obligation, and (three) the origins of value and valuation. These three issues can be decided comparatively independently.

43   Primo Levi, *The Drowned and the Saved*, trans. Raymond Rosenthal (New York: Simon and Schuster, 1988).

44   *ibid.*, p. 86.

45   Friedrich Nietzsche, *Zur Genealogie der Moral* (1887), trans. as *On the Genealogy of Morals*, ed. Walter Kaufmann, trans. Walter Kaufmann and R. J. Hollingdale (New York: Vintage Books, Random House, 1969), Third Essay.

46   Nathaniel Hawthorne, *The Scarlet Letter* (1850).

47   *ibid.*, Chapter VIII.

48   The phenomenology of the imagination and of phantasy here employed derives from Wollheim, *Thread of Life*, Lecture III.

49   J. H. Newman, *Parochial and Plain Sermons* (1838), Vol. IV, 'Chastisement amid Mercy'.

50   *ibid.*, p. 96.

51   For the distinction between persecutory and reparative guilt, see (though the terminology changes) *Klein*, Vol. I, 'A Contribution to the Psychogenesis of Manic-Depressive States', and Vol. III, 'On the Theory of Anxiety and Guilt' (1948), and *Envy and Gratitude*.

52   Reparative desires as Klein and Kleinians think of them need to be distinguished from

the more self-seeking kind of reparative desire that neo-Hegelian thinkers set store by. These latter desires aim at securing from the victim forgiveness for the act of wrongdoing. On this, see Deigh, *Sources of Moral Agency*, pp. 36–38.

53 A philosopher with whom I would find myself in extreme opposition on this point is Adam Smith. Adam Smith, *The Theory of Moral Sentiments* (1759), puts forward the view that the rationality of an emotion is always to be judged externally, or by reference to the feelings of 'the impartial spectator', and, since these feelings also establish the norm of rationality, Smith concludes that all people should, in any given situation, feel the same. Smith's rationale for this odd conclusion is that people want, above all, shared feelings. This seems an exaggeration. For a criticism of Adam Smith, see Gibbard, *Wise Choices, Apt Feelings*, pp. 279–82.

54 Marcel Proust, *À la recherche du temps perdu*, Vol. III, *Le Côté de Guermantes* (1920).

55 See Richard Wollheim, *F. H. Bradley* (Harmondsworth: Penguin Books, 1959), Chapter 6, and *Thread of Life*, Lecture VII.

56 For the notion of psychic force, see Wollheim, *Thread of Life*, Lecture I, n. 14.

57 *Klein*, Vol. I, 'The Psychological Principles of Early Analysis' (1926), and 'Symposium on Child-Analysis' (1927).

58 For the conservatism of the instincts, see *Freud*, Vol. XVIII, *Beyond the Pleasure Principle* (1920), sec. 5, and Vol. XXII, *New Introductory Lectures* (1932), Lecture XXXII.

59 *Freud*, Vol. XIV, 'Some Character-Types Met with in Psychoanalytic Theory: Criminals from a Sense of Guilt' (1916); and *Klein*, Vol. I, 'Criminal Tendencies in Normal Children' (1927), and 'The Early Development of Conscience in the Child' (1933), and Vol. III, 'Some Reflections on *The Oresteia*' (1963). See also Wollheim, 'Crime, Punishment, and 'Pale Criminality'', reprinted in his *The Mind and its Depths* (Cambridge, Mass.: Harvard University Press, 1993).

60 For the projection of the superego, see *Klein*, Vol. I, 'Personification in the Play of Children' (1929), and 'The Importance of Symbol-Formation in the Development of the Ego' (1930).

61 The term that has been coined for relations that a person has towards others in the environment into whom he has projected some of his internal figures is 'narcissistic object-relations'. It is to be found in *Klein*, Vol. III, 'Notes on Some Schizoid Mecha-

nisms' (1946), and there is a whole literature on this topic. Such relations invariably involve a merging, or blurring, between the person and the figure. See, e.g., Rosenfeld, *Psychotic States*, and *Impasse and Interpretation*; and Steiner, *Psychic Retreats*.

62 See Brian Masters, *Killing for Company: The Case of Dennis Nilsen* (London: Jonathan Cape, 1985). For the underlying psychological phenomenon, see *Klein*, Vol. I, 'A Contribution to the Psychogenesis of Manic-Depressive States'.

63 Betty Joseph, 'A Clinical Contribution to the Analysis of a Perversion', in *Psychic Equilibrium*.

64 *Klein*, Vol. III, 'The Development of Mental Functioning' (1958).

65 Jean Racine, *Andromaque* (1667), Act V.

66 When Williams, *Shame and Necessity*, p. 91, writes, 'What people's ethical emotions are depends significantly on what they take them to be', this must not be taken to be a simple endorsement of what might be called self-attributionism. In the first place, 'people' here evidently does not mean individuals. It means a collective, such as a society, or a culture. So he is talking about moments of considerable historical moment when new habits

of thought arise. Secondly, Williams thinks that, when such moments occur, these affect the place that a certain emotion occupies in the life of society, but they do not bring the emotion into being, or constitute it. This can be seen from the subsequent sentence, where he writes, 'The truth about Greek societies, and in particular the Homeric, is not that they failed to recognize any of the reactions that we associate with guilt, but that they did not make of those reactions the special thing that they became when they are separately recognized as guilt.'

67 Two philosophers who have perceived the essential connexion between emotion and narrative, are Ronald de Sousa and Sebastian Gardner: see de Sousa, *The Rationality of Emotion* (Cambridge, Mass.: MIT Press, 1987), particularly Chapters 7 and 12, where he talks of 'paradigm scenarios', and Gardner, 'The Nature and Source of Emotion', in *Psychoanalysis, Mind and Art: Perspectives on Richard Wollheim*, ed. Jim Hopkins' and Anthony Savile (Oxford: Blackwell, 1992). The idea is approved of in Marcia Cavell, *The Psychoanalytic Mind: From Freud to Philosophy*, (Cambridge, Mass.: Harvard University Press, 1993), and in Martha Nuss-

baum, *The Therapy of Desire* (Princeton: Princeton University Press, 1994), p. 508, where it is suggested that the narratives have a social origin. Ludwig Wittgenstein, *Remarks on the Philosophy of Psychology*, ed. G. H. von Wright and Hekki Nyman, trans. C. G. Luckhardt and M. A. E. Ane (Oxford: Blackwell, 1980), Vol. II, sec. 148, says that every emotion has a 'course', which it runs.

INDEX